PERFORMANCE BEHAVIOR

PERFORMANCE BEHAVIOR

The Lean methodology for continuously improving performance behavior

Neil C.W. Webers

More information about this and other editions is available at:

Foras Media, The Publishing Company

www.foras-media.com

©2018 Foras Media, the publishing company

1st Dutch edition May 2010

2nd Dutch edition September 2010

3th Dutch edition April 2011

4th Dutch edition March 2012

1st English edition December 2012

2nd English edition April 2018

Design, cover design and layout: bartistiek Design (www.bartistiek.nl)

ISBN 978-90-820015-4-9

NUR 801

Contents

Preface

The pace of organizational change increases: the lifespan of products becomes increasingly shorter and this causes strategic cycles to become shorter. Change and improvement are no longer a temporary process, but instead take place continuously.

Many organizations struggle with the question of how they can convert continuous improvement structures and systems into different behavior. Behavior that actually results in the expected performance, which gives both the employee and the manager more authority and control over their work.

This requires a specific approach that links behavioral development directly to expected performances in an embedded system. This approach also has consequences for the way in which organizations handle the development of people: behavioral development as a continuous process requires a radically different hr-model. Most organizations have found out that their current job appraisal system, in which job performances are appraised once a year, is not suitable to steer performances appropriately. However, they don't possess any alternatives. Therefore, they attempt to make personal development measurable with "personal objectives", "values" and "competencies".

This development is a dead-end. The development of behavior has to be aligned with the performance and this behavior has to be measured and steered in the same frequency as the delivered performance. Here, it is important that the employee gets maximal space within his own performance responsibility area. In this way, the responsibility and authority will lie at a lower level within the organization and the desired performance is achieved at each level within the organization. This is what performance behavior does.

The past years, I have worked on the continuous development of the performance behavior concept with joy. Each day, new insight is added to the concept and I hope that you, as reader, will also contribute to further developments of performance behavior in your practice.

Many of the things you will read in this book will be common sense. So ask yourself the question: "If they are so common sense, why aren't they common practice?" I hope that reading this book and practicing it, will help you formulating the answer...

1

WHAT IS PERFORMANCE BEHAVIOR?

In this first chapter we introduce you to performance behavior. What is performance behavior? The terms behavior and performance are important here. What does behavior in organizations look like and how is it brought about? How is performance in organizations brought about? And what combination of behavior and performance do you need to achieve performance behavior? In short, the chapter outlines the context of performance behavior.

Behavior

Behavior is the sum of visible and invisible actions of a person, a group of people or an entire company. This book is concerned with the behavior of an employee, a group of employees, or an entire organization. We talk about individual behavior when we discuss an employee and we talk about organizational behavior when we discuss an organization or group. The behavior of an employee might deviate from the behavior of a department and the behavior of a department is not necessarily equal to the behavior of the organization.

When we know what behavior we display ourselves and if we understand the origin of certain behaviors, we are better able to recognize and effectively deal with these behaviors. We can also handle the behavior of others better when we know what behavior we can expect from others and when we know which "ingredients" this behavior contains.

Performance

Performance is the result of all efforts; all desired, but also all undesired results. Performance behavior makes a distinction between personal performances, which concern the performance of an individual, and organizational performances, which concern the performances of a group of employees within an organization.

When we know which actions we need to perform to achieve a performance, we are better able to effectively steer these actions, so that the result is actually achieved. This is both true for steering our own performance as well as steering the performance of others.

Performance behavior

Performance behavior means that a measurable connection is made between result and the behavior that is required to achieve that result. It specifies and measures the behavior that is needed to achieve the desired result. When this connection meets a result or quality standard that was defined in advance, then the performance behavior is secured. Because the performance behavior is secured, the result is guaranteed. There is a difference between performance behavior and performance-oriented behavior. For performance-oriented behavior, the direction is clear, but the result is not secured.

An example of performance behavior is the behavior of Dutch ice skater Sven Kramer. In an interview prior to his golden five kilometers at the Olympics in Vancouver in 2010, he was asked why he had a good chance of becoming Olympic champion. He answered by explaining that he completely controlled all factors he needed for a good time: the starting technique, the lap times, the buildup of the race and his technique. Sven is known for dividing the total performance into manageable parts. He did not only map per component which performance he needed to achieve, but also in which way he had to deliver the performance (behavior) to win. Where his competitors spoke of "performing maximally", Sven had secured his total performance. He broke it down and established a performance and behavioral standard he worked towards in a disciplined way. That is performance behavior.

For Sven Kramer, it was self-evident that he would win. With the aid of performance behavior, performance should become equally self-evident in organizations as it is for Sven Kramer. When all performances at each level within the organization are linked to the necessary behaviors, achieving results is secured.

It is important to secure performance behavior because there are a lot of factors we have little influence over. Sven discovered this during the Olympic ten kilometers in Vancouver when he was sent on the wrong track by a disastrous error of his coach Gerard Kemkers and was subsequently disqualified (despite the fact that he had the best time in the classification round).

1.1 Relationship between performance and behavior

In this subsection, we first examine the relationship between performance and

behavior in practice, and subsequently we further elaborate on the definitions of performance and behavior.

"But why didn't you call me?" team leader Peter asks the operator on duty. "The packing machine has not been operating for half an hour which means that we will not be able to pack the amount of products to achieve our objective today!" Paul, the operator, looks at Peter and after taking a deep breath he answers: "Can't you see what a mess it is? I was glad to have some time to tidy the place up."

This conversation between Peter and Paul illustrates a common situation on the work floor: a problem arises and the employees involved all handle the problem in a different way. Everyone has their own interpretation and therefore chooses their own solution, resulting in misunderstanding or incomprehension about the chosen solution.

For efficient management and a maximal result, we prefer as few misunderstandings as possible, especially regarding the solution of daily problems. To realize this, it is necessary to see the causal relationship between performance and the behavior of people.

The example contains multiple layers of information. The first layer is the layer we see and perceive: Paul, the operator, is tidying up while his machine is turned off. He produces nothing. The second layer, the one we cannot perceive directly, is the trade-off Paul made to arrive at his choice: do I call my team leader because I have no products to package, or do I tidy up?

When we refer to behavior within performance behavior, we refer to all actions a person performs. This "performance" can be subdivided into external actions and internal actions. The fact that Paul trades-off the possibilities and makes a choice is an invisible process that takes place in his head, but this internal action is part of his behavior. That he does not call his team leader is visible behavior. Therefore, this belongs to the category of external actions.

Let us look deeper into this situation and wonder what the basis is for the visible behavior of Paul, the operator. The behavior Paul displays at work has an underlying reason. His response "I was glad I had the time to tidy up" shows that he presumes he was doing the right thing by tidying up. He perceived his environment with his senses (in this case his eyes), he evaluated this environment (there are items that do not belong here) and checked this evaluation with his inner standard: it is too messy here. How did this standard arise? Is Paul also this neat at home? Does Paul have a neat character? Is he trained by the company to be neat? Was it a conscious decision? Or was it subconscious? The standard he developed to evaluate his own environment is determined by his genetic makeup, character, education and social factors.

Let's take a look at what happens after Paul judged his environment to be "too messy". The situation starts with a telephone call Paul receives from his colleague who tells him he has to wait a little longer for the product he needs to pack with his machine. Via his ears, he perceives the situation: I have to shut down my packing machine for a while. Since his colleague gives no indication regarding duration and Paul also does not inquire after this, Paul does not know how long he has to wait. He also has no idea what the reason is he will not receive products to pack. Paul had already ascertained it was too messy in the morning, so the phone call from his colleague is very convenient. On the basis of two signals that Paul receives (no products to pack and a messy department), he makes a decision in a matter of seconds: he takes a broom and trashcan and tidies up.

From this example, we can learn that behavior is influenced by the context. We perceive something and interpret it. Sometimes we leave out information and sometimes we supplement it ourselves. Paul immediately assumes that it will be at least an hour before he will receive products, although no one told him this. He assumes this, because such situations often take an hour to solve. He interprets the signal he receives from his colleague in his own way and on the basis of this he decides to take half an hour to tidy up because in this half an hour he has to wait anyway. Paul also intends to call Peter, his boss, after he is done cleaning so that Peter can take action to make sure the products are received again.

The result of the behavior that Paul displays is largely influenced by the ideas Paul has about certain events, based on previous experiences. He has a "mental representation": the idea that Paul has regarding a tidy department and the idea that Paul has regarding "no products to pack". These ideas determine how Paul interprets the situation and the choices he makes. Figure 1.1 shows what this looks like in a schematic way:

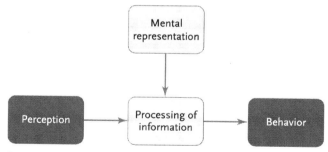

Figure 1.1 *From perception to behavior*

Everyone processes received information on the basis of his own mental representations and makes conscious and subconscious choices that are partly visible and partly invisible to others.

This information processing does not stand alone. It is influenced by colleagues, experiences, managers, instruction signs, e-mails, Internet, newspapers, television and other sources of information. Besides that, there is not always a strict separation between work and private. If Paul has a neat personality ("Even as a child he cleared away his own toys"), he probably needs less structure at work to clean up than someone who has a more chaotic personality. Also, there is a good chance he has everything neatly stored away in his garage at home.

Paul's behavior is largely determined by who he is (personality, intelligence, experiences and interaction), by social factors (the people in his private and work environment), by how he feels (when he spent his entire life in a wheelchair, he will function differently from someone who is a marathon runner), by cultural and geographic factors (if Paul has Asian roots, he will have different values than when he comes from West-Europe) and finally by spiritual factors such as faith and convictions.

Figure 1.2 shows which factors influence information processing.

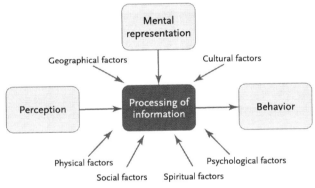

Figure 1.2 *Factors that play a role in the realization of behavior*

There are four basic elements that play a role in the realization of behavior:

1 The physical action needed to allow the behavior to take place;
2 The emotion someone experiences when he displays the behavior;
3 The psychological response that belongs to the behavior;
4 The thoughts that accompany the behavior.

Behavior is under normal circumstances stable and steady, that is: in case of stable environmental factors. However, this may change to a greater or lesser extent due to altering factors in the environment, such as death, emigration or a changed work situation. The effect of changed circumstances and the role the environment plays differs per person. Because everyone interprets the circumstances in a different way, the actions, emotions, psychological reaction and thoughts will also differ per person.

Moreover, the behavior of people, but also their thoughts and feelings, is greatly influenced by situational factors. When these situational factors change, the behavior will usually also change (either temporarily or more permanently). In addition to situational factors, personality also plays an important role in the realization of behavior.

Paul's personality determines the unique way in which he will behave in most situations. This can differ depending on the situation (work or private), because his priorities are different in his private and his work life. Furthermore, in his work situation he will be surrounded and influenced by different people than those in his private situation. Paul might display different behavior at home than he does at work. Subsection 1.2 elaborates more on personality and behavioral profiles.

When you are able to explain behavior, you are also better able to identify the factors that bring about this behavior. The better you can identify behavior, the better you can predict it. The predictability of behavior is directly related to the result of the behavior: the more predictable the behavior, the more predictable the result.

Ideally, the results of an organization should be as predictable as possible. Since the people who work there largely influence the results of an organization, having predictable behavior in employees is an important factor in the predictability of the company results.

An employee's performance is the sum of his efforts and the organizational results are the sum of the performances of all individual employees.

Back to the example of Paul, the operator, and team leader Peter. Paul thought he had achieved the desired result: he tidied up his department. Team leader Peter had a different idea: he assumed the packaging machine was running well and his only purpose in visiting Paul was to have a short talk. When Peter arrived at the machine, he discovered that Paul's result differed from the result he had in mind. Their "result expectations" were clearly different.

1.2   From processing information towards behavior

When people who work together are not in agreement regarding expected results (both vertically: between manager and employee, and horizontally: between employees), everyone will try to achieve the results in their own way. They will each work towards the result they assume to be most desirable. From the example with Paul and Peter, we can see that result expectations can differ greatly. This has to do with the way in which people process new information, as will be clarified below.

Organizing the world with schemas

Do employees work towards their performance consciously, or is this subconscious behavior? A study by psychology professor Ap Dijksterhuis shows that our conscious mind can process no more than 60 bits per second. In contrast, our subconscious mind can process approximately 11 million bits per second. We have a tendency to place our consciousness on a pedestal, believing ourselves to be capable of rational thinking and making autonomous choices. This study shows, however, that the processing capacity of our subconscious mind is approximately 200.000 times as large as that of the conscious mind.

Perhaps that is for the best. Our body is a complex chemical factory and we do not want to be constantly thinking about whether our heart continues to beat or whether our lungs continue to breathe. We assume that our bodily functions "simply" continue to function. Our head works the same way. Our brain carefully filters everything our eyes see. If we have already seen information before, it will not be stored a second time; after all, it is already stored on our "hard disc". When we receive a lot of information all at once, our brain prioritizes for us without us knowing what we do and do not remember. In fact, the brain determines what it wants to remember and what it does not want to remember.

That is why the traumatic childhood event that one tries to forget always manages to resurface. And when I ask you now not to think of a pink elephant, your brain will automatically show you a pink elephant. You cannot "turn off" your thoughts. Your brain does what it wants when it wants to. It does so for a reason. It is in this way that we build up an enormous collection of images, which we "label" from the moment we are born.

For everything, we apply one or more labels that each represent a value. That value can be a feeling (emotion) but can also be an opinion (a standard). When I see a banana peel on the floor, if I have already labeled it as such, I could perceive this as dirty. Someone else, who has just been on a tropical island, eating delicious bananas, could associate it with "holiday".

The world is so complex that our brain classifies all the images, tastes, scents, sounds and other stimuli that our body processes during life. And that is not all: we also build up experience about social interaction with people and things in certain situations. We use this to explain and estimate how certain behavior happens. We call this knowledge of each social interaction a script. The more often a specific social interaction occurs, the more scripts we have for it. For instance, it is likely that we have many scripts for a person who is nervous, but less scripts for someone who walks around naked, since we do not encounter the latter situation as often as the first.

These scripts lead to schemas that provide us with information about how we should interpret our observations. The schemas lead to a "guidebook" for the interpretation of events around us. These schemas are influenced by the culture we live in, our upbringing, our education and the experiences we have over the course of our entire life. This "guidebook" is an important guide in our life, because this continuously provides us with information to help us understand and interpret the rest of the world. There are social schemas, event schemas, specific schemas such as travel schemas and sports schemas and of course work schemas that say something about the way in which we should interpret the activities we perform at work.

It is possible that the schema for "taking the kids to football on Saturday" consists of the schemas "packing up", "loading the car", "driving to the football field", and "arrival at the field". The schema "driving to the football field" has many similarities to driving to work. It is likely that the schemas "driving to work" and "driving to the football field" arose from the same kind of script. It deviates on some points as well. The script "running into an acquaintance in the town centre" occurs more often on Saturday and is more likely part of the schema "driving to the football field" than of "driving to work".

You will be surprised when you run into another parent during work and at a random place. Under normal circumstances, you would only greet him during your kid's football practice on Saturday. This person does not fit in to the "driving to work" schema. He is not a very nice person (label: "rude") so during work it is suddenly hard to say a friendly "good afternoon".

Labels, scripts and schemas subconsciously influence the result of behavior and with that they can influence performance both positively and negatively.

Schemas influence what we remember

Problems can arise when we label our stored observations. In the example in which you drive to the football field, you perceive something that does not match the schema in which you have stored a previous experience. Person x is part of the schema "football field" and not of the schema "work". In this case, it is difficult for us to remember what we have actually perceived.

There are three types of schemas:

1 Consistent schemas;
2 Inconsistent schemas;
3 Irrelevant schemas.

When we find ourselves in a situation we have experienced before, we perceive it as "normal" and therefore know what to expect. This is a consistent schema. Our brain's first response with a consistent schema is: "Right, I already know this: I don't have to process this information."

When we find ourselves in a situation that is "abnormal" and deviates from what we expect, this is an inconsistent schema. This schema does not match the situation we find ourselves in and our brain's response will be to reject it, because the situation is different than we expect.

Finally, we can find ourselves in a situation that our brain can barely make sense of. With such a situation, remembering information is particularly difficult.

This phenomenon is very common with people who have experienced an assault and have seen the attacker. Because most people have never experienced such a situation before and the event occurs completely unexpectedly, vital information is not stored. Eyewitnesses who already have a script of an assault (because of a movie or experience) usually do remember more outstanding details, but the brain does not always store these details correctly. This is because the situation is completely irrelevant to the schema they were occupied with at the moment of the assault.

Different people who experienced the same assault often have different images of the same attacker. Huge variation can occur. Did the attacker wear a red hat or a black one? Did he wear a black or a green coat? Did he have blonde or dark hair? People do remember the event itself, but most details are barely stored or not stored at all, while in other cases several specific details are stored. Our brain largely determines what it does or does not want to remember.

The scripts we build are not actively turned on or off by our brain. They are usually only activated at the moment of perception. If I have just seen a picture of a banana, the script of a banana is turned on. All scripts connected to bananas, such as holiday, monkey, hunger and fruit are also activated in our brain to a lesser extent. The further away other scripts are from the banana script, the less they will be activated in our brain. This mechanism clearly shows why two people can have completely different associations with the same object. The connected scripts are activated in one person because of his specific knowledge and experiences whereas this is not the case for someone else.

Knowledge of situations or problems that are not very common is difficult to activate in situations where we need this knowledge. This can be illustrated by the following example: when steersmen on a ship are surrounded with the most advanced systems, they appear to be the weakest link in case of accidents. More than 80% of shipping accidents are caused by human error (Butter, 2000). In situations that are not-common, the brain tends to have difficulties coping with the situation and keeping focus. For instance, let's look at a captain who makes a bad decision. As long as the next decision is made correctly, the consequence of the bad decision is small and insignificant. However, when a series of situations occur in which the brain is insufficiently capable to reproduce stored information (because the situations concerned are new, do not occur often or because someone is distracted at the moment, or had to go to the bathroom for instance) this series of seemingly insignificant events can eventually end in catastrophe. Usually, not one but multiple causes can be found in case of accidents. The disaster of the Herald of Free Enterprise in 1987, which lead to the death of 193 people, is such an example. Employees were insufficiently trained and therefore no one felt responsible for safety. This resulted in bow doors that remained open. Additionally, a system to ensure that the bow doors closed automatically was not present. The ship was late and wanted to leave as soon as possible. This caused a high bow wave that flowed inside the open bow doors at the stern. Moreover, the Herald of Free Enterprise was not sailing its regular route and the ship did not fit to the loading bridge at the dock. The ship was much too high. The captain managed to compensate for this by filling up the ballast tank with seawater. This deviated from the normal procedure, but did allow the passengers and their vehicles to drive up to the ship via the bridge, so the ship could depart quickly to catch up on lost time. Not one factor but all these factors occurred at the same time, causing the enormous ship to capsize.

Our memory functions within the structure of schemas. As soon as we attempt to store deviations from these schemas, we experience problems. By storing within the structure of schemas it is much easier to recall information at the moments we need it again. The more often we use a schema, the easier we can recall this schema. However, we do not recall all information from the schema, only the information we need at a particular moment. The information we do not need remains unused and stored away in our brain, to slowly fade away and eventually disappear. If we do not need information on a regular base, it becomes increasingly difficult to recall.

We use our schemas not merely to categorize the world, but also as frameworks within which we perceive the world so we can make sense of it. We perceive and interpret all new information on the basis of our current schemas. Because of this, schemas partly determine how we view the world. When we encounter information that is at odds with our convictions (read: schemas), we prefer not to store it since this would mean we would have to adjust our convictions. Information that matches our convictions is much more easily stored since it matches our already existing schemas. In a way, we see and remember mainly what we (subconsciously) want. You hear what you want to hear because this is easier and costs less energy.

When you do not consciously look for a framework or new point of view, it is practically impossible to change your opinion. You have to consciously want this before you are able to do so. This also means that the older you are, the more opinionated and rigid you become and therefore, the more difficult it is to change your point of view. The younger you are, the easier it is to influence your schemas. When you are young, you need more sleep to process all the images you have experienced during the day; older people generally need less sleep because they have added fewer new schemas to the existing collection in their mind.

Learning and developing: adding new schemas

We naturally have a defense mechanism that makes sure our development mechanisms get closed as we grow older.

The defense mechanism will work faster and more effectively as we become older and know more, since the knowledge and experience we have built resulted in the life we live right now, accompanied by all the schemas we have consciously and subconsciously created. This makes it easier to add experiences and knowledge when we are relatively unwritten (younger). We can also turn this defense mechanism on by ourselves, consciously or subconsciously. Our mind is in development mode when we think it could benefit us.

Moreover, research shows that our brain, just like our senses, reacts best to a shift in stimuli. When we are in a warm room, we get used to the warmth, but when we go from a cold room to that same warm room, it feels much warmer. Our brain can also better remember when we vary between information that falls within a schema, for instance French words during French class, and information that falls just outside the schema, such as a French term of abuse. Our brain unfailingly registers that the term of abuse does not really belong in the schema and therefore it pays more attention to it.

As we add schemas, it becomes more difficult to add information to them. This is due to the fact that schemas consist of situations in which certain behavior has been shown to (in the past) yield the same result. That result provides a certainty we prefer to hold onto. That is why we prefer to exhibit the same behavior. We wish to achieve the same result again. Employees who have performed the same activities for a longer period will generally have more difficulty learning new things than people who have just started working. This is a question of age: older schemas are used more often. It is also a question of experience: despite being younger someone can still have more work experience than someone who is older. And finally, it depends on the various behavioral profiles: someone with a behavioral profile that shows more stability and certainty will have more trouble adding new information to schemas than someone with a behavioral profile that shows more curiosity and entrepreneurship.

1.3   Behavioral profiles

Back to the example of team leader Peter and operator Paul. Peter is 52 years old and tried and tested. Paul has been working as an operator for 23 years, and has been on the packing line for over 15 years. Both have a lot of experience in the work they do. Because they have worked at the same organization for such a long time, many of the images they have perceived, and therefore the work schedules they have built up, have probably arisen from the same sources. As they work in the same department, for the most part, they see and hear the same things every day. How is it possible that they do not have the same point of view? Paul decides to tidy up, while Peter would like him to make sure the machine is running.

Apparently, Peter and Paul have interpreted the same information in different ways. Since their environment is nearly the same, you can conclude that the cause of this difference in interpretation lies within the individual. Research shows that the way in which we convert perceived images into behavior is largely determined at birth. During our life, all we can do is refine this process.

In 1921, the psychologist Carl Jung conducted revolutionary research and to this day, we continue to base the way in which we conduct personality tests and assessments on his research. Jung described four behavioral styles, based on how people interact with their environment: *intuition, feeling, thinking and sensation.*

In the 1930's, psychologist William Marston used Jung's work as the basis for further development. He was one of the first psychologists to describe the behavior of healthy people; before, only the behavior of mentally ill people was researched. On the basis of Jung's behavioral styles, Marston established four stable characteristics (profile factors) that can be used to map the behavioral profile that is already present at birth:

1   *Dynamic*: Task-oriented, competitive and fast behavior. Prefers to be goal-oriented and direct. Wants to achieve results and looks for challenges. Is competitive and expects direct answers.
2   *Inspiring*: People-oriented, extraverted and fast behavior. Is very convincing. Likes to make contact with people and is open. Likes to work in a team.
3   *Social*: People-oriented, sensitive and thorough behavior. Prefers to work in a well-organized and structured environment. Is a good listener and enjoys doing things for others.
4   *Correct*: Task-oriented, cautious and thorough behavior. Makes high demands on himself and on his environment. Wants to know what to expect before he starts. Likes to analyze thoroughly.

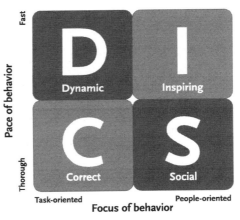

Figure 1.3   *The four profile factors alongside the axes 'pace of behavior' (thorough and fast and 'focus of behavior' (task-oriented or people-oriented)*

Pace and focus

The basis of individual behavioral profiles stems from two different motivators: focus and pace. Focus consists of two components: decision making on the basis of tasks (rational) and decision making on the basis of people (emotional). Someone who focuses on tasks makes rational decisions, is goal-oriented and often finishes his tasks. Someone who focuses on people makes decisions on the basis of relational, human considerations. Relationships are important to these people; "together" is an important word.

Pace as a motivator determines the pace of actions. People with a high pace are active, speak quickly and respond and decide quickly. People with a slow pace are thorough, investigating, walk and speak slower and calmly make their decisions. People with a fast pace are called extraverts according to Jung's behavioral profiles; people with a slow pace are introverts.

 Determine your own behavioral profile via www.profile4free.com.

People with a fast pace and driven by tasks are goal-oriented and direct. They are also dominant, because they want the task to be finished at any cost. They are described as dynamic.

People with a fast pace and people-oriented are described as brisk and easy-going. Such people are often amiable and influential. They are described as inspiring. "Dynamic" and "inspiring" are both extravert profile factors.

People with a slow pace who are people-oriented are social types. Such people are often more passive, but also more stable and resolute. Sensitivity is also an important characteristic.

Correct, calculating and conforming to rules are characteristics belonging to people who are task-oriented and have a slow pace. They are often described as correct and conscientious.

Figure 1.4 uses an axes graph to show typical characteristics per behavioral profile.

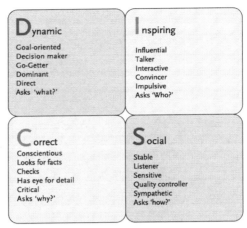

Figure 1.4 *A number of typical characteristics per profile factor*

Combination of profile factors

Everyone has at least one, but no more than three, profile factors. Together, in combination and through interaction with each other, these determine an individual's behavioral profile. You cannot have them all, since you cannot be "everything" at the same time. For example, a thorough method excludes a quick one. And being an introvert person excludes one from being an extravert person. Nevertheless, this does not mean that someone is incapable of displaying different behavior temporarily. However, when the behavior that is inconsistent with the behavior profile lasts too long, tension and even stress can occur. Everyone prefers to display behavior that is consistent with his personality, both at work and in his private life. Our own measurements conducted over a period of ten years also prove that these characteristics are highly constant.

Most people have two profile factors. The extent to which a profile factor is present, but also the combination of other profile factors and a person's awareness of his own behavior usually determine the behavior the person displays.

Team leader Peter has a behavioral profile that contains a certain level of dominance; the profile factor "dynamic". He also prefers to check whether his people stick to their agreements and he is highly critical. These last characteristics are due to his "correct" profile factor. According to his behavioral profile factors, Peter is neither "inspiring" nor "social". Therefore, he tends to exaggerate his critical attitude, which means he does not always take the feelings and opinions of others into account.

Paul, the operator, enjoys entering into discussions with Peter. He is easily distracted, which means he often sees too many things he perceives as important. This is a result of his "inspiring" profile factor. Additionally, Paul appreciates a fixed work place in which preferably no change occurs. He definitely does not want to be transferred to another department, as Peter had planned to do last year. The very thought makes him nervous. This is caused by Paul's "social" profile factor. He derives his self confidence from the experiences he has; this

Daniel D. Ofman (2006). 'Core qualities gateway to human resources.'

gives him confidence, since he knows what to expect. If he does not know what to expect and suddenly finds himself in a new situation, he becomes nervous and will try to get out of the situation as soon as possible.

Research has shown that in Western cultures, the majority of people prefer the profile factor "dynamic" in other people's behavior. This profile factor is seen as most appealing because people with this factor, just like Peter the team leader, are more likely to be leading and steering than the other profile factors. In Asian cultures, the more introvert profile factors are preferred. No profile factor is better or worse than another. Each profile factor has its own qualities and pitfalls. The pitfall is an exaggerated quality. Figure 1.5 clarifies this.

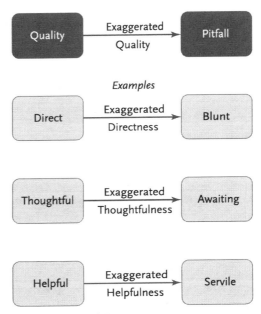

Figure 1.5 *Exaggerated quality as pitfall*

Our own investigation of profiles of over five hundred managers shows that many managers have the profile factors "dynamic" or "inspiring", and in most cases both. Additionally, employees that fulfill roles that require a lot of extraversion, such as management roles, often have more dominance and influence in their behavior profiles. And employees who fulfill roles that require more introversion, such as supporting roles, more often have "social" and "correct" in their behavior profile.

Genetic predisposition

The behavioral profile is already established at birth, or shortly after. Statements such as "I used to be "dynamic", but now I only have "social" in my behavioral profile" are untrue. We have a natural tendency to display predetermined behavior in a certain situation. However, we can learn to handle the qualities and pitfalls in our behavioral profiles. When we know which behavioral profile we have and can understand what brings about certain behavior, we are better able to recognize this and handle it effectively. Moreover, we are better able to handle the behavior of others when we know what we can expect of them and what "ingredients" their behavior contains. It makes the behavior of others predictable, and with that, it becomes easier to influence.

We cannot change the tendencies we get from our behavior profile, but we can influence the way we express these tendencies in our behavior. We can develop the way in which we handle our behavioral profile, without striving to change our behavioral profile to make it better suited to the role we would like to fulfill in life or at work. However, it is a question of intelligence whether people are capable of adjusting their behavior in such a way that they avoid the pitfalls in their behavioral profile.

In order to be able to talk about intelligence, it is important that we understand exactly what intelligence is. We should realize that intelligence and behavior are separate from each other. Two people can have exactly the same behavioral profile, but due to a difference in intelligence can fulfill completely different roles.

Often, intelligence is viewed as a competency in its own right. In reality, intelligence consists of a number of subdivisions that can each be developed in their own way. Intelligence is the capacity to solve problems. This problem solving can take place in four ways:

1   We need analytical intelligence for problems that require decomposition and abstraction. An engineer who wants to build a bridge needs this form of intelligence to determine the right spot for the underwater support pillars;
2   We need creative intelligence for problems that require originality or creativity. The inventor of a new, electrically driven vehicle with which we can drive as far and as comfortably as our current car needs this form of intelligence;
3   We need epistemic intelligence to solve problems that require specific knowledge. A vascular surgeon needs this form of intelligence when he finds more severely clogged vessels during open-heart surgery than he had previously estimated on the basis of the scan;
4   We need facilitating intelligence to combine the previous three intelligence areas. A pilot needs this form of intelligence during an emergency landing where he has to manage the cockpit staff, needs to keep the plane in the air, comfort the passengers, communicate with flight control and keep his own emotions under control.

1.4   Organizational performances

Individual behavior of employees, which is determined by behavioral profiles, plays a crucial role in achieving the organization's results. We define the performance of an organization as follows:

▶▶   *"The performance of an organization is the sum of all desired, but also undesired results, which were brought about by all efforts that were made pos-*

sible within the organization, with the resources that were employed for this purpose. Here, people, machines, materials, methods and management are referred to as resources."

The desired performances of an organization are all the results that add value to the product or the service for the customer. The customer is prepared to pay for this. All undesired performances are the gains that required effort, but that the customer does not really need and is not prepared to pay for. However, these undesired gains cost resources, without adding value. They belong to the category "waste".

Organizations should strive, as much as possible, to achieve only the results that add value and limit waste, or rather: eliminate waste. To be able to achieve only results that add value, the organization can follow the following steps:

1   First, the organization has to make sure that an individual employee knows exactly in which way he can influence the performances and how these performances add value;
2   Subsequently, the department or team in which the employee works also needs to know exactly what the team performance or department performance is and how the team or department can influence this performance. Here, primary activities that directly influence the performance level directly are most important. Secondary activities that have a less direct influence on the performance level (being on time, using a certain standardized work method) are also important, but do not have an immediate impact on the results;
3   Finally, it is necessary to define the goal values and behavioral standards in a clear way.

In performance behavior we distinguish between indicators, goal values, behavioral standards and the standard(s).

Indicators are used to monitor whether or not the organizational objectives will be achieved. These can be qualitative or quantitative. This can be illustrated with the example of an apple producer who monitors his organizational objectives. He could use the qualitative indicator 'quality of apples' for this. However, in addition to the qualitative indicator, the apple producer could also use a quantitative indicator such as production-efficiency. By monitoring these, and possibly more indicators, the apple producer is able to track its performance with regard to the organizational objectives.

Subsequently these indicators are used to derive clear goal values. With goal value we mean the specification of a certain value, for example for the indicator production-efficiency: a specific number of kilos per hectare of apple trees.

A behavioral standard, on the other hand, specifies a behavioral value. For instance, the standard for the value "being on time for a meeting" can be determined by the organization as: "being present at least two minutes before the start of the meeting".

Finally, we define the standard(s) as the standardized way in which work is performed by the employees at the different levels in the organization. In performance behavior the use of standards is fundamental to achieve a performance behavior organization in which continuous improvement is possible. To achieve this state the process of establishing, safeguarding, improving and renewing the standard(s) is critical. We elaborate on this topic further in chapter 2.

In the example of the packing machine, team leader Peter had a specific objective to pack a certain amount of products that day. One possible indicator to monitor the amount of packed products is the downtime of the packing machines. However, the organization has no predetermined specified goal value for the downtime of the packing machine. So Paul has no specific goal value he can work towards. Furthermore there is no standard in place which clarifies what Paul should do in case of downtime. Subsequently Paul starts to employ his own goal value and behavioral standard. He starts cleaning to achieve his own goal value: a tidy work environment. The way in which Paul determines his own goal value and behavioral standard stems from his frame of reference, his behavioral profile, his schemas and other external influences, such as the clutter around him. This usually happens subconsciously.

This example shows conflicting goal values and a lacking standard; employees will set their own goal value when an organization does not establish clear goal values that are derived from indicators that monitor the organizational objectives.

Other examples of conflicting goal values or behavioral standards are:

- The goal value with regard to the time customers have to wait until they are serviced is five minutes at a specific company. Yet, the customer service switchboard operator says to the customer: "You've only been waiting for 10 minutes? That's not so bad; they have staffed too few people today and other customers have had to wait much longer."
- The behavioral standard to pass for your driving license is that you may never drive through a red traffic light. Yet, a road user says after driving through

a red light : "But I was in a hurry, and there was no traffic"
- The goal value with regard to the number of customer complaints at a food manufacturer is zero. Yet, a manager who accounts for his performances is saying: "But isn't it logical that the customers' complaints will increase when we speed up production?"

These examples show that organizations need specific goal values and clear behavioral standards to be able to steer on result. However, many organizations state that they have clear goal values. They work towards "satisfied customers", "higher production" or "as few errors as possible". These goal values might seem very concrete but are, in fact, highly abstract.

In the example we used earlier, an apple producer can use the 'quality of apples' as an indicator for the organizational objectives. However, if the apple producer strives towards the goal value 'the highest quality' of apples, this is a very abstract goal value. This needs to be translated to a specific goal value. High-quality apples can be measured by the physical characteristics of the apple. This could be the number of deviating spots on the apple. So the specific goal value for the quality of apples should be: no deviating spots on the apple. This makes the goal value concrete. Additionally, a goal value should never be "the maximum achievement" even though this is what every manager strives for. The reason for this is that "the maximum achievement" is not a specific goal value. And when this goal value is not completely clear, how is it then possible to steer when there are deviations on the path towards the goal value? Right: it is not possible to steer in that case.

By clarifying each goal value on each level within the organization, we focus on achieving results. And hereby we prevent that a justification is given in hindsight when the results were not achieved. With "hindsight justification" there usually is a "very good reason" that is given for not achieving the desired result. However, there is always a good reason. People are great at explaining, in hindsight, why something went wrong or why something did not work out. But the key to maximizing the performances of organizations is not hindsight clarifications of failure. Organizations should create preconditions and success factors that allow all employees within the organization to proactively focus on an objective that is set by the organization. The employees should be familiar with these. Organizations should steer on deviations in advance instead of explaining the deviations in hindsight, irrespective of the reason for the deviation.

The reality is however, that in organizations, deviations are usually explained in hindsight and that the deviations are not steered upon in advance. This is caused by the following:

1   The explanation of the performance deviation is not compared to a specific goal value, but to a maximum achievable value (the value the manager has in mind) that can "always be higher". This results in a deviation that is insufficiently measurable, and without a specific deviation it is hard to relate possible solutions to the deviation;

2   The goal value is determined on the basis of a performance indicator that is used too high up in the organization. This means that the performance deviation derived from this goal value can't be explained at the lower levels of the organization. An example of this is the number of apples per barrel with a bad spot. The goal value that is derived from this indicator is not clear enough for the employee; how does this relate to his own production? Using goal values that are derived from indicators that are used too high up in the organization will always mean that the check on performance will take place with a lower frequency than the frequency at which the performance comes about. Due to this, it is only possible to explain deviations in hindsight and not to steer on these deviations during the process. A concrete indicator that could be used to derive a concrete goal value for the employee could be: "How many apples need to be checked per fifteen minutes". Now it is possible to steer on these checks and thus to influence the performance: the "number of bad apples per barrel".

Figure 1.6 visualizes cause 1. An imaginary, non-measurable goal value has been established as "maximum value"; as a result, no specific deviation is registered and no specific root cause can be established. Therefore, the only action that is taken is a corrective action; however, this only fights the symptoms.

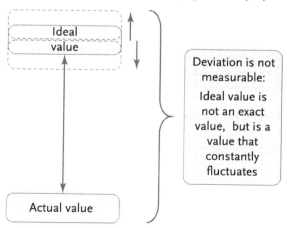

Figure 1.6 *Non-measurable deviation, because the goal value is an ideal value that continuously fluctuates*

Figure 1.7 visualizes the desired situation concerning the establishment of goal values. Here, the desired goal value is not "the highest achievable", but a specific goal value. With this specific goal value it is possible to measure the deviation exactly.

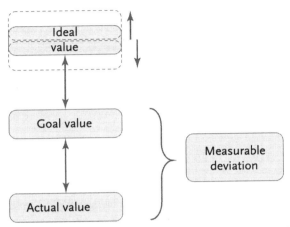

Figure 1.7 *A measurable deviation, because the goal value has a specific value*

Stretch causes development and therefore results

The fewer resources we need to achieve our objectives, the more efficiently we achieve the desired result. This is called result efficiency. Naturally, we strive for a result efficiency that is as high as possible. In theory, the maximum result efficiency is a situation in which we do not need any resources to achieve our objective: the objective is already reached at the moment we formulate it. When this happens, we have to increase our objective so tension arises between the goal and the resources to achieve this new objective. In performance behavior, this tension is called stretch. In this way, we ensure that the bar is raised every time and, within performance behavior, it forms the basis for our continuous improvement system. In this way, continuously creating tension within the organization leads to continuous development and increasing results.

When objectives and resources are balanced, people experience a comfortable state of mind. If the objectives are too high to be realized with the resources available, people who try to achieve these objectives can experience stress or a sense of panic because the objectives are not achievable.

When the goals are so easily reachable that not all available resources are needed, people immediately get the idea they can take it easy; they might sit back and this can eventually lead to boredom.

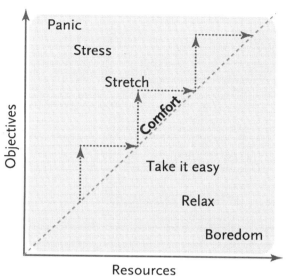

Figure 1.8 *Objectives-resources model*

With dotted lines, the objectives-resources model in figure 1.8 shows the growth of the organization when it continuously makes the step from a comfortable state to one of tension.

Organizations that set unrealistic objectives do not create stretch, but stress. This does not lead to increased productivity but instead to decreased productivity. In practice, people who experience stress either do nothing, because they cannot achieve their objective anyway, or become overworked, because they think they can achieve the objective but eventually find out they cannot.

Organizations that set their objectives too low and therefore offer no challenges eventually create boredom for their employees. In some instances, employees have resorted to vandalism and started to sabotage their work out of pure boredom. They had too little work to do and sought other distractions.

Setting the goal values

Goal values or behavioral standards can arise on the basis of the performances of comparable (other) organizations. We call these benchmarks.

There are different types of benchmarks that we can employ when establishing goal values or behavioral standards:

- The world-class performance behavior benchmark uses a specific organization as reference point. This organization is the best performing organization compared to a number of other organizations that are comparable in terms of process and size. We call this best in class;
- In competitive benchmarking, a comparison between immediate competitors takes place;
- In process benchmarking, the best performing part of a specific process component is investigated;
- In strategic benchmarking, we mainly look at the differentiating capacity with regard to the competition.

These benchmark methods are based on external goal values that are used in other organizations. Additionally, organizations can also establish internal goal values or make a comparison with the previous year's results. The latter, for example, is often used in retail, but in most organizations the goal values are determined on the basis of a budget and comparisons with other companies. Budgets are usually indirectly based on historic values, adjusted for inflations and prognoses.

Translation of objectives from top to bottom

Within each organization, many different goal values can be established and pursued for different indicators. These include goal values for the indicators of company profitability, the service level of bank employees, run time efficiency of products to be auctioned, and the number of beds per nurse per patient with a specific care status. When these goal values are established it is possible to work towards them, but they are valid at different hierarchical levels within the organization. At different hierarchical levels particular performances are monitored. In performance behavior we call these levels performance influencing levels. At the different influencing levels particular performances are measured and possible deviations from the goal value are steered upon at these levels. Chapter 2 elaborates further on this topic and the following examples illustrate the concept of different influencing levels:

In the company profitability example, goal values are established, measured and steered at the highest performance influencing level of the organization: the monitoring level. For the run time efficiency of products to be auctioned a goal value is established that is one level lower than the monitoring level. This is the steering level. And the established goal value for additional sales by clerks is measured and steered at the performance influencing level: the action level.

It is of vital importance that the objectives at the monitoring level are correctly translated into the objectives at the steering level and are subsequently translated from the steering level to the action level. Let us take a closer look at how the levels of monitoring, steering and action are related to the organizational objectives.

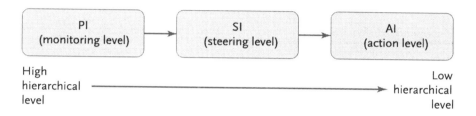

Figure 1.9 *Various performance influencing levels in an organization*

Figure 1.9 shows that the objectives, and the way there is steered towards these objectives, should be viewed within the context of the organization. The organization's mission, vision and strategy influence the model.

- *Mission* answers the question "Why is the organization here?"
- *Vision* answers the question "Where is the organization going?"
- *Strategy* answers the question "What will the organization do to realize its ambitions?"
- *Objectives* answer the question "How will the organization put its strategy into practice?"
- *Performance* indicators answer the question "Which measurement instruments and units make our objectives measurable?"
- *Steer* indicators answer the question "How do we measure the result of the actions that eventually influence the result of our objectives?"
- *Action* indicators answer the question "Which actions are needed to eventually steer our process?"

The organizational objectives are translated from general into specific objectives, until they eventually describe which actions bring about results. The indicators used for this are called performance indicators and the levels at which the performance is influenced are the performance influencing levels. The three performance influencing levels in performance behavior are the monitoring level, steering level and action level. These three levels match the known hierarchical levels; strategic level, tactical level and operational level. Figure 1.10 shows this.

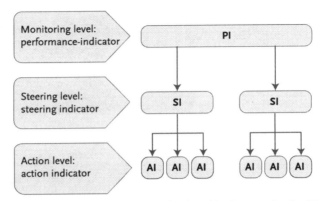

Figure 1.10 *The three performance influencing levels within the organization hierarchy*

Performance indicators are measurable aspects or activities that provide a clue, usually in relation to an established goal value, about the whole, or part of the quality and quantity of a company process. Here, the monitoring level of the performance indicators is the highest level within the organization or department. The steering level is the level at which performance indicators are influenced by the way that management steers and the action level is the level where performances are influenced by actions of employees.

Vertical alignment

Vertical alignment within organizations is necessary to align the objectives and the necessary resources with each other. This vertical alignment of the organizational goals takes place by means of a correct top-down translation of the monitoring level objectives into performance indicators (PIs). The most important performance indicators of an organization are often called the *key performance indicators* (KPIs). Subsequently, the (*key*) performance indicators are broken down into so-called *steer indicators* (SIs) for the middle management, at the steering level. Finally, the steer indicators are translated into action indicators (AIs). These action indicators are for performances at an individual level, at the action level.

The use of PIs and KPIs originated from the theory that performance indicators have to be taken from the organization's critical *success factors* (CSFs). CSF's are those factors at which the organization is already successful. The starting point of the CSF-theory is that when the success factors of the organization indicate the differentiating capacity of the organization, the translation of this differentiating capacity is the basis for achieving the right performance focus in the organization (De Waal, 2001).

> http://www.the-performance-factory.com/en/free-performance-library/performance-management-articles/

Horizontal alignment

Horizontal alignment of the organizational objectives refers to synchronization between the employees who operate on the same hierarchic level. When the goal values for the various employees working towards that value are not derived from the same indicator and are different from each other, it is possible they are working on conflicting objectives. This leads to a loss of effort which does not result in added value or profit and thus the organization is not using its full capacity.

Steer on performances

As mentioned before, all results that contribute to the organization will form the performances of the organization. The nature of these performances can differ, depending on the focus of the organization. The ability to shift the focus is an essential component of the flexibility of the organization; when the market or customer has an altered demand, this should lead to an immediate change in the way in which there will be steered on performance within the organization.

Summarizing, we distinguish the following performance objectives from high to low:

- (K)PI: (key) performance indicator;
- SI: steer indicator;
- AI: action indicator.

Figure 1.11 on page 41 shows these performance objectives in the performance behavior model.

The various levels indicate the distance to the primary process. The closer to the primary process, the more the performance indicators become action indicators. The larger the distance to the primary process, the more action indicators become steer indicators. Even "higher up" in the organization, we speak of (key) performance indicators.

The following overview gives examples of various types of organizations with examples of performance indicators at the monitoring, steering and action level.

Organization / Branch	(Key) performance indicator	Steer indicator	Action indicator
Hospital	Goal is to efficiently make use of the number of available beds	Duration of stay per patient or visitation hours per doctor per day	Number of checked standards during the visitation.
Packing company	Goal is to make as many packages per available time as compared to the established quality standard	Number of correct packages	Number of correctly performed quality checks per line per hour.
Local authority	Goal is to operate in as citizen-oriented a manner as possible	Run time licenses	Average application time per building permit
Production company	Goal is to make optimal use of the machine park	Product efficiency	Number of minutes of technical failures per hour
Gas station	Goal is to maximize the amount paid per customer	Extra turnover	Amount of additional sale in addition to fuel per customer
Nursing home	Goal is to make the residents as satisfied as possible	Residents Satisfaction	Food served at agreed temperature at the appointed time

Organization / Branch	(Key) performance indicator	Steer indicator	Action indicator
Contractor	Goal is delivery time and quality according to agreements	Run time of projects	Timely supply of building materials
Manufacturing	Reliability	Being prepared in a meeting	Showing (the quality of) the preparation before the meeting
Healthcare	Involvement	Asking a client how he is doing	Giving feedback twice a week about the reactions that are given as answers
Oil and Chemicals	Safety	Proactively checking the agreed standards	Giving feedback about the deviations that are measured in the standards; check and set out action to find root cause
Logistics	Flexibility	Keeping enough room in the agenda to resound on situations	Not saying more than twice a week 'saying no' to an additional question
Hospitality	Friendliness	Giving every customer a warm welcome	Minimum of 90% of the mystery shoppers receive the 'hello' welcome when entering the restaurant or shop

Table 1.1   *Examples of various types of organizations with examples of performance indicators at the monitoring, steering and action level*

The achievement of results starts in the primary process. After all, this is the lowest level where it is possible to directly influence the result of the organization. The higher the level at which is steered upon the primary process, the more indirect the result of that steering will be.

Change in the direction of the objective

There are a lot of different situations that can be the cause for improvement. Whether it is about the communication between team leader Peter and operator Paul about priority establishment, or about a new safety procedure that needs to be integrated in the work process of a nursing home to improve flawed communication between supervisors. It can all be a cause for improvement. Every implementation of change has a motive to improve something. However, in most organizations, improvement processes and trajectories are completely separate from daily performance. That is notable. We will elaborate on this topic in chapter 5.

Change means implementing a different course of action that is linked to a change in thinking. In order to change, you need to have an objective. After all, without an objective there is no direction and therefore no focus.

Nearly every management book incorporates the following fragment from Lewis Carroll's 'Alice in Wonderland' (1863), to illustrate the consequences of the lack of an objective:

▶▶   Alice: "Would you tell me, please, which way I ought to go from here?"
       Cat: That depends a good deal on where you want to get to."
       Alice: "I don't much care where."
       Cat: "Then it doesn't matter which way you go."

No matter how old and often cited this fragment is, it remains current and, especially, true. Because when you don't know where you want to go, it doesn't matter how you want to get there. It is as if you want to go on a holiday and you start searching for a nice destination in the travel guide once you are already on the plane. But if it is so logical that the objective determines the road, why do most companies fall prey to the pitfall of choosing a way without first determining where it leads? This happens both on an operational level, when a fast improvement action is carried out without investigating the actual root cause, and on strategic level, when policy choices are made without a matching business case.

From the point of view of change this means: when it is clear where you are now as an organization and you know what result you wish to achieve, you can subsequently determine which objectives and resources you need on the lower performance influencing levels in order to realize the chosen objective. After all, effective improvement is impossible without problem diagnosis and objective setting. "We'll try something and see where it goes" doesn't sound much like a structured improvement process. Therefore, the following chapters will pay attention to making a good diagnosis and subsequently pay attention to prepare appropriately for the change.

The questions "Where am I now?", "How do I reach my objective?" and "What resources do I need for this?" help to shape the change process. Figure 1.11 shows the performance behavior model, the *what & how* model, including the two levels in the steering and improvement process: performance and behavior.

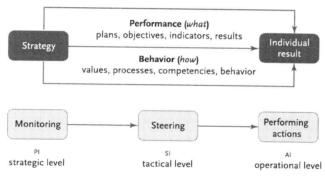

Figure 1.11 *Performance behavior model*

The performance behavior model has two main lines: the performance line that indicates what needs to be achieved, and the behavior line that makes concrete how that should happen. The performance line is mapped first: after all, the eventual objective is the result. Going through the performance behavior model in a structured way leads to the answer to the question many companies barely ask themselves: "What defined behavior do we, as organization, need to achieve specific defined results?" When we have mapped this in detail, we can also steer on it more specifically.

1.5   The performance component of performance behavior

The performance line – or the objectives and desired results you wish to achieve – is established by the organization by means of (measurable) criteria. The most important goal values for the organization are determined and subsequently translated into the three performance influencing levels (monitoring, steering and action). It is important to begin by translating the general organizational objectives into objectives at an increasingly lower level within the organization: the organizational objectives are translated into the objectives for employees via the department objectives. In this way, the strategy for employees isn't a vague and general plan that is established – and usually implemented – by the board, but comes alive by its direct translation into all underlying levels down to the individual employee.

When you wish to test if this translation has been carried out correctly, you can go through the reverse process: the sum of all individual results has to lead to the realization of the departmental objectives that were determined in advance. This sum of the department objectives logically leads to the achievement of the strategy of the organization.

As mentioned before, most organizations distinguish between the following three layers of management:

1   Strategic level (this is the monitoring level in terms of performance behavior);
2   Tactical level (this is the steering level in terms of performance behavior);
3   Operational level (this is the action level in terms of performance behavior).

The way in which this is approached in practice depends on the size of the organization. At multinationals, the middle management or tactical level consists of multiple layers that start with the level that could be a strategic level in a smaller organization. This could include the managers who work at various offices in various countries, the heads of department and the sub-layers of supervisors. The middle management of, for instance, a small hospital consists of the supervising layers immediately below the director, who is at the strategic level. The specific role (tactical, strategic or operational) a manager has in influencing the result strongly depends upon the level at which he operates. This differs greatly between large and smaller organizations, which might make comparing roles at different organizations difficult.

The strategic steering level – the highest hierarchic level of the organization – occupies itself with the questions "Which results do we want to achieve over the next three to five years, with which customers, in which markets?" It is expected of this organizational layer that an internal and external analysis is made and the direction the organization should follow is proactively determined. The strengths and weaknesses, together with possibilities and threats nurture the multiannual plan and the annual plans of the departments, the tactical level. An essential tool to determine if, and when the organization moves towards the right direction is the use of performance indicators. By measuring the various goal values of the performance indicators at the strategic level it is possible to monitor any progress.

The tactical level translates the strategic policy into the organization. It is their job to determine which factors are needed to perform the plans, and to assign people and resources to organizational units that have certain result expectations. This is measured in one or two years. Middle management shapes the tactical level. Middle management is expected to further translate the management's policy (determined at the strategic level) into SIs (steer indicators) and that they structurally solve operational problems. The core competence of the tactical level lies in creating or arranging structures and steering people so the organization functions smoothly.

The operational layer of the organization is responsible for the daily state of affairs. This layer has to actually perform the activities within the framework the tactical level has established. This layer often has positions such as team leader, chef, coordinator or team coach, but also production leader or foreman. This is to ensure that the group size remains easy to handle. At this level, plans are shorter than a year. The performance indicators are an essential tool for the operational layer in order to determine whether and when it moves in the right direction. These measure the various goal values at the action (operational) level.

This level also observes the activities performed by each employee to execute the department plan as spelled out in the chosen policy. This is expressed in personal goal values. There are organizations that don't work with personal goal values, but with team goal values.

Because different goal values of different indicators have to be realized at each organizational level, the activities at each of the three levels differ greatly. This is the reason that the specific goal values of the indicators – the performance objectives of the performance behavior model – also differ on each level.

Performance management

In order to add structure to the process of steering towards specific goal values at each level, a performance management structure is needed. Performance management is part of performance behavior. It is a process that focuses on deviations from the goal values at the performance influencing levels: from action indicators (at the 'real time' action level) to steer indicators (at the steering level) to performance indicators (at the monitoring level) as were worked out from the strategic objectives of the organization.

The performance management method is part of the PDCA-cycle of an organization (figure 1.12). PDCA stands for Plan, Do, Check, Act. This model is also known as the Deming Wheel. However, something important should precede the PDCA-cycle: determining an objective or specific goal value. Making a plan without an objective is like buying a travel guide without choosing a destination.

Determining the goal values for each performance influencing level is the starting point for performance behavior, because without a specific goal value you can't steer on the deviations that occur between the actual performance value and the goal value. This all begins with formulating the objectives over the long term. These long-term objectives have been drastically shortened in the past ten years because the life cycles of organizations now follow each other more rapidly. In the previous century, a long-term policy covered ten years; now most organizations are lucky when they can plan ahead for three years. Even though the terms have grown shorter, each organization still needs a long term policy as the basis for choices regarding objectives and resources.

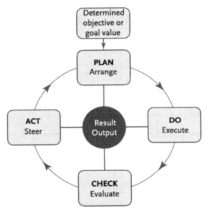

Figure 1.12 *Determining a goal value is part of the PDCA-cycle*

Translation to action indicators

Translating performance indicators into steer indicators and action indicators is not merely translating strategy into various performance influencing levels, but also aligning the various objectives with each other. The organization has to be able to understand the meaning of the strategy, to steer and to contribute to the objectives by means of performance management. The aim is to be able to indicate, at each level within the organization, what the specific contribution of each objective is to the strategic objectives of the organization. This is called a breakdown: breaking down objectives at the strategic level so that they work at even the deepest objective level. In performance behavior, we call this cascading objectives towards the action level. Compare it to the carnival attraction high striker (figure 1.13).

Figure 1.13 *High striker*

The high striker has three main components:

1   The pin you have to hit with the hammer;
2   The pole with the vertical scale;
3   The bell.

The person performing the behavior uses the hammer to hit the pin. Because of this, the cube flies up the pole. The scale starts at the bottom with "wimp" and ends at the top with "bruiser", and the maximum performance can be achieved when the cube hits the bell at the top of the pole. When the person with the hammer slams the pin, the effort is complete and it becomes a wait and see situation. How high will the cube go and will it or will it not eventually hit the bell?

When we make the comparison to an organization, the effort of the person with the hammer is the primary process, the positions of the scale are the steer indicators and the bell is the monitoring indicator for this action. However, an organization would like to know for sure if they are going to hit the bell – every time, every day, independent of the person who holds the hammer. However, in most organizations this is not guaranteed. They might think so and they certainly hope so, but they have not really secured it. This is exactly the objective of performance behavior. It answers the question "How do I ensure the behavior that leads to the desired performance?"

To answer this question, we will continue to use the metaphor of the high striker. What behavior is needed for the desired performance? We name a few elements:

- Lifting the hammer high enough;
- Standing right in front of the pin;
- Holding the hammer in the right way;
- Hitting the pin hard enough with the hammer;
- Checking if all parts are greased so the cube can move smoothly;
- Making the blow with the hammer correctly;
- The right position of the back and the head;
- Concentrating thoughts on reaching the objective;
- Checking if there is damage to the hammerhead;

And probably many more behavioral aspects that can influence the result.

Curious about the continuation? This example continues on page 51.

> Performance behavior translates the strategic objectives from the monitoring level into specific objectives at the steering and action level. This translation takes place within a secured performance management structure in which the behavior of employees – the behavior with which they achieve performance – is facilitated.

The way we make the results measurable is the most important aspect of performance management. Making the results measurable means that we can measure the actual values of a performance. If we can measure these, we can also compare and improve them. Additionally, we can set objectives and compare the actual values to the goal values. We can steer on a possible difference between the goal value and the actual value.

Financial prefixes have often been used as the basis for steering. Yet, from a contemporary perspective, this form of performance management does not provide the means to be able to steer on performance to make sure the organization is competitive within the market. The life cycles of products, services and also of organizations are becoming shorter. Buyers demand increasingly more and information technology is increasingly important in all sectors. Under such circumstances, the results from the past offer no guarantee for the future. Moreover, if the Credit Crisis of 2008 that hit both the United States and the European Union has taught us anything, it is that we need more than merely financial data.

In addition, we also observe a change in the way many organizations steer: previously, we looked at historic data, whereas nowadays we look at budgets and plans that are substantiated with a future view. With this, performance management became more than "measuring is knowing"; measuring with performance indicators is immediately placed within a broader perspective than one that is solely financial. In recent years values, behavior, responsibility and leadership have become key terms in response to the decline of both highly successful organizations and seemingly untouchable banks. Driven by stakeholders and focusing only on financial indicators, banks have gone bankrupt one by one.

Within performance management, the following rules apply to the translation of objectives:

1 Connections between the discussed strategic objectives and the action objectives have to be visible. Every objective needs to contribute to the strategy of the organization at every performance influencing level (monitoring, steering and action) and the connections between the objectives at different influencing levels can be derived from the strategic choices of the organization;
2 A correct and complete breakdown of each (key) performance indicators has to have been made: from (key) performance indicators at the monitoring level to steer indicators at the steering level to action indicators at the action level;
3 There has to be a connection between the (financial) performances and the behavior that brings about these performances.

The second principle is crucial to be able to influence the (key) performance indicators and to eventually achieve the objectives that are set at the strategic level. In organizations there are multiple (K)PI's that are monitored at the strategic level. To be able to influence these (K)PI's it is necessary to make a complete breakdown for every (K)PI. With this breakdown the organization determines which actions at the action level influence the (key) performance indicators and how these actions can be followed at the steering level with the help of steer indicators.

A high quality breakdown specifies the (K)PI, the underlying steer indicators and subsequently the action indicators that are followed by the steer indicators. Usually the breakdown is narrow at the top and widens towards the bottom as every indicator is influenced by multiple other indicators at the lower levels. Figure 1.10 illustrates this.

Besides an overview of the influencers of the (K)PI's, the breakdowns of every

(K)PI also show the structure that indicates how many indicators and which indicators should be discussed at each level in the organization (at the monitoring level, steering level and action level). Beacause the breakdown has a pyramid shape, the action level has the most indicators that need to be discussed, followed by the steering level. At this level indicators are discussed that are used to steer the action level. Finally at the monitoring level the few critical key performance indicators are discussed.

The third principle opts for further elaboration of the performance behavior model: the behavioral component.

1.6   The behavioral component of performance behavior

When the objectives of the performance component have been determined, the next step is to determine the objectives of the behavioral component. The performance component of the performance behavioral model is aimed at content; the behavioral component is aimed at development. Again, it is true that the way in which the translation takes place differs at every level. Therefore, we should take a close look at both the desired behavior at the lower levels of the organization, but also at the level of the collective values of the organization. All these levels should be aligned.

An illustration of the importance of this alignment is shown by the example of a big logistics organization. This specific organization had defined their core value as flexibility, while in fact their clients preferred reliability over flexibility. The core value has been communicated within the company for years, which led to the fact that only very few employees were actually working according to the standards because of the perceived need of flexibility. In this case there is a clear misfit between the behavior that is desired in the process and the behavior that is desirable from the perspective of the values of the organization. The organization had no emphasis on working according to the standards and was focused on flexibility, while the clients were demanding a reliable process in which the standards are safeguarded, the work planning has as little deviations as possible and the output is as reliable as possible.

After the misfit was identified by the organization a change initiative was started in which the desired behavior at the lower levels in the organization was redefined. Action indicators such as deviations in work planning, and variation in output were embedded in the daily work to increase reliability. Eight months into the change initiative a real contrast was visible compared to the starting situation. There was less deviation in planning, less variation in output, and almost all employees within the organization were now safeguarding the standard. These changes significantly increased the reliability of the process. More-over, this focus on reliability also had other positive side effects:

Because of the increased reliability there were fewer interruptions in the pro-cess. This resulted in the fact that there was more room to be flexible towards clients. So in the end, the identification of the misfit between desired behavior at the lower levels of the organization and the values of the organization led to a change initiative that made the supply chain more reliable, which led to a more commercially flexible organization.

To make sure that there will be a fit between the desired behavior at the lower levels of the organization and the values of the organization it is necessary to develop the behavioral component of the performance behavioral model of an organization (see figure 1.11 on page 41). This starts with defining the values of the organization at a strategic level. If an organization has no shared values, every individual brings his own values to the organization. The values which people recognize in themselves then become the values of the organization.

Naturally, every individual always brings his own values to work, but when the organization clearly and transparently presents its values, every individual can determine beforehand to what extent he recognizes these and can choose whether or not he wishes to conform to those values and whether or not he would like to work for the organization. Should he decide to work for the orga-nization, an organization can also expect of him that he will perform his work in conformity with these shared values. When there are no shared values within an organization, the bystander effect can occur: the larger the group of people, the less action the individual will display. Responsibility is then "divided" by the number of people present within a group. In various experiments, it has been shown that the presence of other people inhibits the willingness to act. The re-verse is also true: when less people are present, the larger the willingness to act.

In most cases, the experiments involve everyday situations: helping others in an emergency situation in which immediate action is sometimes necessary. The more bystanders, the longer it takes for anyone to help, since everyone thinks: "someone else will act". However, if you are alone and if you encounter an emergency situation, you will likely act sooner since there is no one else who can respond to the situation.

Another reason that people are passive in the presence of others lies in the fact that the actions of others serve as an example for us: since no one acts, action is apparently not necessary. In this case, it is also true that when the mass of the group increases, the measured effect is stronger.

As a final reason, it can be stated that people often think that another person will be able to do it better than them, and use this to justify to themselves that action is not necessary. The bystander effect is often phrased as follows: when everyone is responsible, no one is.

When the shared values within an organization are made explicit at the action level, there is more accordance with the action within the defined values.

The bystander effect explains why it is necessary to have clearly defined and explicit common values within an organization. But when common values are defined within an organization, employees often do not act upon them or do not act upon them in the right way. This occurs due to the fact that many organizations fail to translate the values of the organization into the desired behavior belonging to these values. If this translation does not occur, people logically provide their own interpretation of the behavior that, according to them, belongs to the values, based on their own mental representations (see paragraph 1.1).

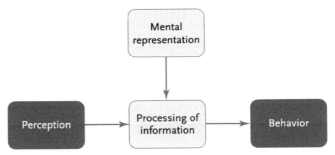

Figure 1.14 *From perception to behavior*

Let's return to the behavioral component of the performance behavior model. At the monitoring level, the top-management has to determine what the values are that it would like to use to achieve the objectives. Values indicate what an organization would like to disseminate in the social and societal field: the ideals and motives that an organization pursues. The behavioral standards that result from the values are the guidelines for actions that influence daily social communication within the organization. This adds substance to the values.

At the steering level, behavioral standards are translated into competencies: what should the employees know, be able to do and what attitude is desired to achieve the specific goal values that are established in the performance component of the performance behavior model? Subsequently, the behavior that individual employees show has to be measurable, so it can be determined whether or not they meet the desired behavior. To be able to measure this, it is necessary to create behavioral criteria that describe, at the action level, which specific behavior is needed to achieve a specific performance.

The next step is to evaluate, on a person-to-person basis, to what extent current knowledge, attitudes and competencies are sufficient to perform the work. The gap between the current and required knowledge, competencies and attitudes is equal to the personal development that the employee will have to go through to be able to contribute to the result of the organization.

A link between the performance objectives and the behavioral objectives exists in every performance influencing level of the organization. For the monitoring level, the (key) performance indicators for the yearly plans have to be brought into agreement with the values and the behavioral standards that have been established. For the steering level, the competencies have to be linked to the steer indicators. For the action level, the behavioral criteria are linked to the action indicators.

The example of the high striker on page 45 continues here. We hit the pin with the hammer at random and hope for the desired performance. By measuring the various behavioral aspects of this effort, we should be able to discover why this behavior does not result in achieving the desired performance. For example: when the cause lies in the physical inability of the person to correctly swing the hammer, we can focus on the development of his muscle strength. However, before we can discover the causes, we first have to determine which behavioral aspects we can measure. We map the behavior via observation and then name the most important influencers. The three main influences are:

1   Position in front of the pin;
2   Swinging in combination with physical strength;
3   Holding the hammer.

However, we would like to be able to influence behavior before performance is achieved. Therefore, in this case, we will place a camera near the person and a screen next to the pin so the individual can see both the pin he has to hit and the screen. Moreover, we store all the footage, so we can analyze a behavioral pattern for how the person swings the hammer. On the screen, he can see his own position and through the screen he receives a direct warning if he does not hit correctly. Also, when the swing is not in conformity with the specification, he receives a direct signal through the screen and when he does not hold the hammer correctly, he will hear a whistling signal.

In this (imaginary) example, we now have:

- Named action indicators;
- Made a feedback system through which the individual receives feedback about his behavior;
- Collected information about the number of strikes, the different people and their specific development points regarding behavior.

This leads to hitting the pin better and more often, meaning the bell rings more often. In short: it leads to better performance.

We can go even further and evaluate the standards that are in place (how frequently and in which way does the hammerhead have to be checked?) or observe the training schedule at the gym in order to increase physical strength. These are all interventions that we can only employ when we have set an objective, when we have measured that the current value deviates from the goal value and when we have identified what the root cause for this deviation is.

In short, it is very important that strategy is translated into objectives and results, both on a departmental level and on an individual level. Moreover, a plan has to be made to achieve those results. In this way, it becomes possible to make employees personally responsible for achieving their own objectives and the objectives of the organization.

Attribution and stimulating desired behavior

Behavior occurs within context. Someone who performs his actions exactly in conformity with the behavioral standard, but is distracted at the exact moment he has to hit, will probably not achieve the desired result. The cause of not achieving the desired result can be found within the person itself, but also within the context. This raises the question: is performance and failure always attributed to the right person or cause?

We can explain our own behavior by looking at ourselves ("I have tidied up my work space because I thought it was the right decision") or at the world around us ("I display this behavior because I was encouraged by my colleague"). The first is called *internal attribution*, the second is called *external attribution*. However, this division does not always work; we often make attribution errors. We attribute "good" behavior to ourselves, whereas we attribute faulty behavior to others. Conversely, we have a tendency to attribute faulty behavior of others to their "character", whereas we attribute good behavior of others to situational factors.

The attribution error is less common in performance behavior. When performance is measurable and concrete and the link with behavior is made explicit, as happens with performance behavior, the achieved performance can clearly be attributed to one's own actions.

Correct and specific feedback of behavior in relation to the achieved performance of employees is one of the anchors within the system of performance behavior. First, the manager attributes the right behavior to someone. This means that he establishes the specific behavior this person has displayed that has actually led to the achieved performance. Subsequently, he validates the attributed behavior by indicating that the displayed behavior is the desired behavior (stimulating). Attributing behavior in combination with stimulating desired behavior, as close to the moment the behavior occurs as possible, is the most effective way to validate desired behavior and to secure it in your organization.

1.7   Steering and accountability of behavior and performance

Achieving a performance is related to the behavior that brings about the performance. When we wish to influence the performance (read: increase), we will have to specify both the performance and the behavior that brings about the performance at the right level. The next step is to account for the delivered performance and for possible deviations from the goal value. In the final step, the desired behavior is rewarded so the behavior that brought about the performance is stimulated. This results in the following steps within performance behavior:

Step 1   Specify the performance and the behavior that is needed to achieve the performance.
Step 2   Set up a system for the accountability of the performance results, so that it is possible to steer on the deviations from the goal value of the performance. Here, the frequency of the performance measurement (the number of times the performance measurement should be executed within a certain time) has to be aligned with the behavior frequency (how often the behavior is displayed to arrive at the performance).
Step 3   Confirm desired performances and behavior and steer undesired performances and behavior: correctively and preventively.

When this happens at every performance influencing level within the organization, this is called a secured steering and accountability structure.

This is shown in figure 1.15:

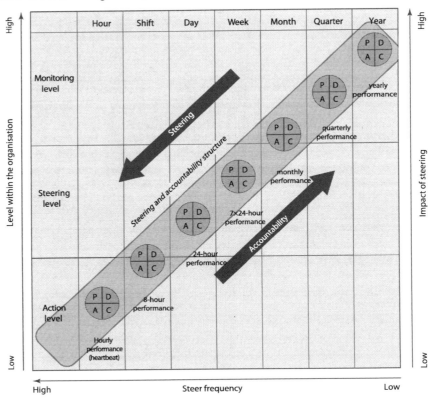

Figure 1.15 *Secured steering and accountability moments in a secured PDCA-cascading top-down and bottom-up*

The performance frequency at the action level is higher than at the monitoring level. However, the impact of the result at the monitoring level is larger than at the action level.

Goal values and the actual performance values are looped back in the appropriate frequency: the closer to the primary process, the more often the goal and performance values will be looped back. The further away from the primary process, the less frequent.

In order to steer performance in combination with behavior, a system within the organization is needed which steers behaviors in such a way that the results are actually achieved. The foundation of this system is safeguarding the established standard(s), where the result is accounted for and deviations from the goal values are addressed. This is the topic of the next chapter.

2

SAFEGUARDING THE STANDARD: STEER AND ACCOUNT

In performance behavior, at the level of safeguarding the standard, steering and accounting is the method that is used to account for results and to steer on deviations from the set goal values. This chapter elaborates on the steps that must be taken to allow steering and accountability to take place in your organization. For each step will be explained what the goal of this step is and how it contributes to safeguard and steer on the performance behavior standard.

2.1   Safeguarding the standard in five routine steps

Standards

Safeguarding the standard is a crucial activity in the realization of the strategy. In order to achieve this we work with the three steering levels mentioned earlier: strategic/monitoring, tactical/steering and operational/acting. Without standards, it is impossible to steer. A standard has to be in place and the work within the organization has to meet this standard. An organization can only start improving a standard when it has and safeguards a standard. However, all too often, companies begin work on improvement while no standard exists. How can you build a house and decorate the rooms if there is not yet a foundation?

> In practice it appears that more than 80% of organizations currently are not ready for continuous improvement, as the level of safeguarding the standard within their organization is for less than 20% in place.

Both the word safeguard and the word standard often evoke resistance in organizations. People have the tendency to think they know what is best for them. This makes it especially hard to make sure that standards are followed. Standards also evoke resistance because they ensure that both qualitative and quantitative measurements are possible, through which organizations can obtain information about both the performance and the behavioral component. Many employees experience this as threatening. They think that employing standards equals working harder, or producing more, or performing the same work with less support. However, this fear is unfounded. The top down transparency in objectives and behavior brings about a more efficient management, which results in an increased competitive advantage, even in the short term. The alleged threat actually provides more security for employees in the long term.

The standards in an organization are extracted from the knowledge and experiences of employees who have contributed to the result: how did the result come about, what went well? These methods are clustered and recorded so everyone can apply them in the same way; everyone profits from the best idea, the best method. The more an organization works in conformity with the standards, the more there is a general routine, the larger the predictability of the work process and therefore also the results. And what do organizations want? A predictable and reliable process so they can meet the customer's wishes as much as possible with as little waste – costs the customer doesn't want to pay for – as possible.

Standards bring about a work environment in which the starting point is to work in the most efficient and safe way. Additionally, the standards offer the possibility for improvement. This makes the organization more efficiently equipped to serve the customer. After all, the customer wants the highest quality for the lowest possible price. In the most optimal situation, an organization that safeguards the standards adds pure value to the product without any waste.

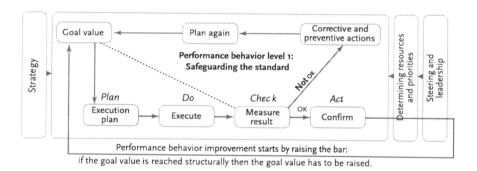

Figure 2.1 *Performance behavior cycle on the level of safeguarding the standard*

Continuous improvement: safeguarding, improving or renewing the standard?

Before we elaborate further on safeguarding the standard, we will discuss how safeguarding the standard relates to improving and renewing the standard:

Safeguarding the standard means that we check whether the work is performed in conformity with the standard and whether the objectives are achieved. We intervene in case of deviations.

We often have to mark time as part of safeguarding the standard, before we can actually safeguard the standard. We first have to establish and implement the standard. In performance behavior, this step is considered part of safeguarding the standard, but in practice this is sometimes a separate first phase, because the standards are completely absent.

We improve the standard when the current standard doesn't suffice in order to achieve a specific objective. Then, we adjust a procedure, using the current procedure as the basis, and this adjusted procedure becomes the improved standard.

We renew the standard when the current standard is useless in achieving a specific goal. A completely new standard is needed.

When Porsche AG, the famous German car manufacturer, implemented the lean-method in 1991 (which we will revisit in chapters 5 and 7), the company first scrutinized the delivery of parts by suppliers. By 1997, they had reduced the number of parts with errors by 90%. The level safeguarding the standard was under control, since Porsche was able to deliver the parts according to the agreed-upon specification. Subsequently, they found that the standards that had to ensure that all internal processes were performed first time right were now open to improvement. The many projects that worked on improving the standard resulted in a reduction of internal errors by 55% in a period of five years. Finally, Porsche wanted to drastically shorten the run time from part to new car from six weeks to less than a week. This required a completely new design of the value stream. This process, which took more than six years, eventually lead to a total process run time of three days between the order of the customer and delivering a custom-made Porsche. They realized a reduction of the runtime of no less than 93%.

This example illustrates how an organization sets the improvement process in motion by first implementing the level of safeguarding the current standards. When this level is in place sufficiently an organization is able to improve the standards in a structured way and is finally able to develop new standards that are needed to make a huge improvement leap: bridging the gap between the current state and future state.

There is a natural path that leads from safeguarding the standard to improving the standard to renewing the standard. Organizations that follow this path continuously improve themselves. But it can also be necessary to improve or renew the standard when new objectives are established that require another standard.

Plan, Do, Check and Act as operational cycle

The PDCA-cycle is the process cycle that became famous due to William Edwards Deming, who caused a frenzy during World War II with his product optimization methods. The PDCA-cycle consists of the following steps:

- *Plan*: establish a plan for the change you wish to bring about;
- *Do*: execute the established plan;
- *Check*: measure the results of the plan;
- *Act*: adjust the results on the basis of the deviations found in the measurement. (And continue with the plan when an adjustment should take place).

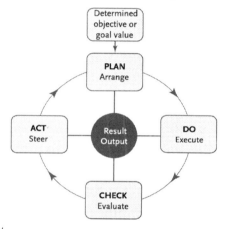

Figure 2.2 *PDCA-cycle*

This PDCA-cycle is still used often, but dates back to a period in which Ford only made black TFords and Ford was the only mass producer of cars. In this period of industrialization, people mainly focused on efficiency. The statistician Dr. Deming provided the basis for measuring performance. He was also one of the first to acknowledge the importance of the right competencies for the right tasks. However, we should place his work in context before using it in performance behavior.

First, Deming introduced the model as a process-modeling instrument at the monitoring level, while the model is now also used at the action level to ensure improvements are put into action. But, according to the performance behavior philosophy, the most important first step is missing: determining the goal value.

Secondly, the commitment model of, among others, Winograd and Flored caught up with the PDCA-cycle as a process-modeling instrument. The interaction between "customer" and "supplier" is important here. In this model, the supplier is the system that is operated while the customer is the operating system. The latter matches better with the pull-method, which is used within the lean-philosophy: the customer as operating system "pulls" the demand of the supplier in the value stream.

Therefore, we use a modern version of the PDCA-cycle within performance behavior. This cycle is not used only at the first level of performance behavior, safeguarding the standard, but also at the other levels: improving and renewing the standard.

> A winner has a plan. A loser has an excuse

The starting point for safeguarding the standard within an organization is the objective to be achieved. When the objectives are achieved and there is no difference between the goal and the measured value, there is no reason for action since there is no deviation. The initial improvement impulse arises from the deviation between the goal and the current value. When the standards are in place and the current value meets the goal value, the goal value can be increased. When you set a higher goal value, a deviation between the current value and goal value immediately arises. The next step is that the organization investigates what causes the difference between the goal value and the measured value. In terms of improvement: what is stopping us from achieving the new goal value? When that has been determined, the organization can take action.

PRSS: Performance deviation, Root cause, Solutions, Specific improvement objective

The PDCA-cycle is intended to implement change, to measure whether this change achieves the desired results and, if necessary, to be able to steer But when the measured results deviate from the desired results, what is the right intervention? In order to determine this, you can use the PRSS-steps. PRSS stands for:

- *Performance deviation*
  The deviation, the difference between the current value and the goal value.
- *Root cause*
  What actually caused the deviation? How often and where?

- Solution

  All possible solutions can only be mapped when the root cause has been found. These include, at the level of safeguarding the standard, both corrective actions that can be performed directly and preventive actions that have to ensure the deviation doesn't occur again. The best solution will be selected.

- *Specific improvement objective*

  The specific improvement goal will be determined when the root causes have been found. This makes explicit which improvement is desired. Since in most cases the deviation between the current value and the goal value cannot be bridged at once because there are multiple root causes, the improvement objective is a (small) part of bridging the total gap between the current value and goal value. By determining a specific improvement objective in this step, measuring whether (part of) the gap has actually been bridged can be done more accurately.

When the improvement objective has been determined, the PDCA-cycle starts and the plan is established.

A plan could include a major report with a time line and resources, but for safeguarding the standard this is usually not necessary. A short and concise plan concerning a specific objective is usually sufficient, especially for preventive actions, so it is possible to measure whether the preventive action actually had the desired effect afterwards. This plan also includes the (run)time and required resources. In 95% of all cases, the plan can be summarized on half a sheet of paper.

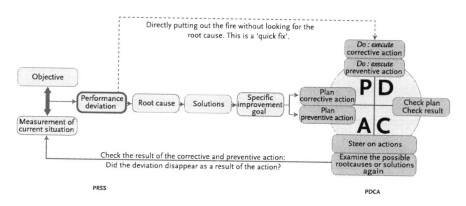

Figure 2.3 *PRSS-steps and PDCA-cycle form the PRSS-PDCA-cycle together*

Figure 2.3 pictures the combination of the PDCA-cycle and the PRSS-cycle.

Deviations: a significant deviation or not?

In performance behavior the PRSS-PDCA-cycle is used to reach a specific improvement goal or a specific goal value. When the current value is different from the goal value there is a performance deviation that needs to be addressed in order to reach the goal value. However, it is important to assess whether a deviation is significant or not to be able to decide whether action is needed. When a deviation is not significant and action is undertaken this could mean that resources are wasted and potentially even that the deviation gets bigger.

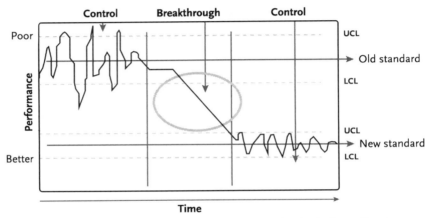

Figure 2.4 *A control chart that depicts performance at the levels of safeguarding the standard on the left, and renewing the standard on the right*

To assess deviations, the notion of control and breakthrough in the context of change that is described in Juran's book 'Managerial Breakthrough: The classic book on improving management performance' is useful. Juran defines breakthrough as 'dynamic change'. Contrary to this situation of breakthrough Juran describes a situation of control, which he defines as a "lack of change; and maintaining the status quo". These two situations can be linked to the different performance behavior levels in which the situation of control corresponds to the level of safeguarding the standard, and the situation of breakthrough corresponds to renewing the standard. Juran describes that the situations of breakthrough and control are mutually exclusive; it is impossible that both situations occur at the same time.

In performance behavior we always start at the level of safeguarding the standard, or in Juran's terms: in a situation of control. This situation can be best understood with the help of control charts to be able to assess any possible deviations. A control chart is a tool that shows the process variation around the average process performance. This tool can be used to separate 'natural' variation from variation that results from a 'special' cause.

On the left hand side of figure 2.4 we see the situation at the level of safeguarding the standard (Juran's controlled situation). The figure shows that in this situation the current performance is moving in an area around the goal value of the 'old standard'. So, basically it happens often that a deviation occurs. However, is it also necessary to act on all of these deviations? The control chart is the tool that has the answer to that question: If the process variation is within the bandwidth of the upper and lower control limit (UCL and LCL), than the variation should be interpreted as 'normal' variation. If you are going to act on a deviation that is between the control limits than 'acting' is going to be a disturbance in itself. This disturbance will lead to a bigger deviation and thus to a bigger performance gap. So only when the deviation lies outside the upper or lower control limit it is required to act upon this deviation.

Figure 2.4 shows that control and breakthrough are part of an improvement system. At first there is a controlled situation in which the standard is safeguarded and a specific goal value is attained. Subsequently the goal value is raised which requires change to be able to attain this new goal value. This situation of breakthrough, in which changes are undertaken to improve performance, corresponds to the performance behavior level of renewing the standard. After this breakthrough is realized by change, a new situation of control is established in which the standard is being safeguarded again. However, this new situation of control now has achieved performance on a much higher level that conforms to the new standard.

Although the two situations of control and breakthrough initially may appear to contradict each other, it shows that when they are used in a subsequent way they become a basic roadmap for improvement of performance.

Management and operator controllable errors

The insights from Juran can also become useful when we want to analyze the reasons that underlie the deviations in performance. His division between 'management-controllable errors' and 'operator-controllable errors' contributes to this analysis.

Juran considers defects and deviations to be 'operator-controllable' if workers have working arrangements that enable them to meet quality standards. This means the operators must have:

1   A means of knowing what is expected of them;
2   A means of knowing what their actual performance is;
3   The means for regulating their output, to reach conformance.

If any of these criteria have not been met, Juran concludes that management's job is not complete, and the resulting defects and deviations are "management-controllable". In practice, the general belief among managers is that most of the defects and deviations are operator-controllable. However, Juran's research (and that of others) shows that over 80% of the defects are management controllable errors and that fewer than 20% of the defects are operator controllable.

So when an organization is involved in improving its performance and reducing its errors and deviations, and it finds that the defects lie within the domain of management-controllable errors, then the subsequent diagnosis should involve the examination of the system; the processes, the methods, the policies, the equipment, the materials - the things that only management can change.

Regarding this distribution of operator-controllable and management-controllable errors, Deming said: 'I should estimate that in my experience most trouble and most possibilities for improvement add up to proportions something like this: 94% belong to the system (responsibility of management) and 6% to the people who work within the system.'[1] He later even revised these figures to 98% and 2%. This is a semantic discussion: if the system fails, than the operator will not use all the tools that are able to help him within the system. Human failure is almost (I agree with the 98% of Juran on this one) always a symptom of system failure. We have to design a system that works like a custom-made suit. Some people will more like the metaphor of the armor, but the message is: If you want to create desired behavior, the foundation is a system that leads the way.

Juran states that "If the managers have met the criteria, then the means for doing good work are clearly within the hands of the operators." So why isn't this always the case? Juran dismisses the "Zero defects movement" as a fallacy that assumes that all human error could be abolished if proper motivation is applied. For instance, golfers don't always hit par, but no one (I assume) could accuse them of lacking motivation. We see this is the theory of TWI (which will

---

1   *Page 315 of 'Out of the crisis' by Deming, E.W.*

be discussed in section 2.6): it is not the instructed, but the instructor who can be blamed when the instruction failed. Juran differentiates between the following Operator-Controllable errors:

1 Inadvertent errors;
2 Technique errors;
3 Willful errors.

Sub 1 Inadvertent errors come from workers' inability to maintain attention. The errors are unintentional, unwitting, and unpredictable (they exhibit randomness). The bulk of remedies lay in getting the system 'poka yoke'.

Sub 2 Technique errors arise because the worker lacks some essential technique, skill, or knowledge needed to prevent the error from happening. They are typically unintentional, specific, consistent, and unavoidable. Remedies here often require the discovery (using the diagnostic techniques) of differences of technique which represent the beneficial "knack" that produces superior results, and then training others or changing the process to embody the better method. With both inadvertent errors and technique errors, usually workers cannot find the reasons for defects themselves, and therefore they will keep on doing what they have been doing. Hence they will keep on producing defects. This will go on until they get the help they need from management.

Sub 3 Willful errors are witting, intentional, and persistent. Juran says that some will come from anti-social elements whose actions will not be defended even by fellow employees and unions. Even so, many seemingly willful errors are still the fault of management; e.g. shifting priorities of delivery versus quality; workers hiding scrap because managers are using scrap figures to blame; posting production scores and not quality scores; shipping non-conforming products even after quarantining; exhortation campaigns causing cynicism. Thus, apart from the "anti-social category" mentioned above, Juran's remedies here again have to do with the management of the system and the style of leadership. So even for Operator-Controllable errors, improvement will only come from management working on the system. (Nigel Clements, 2010)[2]

To conclude this subsection on deviations, it is important to assess whether a deviation is within the statistical controlled bandwidth of the upper and lower control limit. Only if the deviation is outside this bandwidth action should be undertaken. When, for example, an operator still takes action (within the oper-

---

2 prism-nigel.blogspot.com

ator controllable area) while there is a statistical controlled situation than the deviation will get out of control because of this action that is undertaken. Action should only be taken when the measured deviation is above or below the control limit of the control chart. Furthermore, it is important to assess whether the (statistical significant) deviation can be attributed to the operator-controllable area or the management-controllable area to be able to make the appropriate interventions to solve the deviation.

The five steps for safeguarding the daily standard

Back to the five steps in the performance behavioral cycle at the level of safeguarding the standard (figure 2.1 on page 59).

Step 1   Get the (improvement) objective focused
Make the objective SMART (Specific, Measurable, Acceptable, Realistic, Time-specific), ensuring that the goal value causes some stretch for the person who wants to achieve it.

Step 2   Establish an execution plan that includes all standards
After all, without standards you can't steer. Further on in this chapter, we explain which standards you can specifically apply.

Step 3   Execute the plan in accordance with the standards
The daily work should consist of executing the plan in accordance with the established standards.

Step 4   Measure the result
Measure the results on all levels (monitoring, steering and action level).

Step 5   Confirm the result when the result is equal to the objective (or specific improvement objective as part of the goal value), and steer using the PRSS-PDCA-cycle when the result deviates from the goal value.
When the result is achieved: celebrate the success and raise the bar a little to create stretch. You now have arrived at step 1 again.

When the result is not equal to the goal value, it is necessary to steer. In this case, corrective or preventive action has to be taken. When a corrective action suffices, the action remains on the level of safeguarding the standard. However, when a preventive action is required, due to a recurrent problem, a more thorough analysis is needed. This automatically brings you to the level of standard improvement: part of the preventive action will be at the level of safeguarding the standard, but in practice, action is also necessary to improve the standard. An example can help to clarify this.

An employee at an external cleaning company wants to enter a company building to clean it, but his access pass fails. This happens during a holiday. Someone has to leave home to go to the office specifically to let the employee in and deactivate the alarm. This is a corrective action.

A preventive action at the level of safeguarding the standard also exists: the checklist that had to ensure that the access pass worked before it was handed to the external cleaner was not used. It was decided to include the use of the checklist as an indicator in the steering and accountability moment of the IT-department (see figure 1.15 on page 77). This guarantees the standard (the checklist) at the action level.

But preventive action is also needed at the level of standard improvement. How is it possible that the pass didn't work? Apparently, the current standard stipulating that the pass has to be checked is not sufficiently secured. Further analysis shows that it hasn't been determined who is responsible for checking the passes in case of an employee's illness. Moreover, passes are not checked when issued; people simply assume that the IT-department has programmed the passes correctly. This is eventually discovered as the root cause. One of the passes hadn't been programmed correctly causing the employee to be refused entrance. This was the result of an experienced IT-employee's sloppiness. Eventually, the standard check performed at the IT-department has been improved, which excludes the chance of repetition. This is a preventive action on the standard improvement level.

In this way, smaller PDCA-cycles can be found within each PDCA-cycle which ensure that the actions performed at the lower level are checked by the higher levels. That is why the example of the access pass includes both content-related actions, such as correctly programming the passes, and process actions: why didn't the procedure work, or why wasn't the check performed? Ultimately, it is critically important that the check of the action takes place at the level immediately above it (action, steering and monitoring) and that the organization responds correctly in order to achieve the established goal values, namely via the PRSS-PDCA-cycle.

The five steps are explained in further detail in the following sections.

2.2   Step 1 Get the (improvement) objective focused

The result of step 1 is a crystal-clear objective. In the PRSS-PDCA-cycle, this is the step that follows after the solutions have been mapped. The sharper, clearer, and more measurable the objective, the greater the chance is to achieve this objective. The vaguer the descriptions are of the objective to be met, the less concrete the gain. This sounds simple, but in practice it proves to be harder.

Establishing an objective is difficult because we often feel we have formulated the objective concretely, while this is actually not the case. A critical (self) test is a good tool to focus the objective as much as possible. The best-known tool to set an objective is the SMART principle. SMART stands for Specific, Measurable, Acceptable, Realistic and Time-specific. When the objective meets each of these five criteria, it is concrete enough.

When determining objectives, two areas have to be formulated as specifically as possible:

- *Performance objectives*
  What is the exact goal value we wish to measure so we can measure the gain and adjust the goal value if necessary? The goal value and the steer indicators within the performance behavior concept, ensure that it is possible to steer on the performance deviations.
- *Behavior objectives*
  What behavior is needed to achieve the objective? In the performance behavior concept it is necessary to steer when the actual behavior deviates from the desired behavior. This desired behavior is made concrete by setting specific behavioral standards.

When translating the performance and behavior objectives at an organizational level into the individual objectives, long cycle, low frequency objectives are often used by organizations as the starting point. For example, an increase of the turnover by 10% in the next year. However, the behavior that is needed to achieve this objective has a short cycle and is performed at a high frequency. Think of a telephone operator, for instance: she has conversations of a few minutes (short cycle) and does that many times a day (high frequency).

A translation from long cycle, low frequency objectives into short cycle, high frequency objectives is needed, because this increases the chance of actually achieving the result, if however the objective is formulated clearly.

Most professional sportsmen have a clear objective and visualize it in order to be able to work towards this as efficiently and effectively as possible. For example, they imagine how they skate the 10 kilometer race in 12.49 minutes and how they come across the finish-line. They also imagine the feelings that accompany winning. Their imagination is life-like, with moving images in color and sound. Some even feel the cold air on their face. From this clear visualization, they subsequently reason: "What do I have to do to win?" The big objective is chopped up into smaller pieces (lap times, start, movements) until it is clear what has to happen each week and even each day in order to achieve the objective. Sven

Kramer had a video of his best race on his phone. In the week before he had to skate that same distance again, he watched it regularly to see and experience what a race, in which everything goes perfectly and in which all actions that influence the result are under control, looks like.

An objective is the same as the means or resources. This might sound odd, since means or resources are used to achieve an objective. Yet, this statement is true: it depends on the level at which you view the objective. For many company shareholders, it is important to create shareholder value in the short and long term. In order to achieve this, the management works with a strategic plan. The objectives in this strategic plan are the most important objectives for the employees of the company, while for the shareholders these are merely the means to make more money, in the short and long term, than they would receive if they put their money in the bank. The efforts the employees perform are only means for the management to achieve their more important objective, the right execution of the strategic plan. In this way, we can subdivide objectives, resources and efforts and evaluate them differently at each level.

When formulating a crystal-clear objective and safeguarding the standard, we can look at three levels:

1   The objective itself;
2   The necessary behavior (the effort);
3   The available resources.

The objective itself is the performance objective, while the necessary efforts are equal to the behavioral objective.

Subsequently, we can test the three levels of the objective by using the following criteria, which partly overlap with the SMART-principle but extricate the performance and behavior components more specifically:

- Performance-oriented;
- Behavior-oriented;
- Pace;
- Feasibility;
- Efficiency;
- Flexibility.[3]

Table 2.1 shows the steering model that arises by linking these criteria to the

3   *Van der Talk & Wijnen (2006).*

various objective levels.

In order to measure performances at each level, the organization will have to make a breakdown from the monitoring indicators (KPIs on the monitoring level) to steer indicators (SIs) for the middle management (steering level) and finally to action indicators (AIs) at the lowest level, the action level. Subsequently, the standards that have to be followed need to be established at those same levels.

It is often the case that the KPIs are known within the organization, but that individual employees have no idea how to (positively) influence the result at their own level, via their own activities. Therefore, the KPIs have to be translated (cascaded) into the activities of all underlying levels. Does an operator working with a machine know what his goal value is for the number of kilograms he has to produce per hour? Does a data-typist know how many words per hour she has to type? Does a mechanic know how long he can take to solve a failure before he should call an expert? And when this standard is known, do the operator, data-typist and mechanic know which steps to take when they deviate from the standard?

Criterion	Performance-oriented	Behavior-oriented	Speed	Feasibility	Efficiency	Flexibility
Goal	Does the goal contribute to the achievement of the desired performance?	Does the goal contribute to the achievement of the desired behavior?	Are the goals realized within the time set for it?	Are the goals feasible?	What value do the goals add with regard to the effort?	Can the goals be adjusted?
Effort	Does the effort contribute sufficiently to the achievement of the desired performance?	Does the effort contribute sufficiently to the achievement of the desired behavior?	Are the efforts realized within the time set for it?	Are the efforts feasible?	How profitable are the efforts?	Can the efforts be adjusted?

Criterion	Performance-oriented	Behavior-oriented	Speed	Feasibility	Efficiency	Flexibility
Re-sources	Do the resources sufficiently contribute to achieving the performance?	Do the resources sufficiently contribute to achieving the desired behavior?	Are the resources available in time?	Are the resources available?	Do the resources require many sacrifices?	Can the resources be allocated?

Table 2.1   *Model for steering at the three goal levels*

2.3   Step 2 Establish an execution plan that includes all standards

The result of step 2 is a practical execution plan in which objectives and resources have been placed within a certain time frame. This is the corrective and preventive plan in the PRSS-PDCA-cycle.

Formulating an execution plan

The execution plan is merely a few pages long and shows which objectives you have, which activities you have planned and which priorities you can set within these activities. An execution plan is usually a yearly plan. In practice, most yearly plans contain too much information. This makes them difficult to work with. Therefore, it is important that your plan is a work document that you update weekly. This allows you to steer the process in addition to the content.

The execution plan contains the following components:

1 SMART-objectives for performance and behavior;
2 What result you concretely deliver;
3 Milestones that show when you want to have achieved each result;
4 Resources you employ to achieve your objectives;
5 Plans that show who performs what and when;
6 The way in which you will measure and discuss each objective;
7 The way in which you steer your plan in daily practice.

With the execution plan, you know what you will do, in practice. It allows you to account for the achieved results and to steer when the result deviates from the objective. It contains important process steps that add value to your result.

Experience teaches us that most plans are correct content-wise, but generally too little attention has been paid to the organizational behavior needed to achieve the result. This concerns the process information, which tells more about the way in which the plan actually becomes successful. How much time will the manager spend on the management of this plan? How is progress of the plan measured? How is this plan embedded in the three levels within the performance behavioral structure: monitoring level, steering level and action level? Who needs to report to whom, how often and at what level? How do we manage the resources needed to make the plan successful? These are all questions that are not related to the content, but instead concern organizational behavior. To a large extent, these aspects are responsible for bringing about the content results.

Sometimes, the execution plan is a year plan that serves as the total plan, but when something changes along the way – which is not uncommon – it can also be helpful to make a shorter execution plan.

Many continuous improvement paths take place more or less organically. There is little or no programmed steering which is organized. This means that a program is not established on the basis of a pattern analysis. That's a shame, because the programmed route, with a plan and the ability to steer the plan, is the most effective way to steer continuous improvement within your organization.

Determining standards

To be able to measure and improve the deviation from the goal value as specifically as possible, it is important to standardize the processes that lead to the performance. By doing this the result is secured and therefore reproducible.

There are two types of standards in the performance-behavior management model.

1   *Performance standards*
    The performance standards are the standards the performance has to meet. The performance standard is applied in the same way as the goal value. Norm value is also often used, but the norm value is not necessarily a goal value. For instance, think of the norm value for accidents or pollution. Another example is the number of patients who die during open heart surgery. The norm value that is set by the hospital could be a maximum of five deaths per year. However this value is naturally not the goal value since the hospital will strive towards zero deaths per year.

2 *Behavioral standards*

These standards clarify which behavior is needed to bring about the performance. For instance: how much time can a nurse take for administering medication to a patient and how does she record the quality of her work so that, in the next shift, her colleague can see that the activity was performed correctly (correct medication, correct amount, right time, right patient)? The behavioral standards serve to anchor the processes (and the way we behave within those processes).

Examples of behavioral standards are work processes, instructions, protocols, communication frameworks, conference frameworks, improvement structures, one-point lessons (short, development-oriented descriptions of processes), guidelines, procedures, manuals, instructions, out of control action plans (OCAPs) and standard operating procedures (SOPs).

2.4   Step 3 Execute the plan in accordance with the standards

The result of step 3 is that the plan is executed in accordance with the included standards. In the PRSS-PDCA-cycle; this is "Do", or performing the activities.

When there is a higher level of standardization, the routine level of the organization also increases, as does the predictability of the result. As there are more deviations from the standard, the larger the risk of deviations from the result. Figure 2.4 illustrates this.

In his book, the famous lean-consultant Maasaki Imai describes the visit of four Japanese technicians who came to the US to study a production line, to be able to implement it in their own factory. The factory was proud of the 98% production reliability that was achieved at the twenty production lines that worked in three shifts. Merely 2% of products were declined. When the same production lines were included in Japan a year later, the management of the US factory received a thank-you letter from the Japanese management thanking the US management for their hospitality and for the high-quality lines they were using, with an effectiveness of 99,2%. The management was dumbstruck. They immediately travelled to Japan to see how it was possible that the Japanese had realized this enormous improvement within a year. The answer the Japanese management gave was simple and clear: in your factory in California, you have sixty different procedures with twenty production lines in three shifts. Our four technicians have analyzed your processes and together with them we have selected the best procedures and made these our standard.

'Which standards are applied by the municipality during the process of requesting permits?', asked a performance-behavior specialist during the diagnostic phase at a large municipality. The secretary replied: 'We have standards for this process, however, we particularly focus on specific demands of citizens. The performance-behavior specialist was surprised. 'When there are no standards, how is the manager able to manage?', he asked. The secretary looked around and replied: 'But we are especially flexible for a municipality'. By maximally anticipating on the demands of the citizen, we deliver what the citizen wants. We have flexibility as one of our core values. We expect that each civil servant has a flexible attitude towards the citizens." The performance behavior specialist interrupted him: "And does the citizen want a flexible government or a reliable government? Would the citizen prefer his permit with 100% certainty on the agreed-upon time? Or would he prefer 60% certainty, but flexibility with regard to his wishes and the wishes of all other citizens who have requested a permit? "The municipal secretary frowned. "Well, that's a good point. The run time of our permits is nearly longer than our guideline, but that is due to all of the different wishes."

The results the municipal secretary receives are in conformity with the process he created. But when this municipality is maximally flexible, it actually loses all flexibility. The municipality can only become flexible when each step that is taken in the permit process actually adds value for the citizens and all steps that do not add value are removed from the process. The steps that add value are executed in accordance with the standards. The space that arises when this has been achieved is destined for the customer's wishes on the content level (the permit itself). The run time was reduced by 18% for this municipality. The number of permits that were immediately issued correctly increased with 43% and the content flexibility of the permit itself could be extended at the same time. This resulted in satisfied citizens, lower licensing costs, reduced failure costs and less workload.

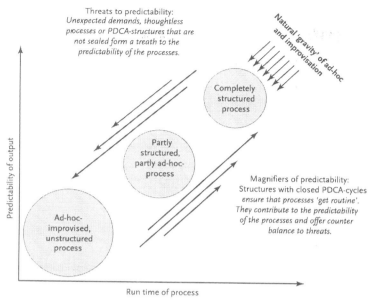

Figure 2.5 *Predictability in time*

Standard Work Organization

Standard Work Organization (SWO) is a way of organizing when a number of fixed standards form the basis for work. The SWO standards are:

- *Process standards*

  Here, we describe how we organize our work. All possible agreements that are separate from the content can be documented in process standards. Here, performance behavior comes in: When does the morning meeting start each day? How long can a meeting take? What is the role of the chairman? How do we prepare for a meeting? How are deviations from the standard considered and discussed? How do we note down the actions that are linked to the deviation?

- *Protocols and instruction*

  Here, we describe how services, structures or machines should run, under normal circumstances. Also, special protocol instructions can exist for deviations. OCAPs (out of control action plans), for instance, are special protocols that are used for specific, common deviations. One-point lessons, for example, are specific instructions on one sheet of paper regarding serving, cleaning or work agreements.

○ *Content standards*
  Here, we describe which criteria a (sub)product or service has to meet. An example of a content standard is the comparison between Robusta and Arabica beans in order to determine the flavor of coffee. Another is the criterion that a cleaning service has to meet. The goal value for the agreed-upon standard for the service is often established in an agreement: the service level agreement.

It is fundamentally important to execute the plan in accordance with a safeguarded standard because people have a tendency to think that they have more, and a better influence on the result than they actually have. This is due to the fact that we are prone to attribute positive results to our own actions. This attribution error phenomenon has been described in the first chapter. Working in conformity with standards rules out personal initiatives that are less productive. Moreover, most people focus on short-term actions: after all, fixing the problem immediately feels better than first spending a lot of time on finding the real cause. But without knowing the real cause, we cannot provide a lasting solution. Working in accordance with a standard, rather than using individual improvement ideas from individual employees, is the foundation for structured improvement of the standard.

Short term action-orientation is independent of the hierarchical level of the employee within the organization. This becomes clear from the statement of a production manager who manages an organization of 450 employees: "It is useless to spend time on finding an explanation for why we are not achieving our objective. I should spend this time on solving the problems I have now."

The following example shows that people have difficulty conforming to the standards on all levels, both on the board level and the work floor.

This example clearly displays people's natural behavior: we want to be able to influence our performance even though we are not completely sure what the relationship is between our behavior and the performance we wish to achieve. In most cases, the effort proves to be more important than the result: when we feel that we have exerted ourselves to achieve a result, we think we did a good job even when we didn't achieve the desired result. There are plenty of examples that show that people try to influence results even when there is no proven relationship between behavior and results. People generally don't connect well with standards. They think they know better than the proven best standard. We can usually observe this behavior from performances: when the actual performance deviates significantly from the desired performance this is often due to a lack of standards. This can also be caused by standards that are not sufficiently secured as action indicators. In this case there is no check whether the standard is used and in case of deviations from the standard there is no steering towards using the standard. As a result, the standard is not (always, and in the right way) applied.

Philips (the company, which provided the new LED lights on the Empire State Building) executed a study was conducted that examined the relation between human interaction and the specific functions of machines. The study was conducted in a factory where the employees that operated the machines work in shifts. For this study a new machine was placed in the factory which was easy to operate so that employees would be able to quickly operate the machine without any support. To be able to do this, the operators got instructions and an elaborate explanation of the function of the machine within the production process. What the operators didn't know was that a few buttons of this machine had no function at all. These buttons looked completely realistic: they were connected to meters on the dashboard, some were a bit more rigid, for instance, and the operator had to turn others a lot before some change became visible on the meter. However, they all had one thing in common: no relationship existed between the button and the machine. The fake buttons did not in any way influence the process that took place within the machine. During the education and instruction process, which the operators all followed in exactly the same way, they were taught not to touch the fake buttons. They were told that these buttons were tuned exactly right and did not require any further adjustment. And that was how the operators worked with the new machine.

In the first week, all operators followed all instructions exactly, but in the weeks that followed more and more operators started turning the fake buttons. One operator in shift A turned the button a little to the right and another operator in the next shift turned it a little to the left without this having any effect on the result. After a while, most operators were turning most of the fake buttons.

After several weeks, the study was stopped due to great success: almost all operators had used the useless buttons to 'operate' the machine. Almost all operators were convinced that these buttons actually influenced the outcome, even after the researchers showed that the buttons were only attached to the gauges on the dashboard and had absolutely no influence on the operation of the machine.

All in all, standardization of the work organization is an important pillar within performance behavior in order to establish performances within a structure and realize the desired responsible behavior with people. It is not a rigid attempt to make the organization unchangeable. Once, there was a TV-commercial with a manager who controlled his employees via strings, like puppets. This image has nothing to do with standardization. A better comparison would be a traffic light. A traffic light only works when everyone understands what a red light means and if everyone actually stops for a red light. When this system no longer works, complementary measures are needed, such as a red light camera to prevent that people run a red light.

2.5   Step 4 Measure the result

The result of step 4 is the gain, expressed in measurable facts and numbers. This is "Check" in the PRSS-PDCA model. Here, both the content and the process that brought about the result are checked.

Performance measurement

The result, or performance measurement, presents the current value of the performance, but that value doesn't provide much information; that value needs to be compared to a goal value. The goal value tells you which concrete value or amount the performance has to meet. No performance improvement is possible without this goal value, because the deviation between the goal value and the current value is the first step towards improvement. In practice, this works as follows:

> When performance ◑ goal value = no action is necessary ☀
>
> (reasoning from positive goal value performance)
>
> When performance ◐ goal value = action is necessary ☺
>
> (reasoning from a positive goal value performance)

- A *positive goal value performance* is a performance that improves as the measured value *increases*. An example of a positive goal value performance is customer satisfaction. As more customers are satisfied, this situation improves for the organization;
- A *negative goal value performance* is a performance that improves when the measured value *decreases*. An example of a negative goal value performance is absence through illness. As fewer employees are absent, the better this is for the organization.

The first action you have to undertake when performance is below the goal value is to investigate the root causes of this deviation. You should not try to solve the problem ad hoc, since that usually does not address the real cause, meaning the problem will continue to occur.

Make sure to measure the results at all levels (monitoring, steering and action). When the frequency with which the results are produced is lower, the frequency of reporting the measurements and deviations is also lower and when the performance frequency is higher, the need for reporting is also higher. When this is hourly, measurement should take place hourly (see figure 1.15 on page 77).

The responsibility for each performance measurement should be at the level of the performance itself. The monitoring level is responsible for measuring performance at the monitoring level, the steering level measures performance at the steering level and the action level measures performance at the action level.

Measurement of behavior

When measurements do occur, most organizations have a tendency to measure only the performance component, the 'what' component from the performance behavior model (figure 1.11 on page 43), the "hard" results. However, within performance behavior this does not suffice. The measurement of the behavioral component as compared to the behavioral standard for the desired performance behavior is just as crucial as conducting a performance measurement. After all, the performance behavior of the employees makes sure that the results are achieved.

Here again, the responsibility of the measurement of behavior should lie at the level at which the behavior is measured, from monitoring level to action level. And, when this behavior is displayed more often it should also be measured more often to allow to steer on possible deviations in the required performance behavior. When this is hourly, measurements should take place hourly, as is true for the measurement of performance.

However, in order to measure performance behavior, the organization will first have to perform a breakdown of the required performance behavior of the organization (at the monitoring level) into performance behavior for the middle management (steering level) and finally into performance behavior at the lowest level, the action level. Subsequently, the standards can be established on those same levels.

Both performances and behavior will have to be measured and compared to the standards that are in place in order to steer on the deviations in the required performance behavior. A supervisor at each hierarchic level can measure the performance behavior, but this can also be done by a colleague who receives the role of auditor, or by an improvement manager. They attend various meetings, observe the behavior by means of a checklist that lists the behavioral standards and then tick off whether everyone behaves in conformity with these behavioral standards. If there is any deviation compared to the behavioral standards, the auditor will note these deviations For example: does the chairman begin by discussing the agenda and does he address latecomers? When the staff official of the Department of Quality, Health and Welfare and Environment has to report about an improvement action, does he base his story on facts and is he specific? Does the mechanic in technical service ask enough questions regarding a problem he will have to handle, so he has all the information he needs to take action? By structurally and continuously measuring the behavior during all consultations in which performance is discussed, the development gaps in performance behavior will become clear immediately. This makes it possible to take action to improve the standard performance behavior. Chapter 6 further elaborates on the methods and instruments to define and further develop desired behavior.

2.6 Step 5 Confirm the result when it is equal to the objective, or steer when it deviates

The result of this step is to give compliments when the objective is achieved or to steer when the objective is not yet been achieved. When the objective is achieved, giving compliments will stimulate the desired behavior. When the objective is not yet achieved an action has to be formulated to steer on the deviation. This is step "Act" in the PRSS-PDCA model. When the desired result is achieved it is important to secure the standards in the organization. By ensuring that the standard is applied company-wide, the variety in work processes will reduce and thus variety in the result will also reduce.

Confirm desired result

The literature pays a lot of attention to sanctions we should impose when the desired result is not achieved – but what should we do when the result is equal to the objective? Nothing is as powerful in reinforcing the desired behavior as the confirmation of it, for instance by giving a compliment. This is most effective when the confirmation of behavior takes place as soon as possible after the moment the desired behavior was displayed.

This is the reason that high-frequency result behavior should also be measured and steered on in high frequency. Only then can the behavior be developed in small, but certain, steps. Celebrate success, but always raise the bar slightly to create tension (also see figure 1.8 on page 35).

Steer on deviations

When the result does not meet the goal value, the following steer mechanism takes effect:

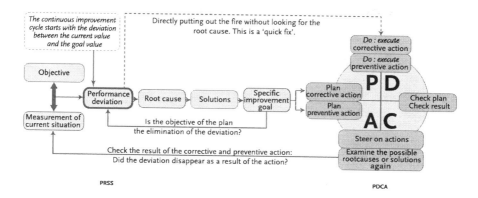

Figure 2.6 *PRSS-PDCA cycle*

This is the combination of the PDCA-cycle and the PRSS-steps, that was explained in section 2.1.

Training Within Industry

At the level of safeguarding the standard it is important to ensure that the proven standards are deployed within the organization to reduce the variety in the work processes, and thus the variety in results. The Training Within Industry (TWI) concept provides guidelines to ensure deployment of the proven standards. The concept was originally developed during World War II to increase the war production by means of standardized techniques, training, and continuous improvements to maximize the potential of every worker. After World War II TWI was applied by firms and became especially appreciated in Japan at Toyota. In this way TWI had a direct impact on the development and use of kaizen and standard work at Toyota.

At the level of safeguarding the standard TWI is especially useful by offering the Job Instruction program. This Job Instruction program provides a structure to effectively train employees to be able to apply the standards. Supervisors train the employees to apply the standards by breaking down the jobs into defined steps, by showing the procedures and by explaining the Key Points and reasons for these Key Points. Subsequently the employees attempt the application of the standard under close coaching until the employee masters the execution.

The main point of the TWI method is the 'What-How-Why' approach, which 'tells the story' in every instruction; 'What sort of task or job has to be done, How the task or job has to be done and Why it has to be done. To be able to effectively instruct the employees the coach or supervisor should first get ready to instruct. TWI describes the following elements that should be considered during the preparation for instructing:4

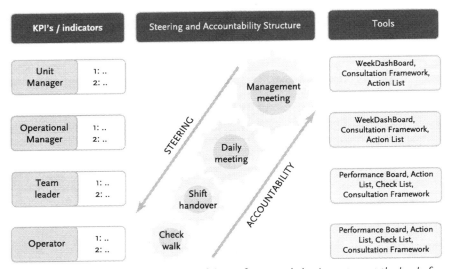

Figure 2.7 *The integrated components of the performance behavior system at the level of safeguarding the standard*

To get ready for instructing, there are four steps to follow within the TWI method:

1   *Set up a proper time table;*
    Skills you expect each person to have by what date
2   *Break down the job;*
    Within performance behavior, this is an important step. The job breakdown has to be made all the way down to the action level so the operator can measure his actions with the help of action indicators. Furthermore in the job breakdown the actions, steps and work processes should be listed. And finally, the breakdown should contain the key points and the reasons (Why?). The final result is a complete job breakdown sheet accompanied by action

4   *War manpower commission Job Instruction: Session Outline and Reference Material, Washington DC (1944)*

indicators.

3 *Have everything ready;*
   This step ensures that everything is in place to be able to successfully instruct. Some examples that need to be considered are: Is the right equipment available and working? Are the right materials available at the right place? Are the right supplies available at the right time?

4 *Properly arrange the workplace*
   Ensure that the workplace is arranged in the same way as the employee is expected to keep it (5S work place).

When the supervisor or coach is properly prepared he is ready to start instructing according to the four steps defined by the Job Instruction program of TWI[5]:

Step 1 Prepare the employee
   - Put the person at ease
   - Describe the job and find out what they already know
   - Get the person interested in learning the job
   - Place the person in the correct position

Step 2 Present the operation
   - Tell, show, and illustrate one important step at a time
   - Stress each key point & reason
   - Instruct clearly, completely, and patiently
   - Do not give more information than the person can master at one time

Step 3 Try out performance
   - Have the person do the job – correct errors
   - Have the person explain each important step, key point & reason as they do the job again
   - Make sure the person understands
   - Continue until you know the person knows

Step 4 Follow up
   - Put the person on their own
   - Designate to whom they can go for help
   - Check frequently – encourage questions
   - Taper off extra coaching and close follow up

By following this Job Instruction approach of TWI it is possible to ensure that the proven standards will be deployed within the organization. In TWI the emphasis is on the coach and supervisor as educator. This is illustrated by the Job Instruction motto: "If the person hasn't learned, the instructor hasn't taught".

---

5 *Sort (seiri)*

Figure 2.7 illustrates the integration of all the components that are needed at the level of safeguarding the standard in one figure. It shows the right KPI's on the right level, with a breakdown all the way down to action indicator or handling indicator level. At the action or handling level also a proper job breakdown is included. Furthermore the figure shows the steering and accountability structure with the different levels that are accountable for the different KPI's, SI's and AI's. Also the standard tools that are used at each level are included in the figure. These tools are used to identify and tackle deviations in an appropriate way. For example by logging actions. All these components together make the performance behavior system work at the level of safeguarding the standard.

2.7 Five S (5S) as example for safeguarding the standard

5S is a tool to tidy up and standardize the work place. This creates a safe, efficient and productive work environment. The system was developed by Toyota and the term 5S refers to five Japanese words that begin with an S.

In Western European cultures, 5S is often viewed as an objective and not as means. Employees and managers think that it helps them to finally clean up their mess. However, it is a tool to establish standards and a tool that facilitates the PRSS-PDCA-cycle to take action upon deviations within the steering and accountability structure. This fits perfectly with the principle of safeguarding the standard. In English, the Japanese S that stands for shitsuke is often translated as "sustain" while the literal translation is "discipline". It is not simply because of the fact that ""sustain" begins with an S that we prefer this word to discipline...

In English, the 5S are usually translated as follows:

1 *Sort(seiri)*
   Remove all non-essential instruments and materials from the work place. Keep only what you need.
2 *Stabilize (seiton)*
   Order all necessary instruments and materials and place each one at an optimal spot.
3 *Sanitize or shine (seiso)*
   Clean the work place and equipment regularly.
4 *Standardize (seiketsu)*
   Use standard procedures and checklists to keep the work place orderly, clean and functional.
5 *Sustain (shitsuke)*

The previous four points need to be rooted in the performance behavior structure of steering and accountability (see figure 1.15 on page 77) to ensure that there will be steered on deviations within 5S and to ensure the system is structurally improved and becomes part of the organizational culture.

In addition to the 'classic' 5S phases, sometimes additional phases are added. These phases are:

6 *Safety*
   This phase can promote safety by explicitly stating safety as a value or it can promote safety when, for example, an existing safety program is undermined and more attention needs to be directed towards it.
7 *Security*
   This possible seventh phase identifies and addresses risks to key business categories such as plant, property and equipment, material, human capital, brand equity, intellectual property and information technology.
8 *Satisfaction*
   This possible eighth phase focuses on employee satisfaction and engagement in continuous improvement efforts to ensure that improvements will be secured within the organization and new improvement efforts will arise.

5S as a program is often effective, but securing 5S within the organization proves to be extremely difficult. This is a shame, since a measurable relationship exists between the level of discipline on the work floor and the number of errors and the number of times work has to be redone in the primary process. A correctly implemented 5S-program delivers an immediate contribution to the productivity. Additionally, 5S contributes to the identification and elimination of hidden losses that can be present in an organization. When the instruments and tools have been arranged and standardized correctly, the employees no longer have to waste energy looking for them.

3

IMPROVE THE STANDARD: DEVIATION OF THE GOAL VALUE AS IMPROVEMENT TRIGGER

Within performance behavior, steering and accountability is the method used to steer on deviations from goal values and to account for the results (see figure 1.15 on page 56). Once safeguarding the standard has been secured, the next step can take place: improving the standard. This chapter discusses the steps needed to improve the standard. The objectives of each step and the contribution to the improvement of the performance behavior standard are explained.

Important topics of this chapter:

- Set your target: what is the objective you want to work on?
- The integration of improvement and safeguarding: how do you turn corrective and preventive actions into an improvement initiative?
- Description of the continuous improvement process: subject – objective – diagnosis – solutions – choice – implementation plan – implementation – result measurement – secure.

3.1 From safeguarding the standard to improving the standard in ten improvement steps

In cases of deviation between the current value and the goal value of a performance, you can take corrective and preventive action. The corrective action takes place at the level of safeguarding the standard. If we use fire as a metaphor, the corrective action is putting out the fire. Preventive actions, such as arresting a pyromaniac, are measures taken to prevent future fires. Preventive actions can take place both at the level of safeguarding the standard and at the level of improving the standard.

Improving the standard is the next step in the process of continuous improvement, after safeguarding the standard, which was the topic of chapter 2. When the current value of a performance is equal to the goal value, no action is needed at the level of safeguarding the standard. Using the fire metaphor: what if a fire occurs four times a year, three of which are caused by a pyromaniac (the example will become slightly more surreal, but we will continue with it nonetheless). In this case, putting out the fire and arresting the pyromaniac are the right actions to reduce the fires from four times a year to once a year, since the pyromaniac caused the fire three out of four times. You could stop here, but you could also establish a new goal value: "in the future, not a single fire should break out". This new goal value makes new analysis necessary. What caused the one fire not lit by the pyromaniac? This leads to searching for root causes and creating solutions to deal with the last potential fire. By increasing the goal value (from four to one to zero fires a year), you create a new deviation between the goal value and current value.

> Increasing the goal value when the goal value has been structurally achieved is the first step in the process of continuous improvement.

At the level of safeguarding the standard, both corrective and preventive actions can be taken to once again meet the established goal value. When these corrective and preventive actions don't succeed in achieving the goal value, an improvement action is necessary. Using the fire metaphor, an example of a preventive action at the level of safeguarding the standard is catching the pyromaniac. This will only happen after the corrective action, putting out the fire, took place. But if we also want to prevent future fires, we will have to come up with a plan to ensure that the pyromaniac no longer has access to the building, or that no flammable materials are present. This leads to an improvement of the present standards.

The run time of the whole improvement process is dependent upon the size and complexity of the deviation. The process consists of ten steps:

1   Define the specific improvement objective.
    Result: the SMART-objective is defined (what is and is not allowed).
2   Collect measureable improvement data.
    Result: everything that can be measured is measured.
3   Analyze the data and get the subsequent improvement information.
    Result: the root causes are known.
4   Map all possible solutions without ranking
    Result: an overview of all possible solutions.
5   Choose the best solution(s): corrective and preventive actions.
    Result: list of priorities of quick fixes on the basis of costs/effort/run time that are implemented in step 6, and a list of priorities of corrective and preventive actions on the basis of costs/effort/run time that are described in a detailed plan in step 6. The quick fixes run parallel to the corrective and preventive actions.
6   Plan the improvement actions in detail.
    Result: implementation plan for corrective and preventive actions.
7   Execute the improvement plan exactly as it was planned.
    Result: plan executed.
8   Measure the results of the improvement actions.
    Result: after improvement actions are taken, measurements of current values are made and compared to the goal values that were the objective of the improvement actions.
9   Confirm the result and secure it by adjusting the daily standard.

Result: an improvement of the current standard that is safeguarded during steering and accountability moments.

10 Steer based on deviations.

Result: take action to secure the improvement action in the daily steering and accountability structure, or steer based on the deviation from the improvement objective. In case of the latter, you should go back one step in the plan each time to locate the problem.

Figure 3.1 displays the performance behavior cycle at the level of safeguarding and improving the standard. The model below shows the location of the ten steps with the standard improvement process.

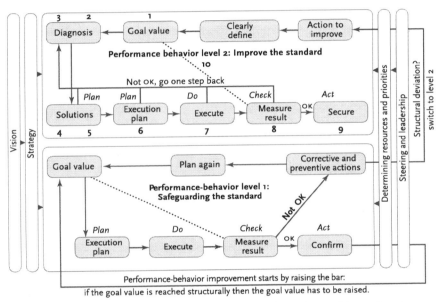

Figure 3.1 *Performance behavior cycle on the level of safeguarding and improving the standard*

These steps to improvement apply when the root causes of the deviation are known, but the solutions are difficult to implement. They also apply when the root causes are unknown, but the solutions are easy to implement. When the root causes are known and the solutions are easy to implement, the problem is dealt with during the daily performance behavior cycle at the level of safeguarding the standard. And when the root causes are unknown and the solutions are difficult to implement, it is time to renew the standard.

3.2   Step 1 Define the specific improvement objective

When defining the subject and converting it into an improvement objective, it is important to investigate which components belong to the subject. In order to discover this, it helps when you ask yourself which components definitely do not belong to the subject.

When you have established what does and does not belong to the subject, you should define the problem definition correctly. You can use the 5xW+H-method for this. 5xW+H stands for five questions that start with a w and one question that begins with an h. Essentially, this method means that you answer the questions in detail. This is not merely a verbal exercise; it also requires measurements, assumptions and verifications. Ask yourself the following questions:

1   *What* exactly is the problem?
    Result: the definition of a problem.
    What is the deviation, what are the characteristics of the problem, what are the consequences of this problem, how urgent is this problem within the whole process and what are the risks or impact to the process?
2   *Where* is the problem located?
    Result: the location of the problem
    Where in the process does the deviation take place, where else in our organization does this problem occur, where exactly are the consequences of this problem located?
3   *When* does the problem take place?
    Result: the duration of the problem.
    Since when is this deviation measured or observed, when did the problem occur exactly, when did this deviation occur again, when was this deviation measured for the first time?
4   *Which* problems occur exactly?
    Result: the size of the problem.
    Which patterns in this deviation can you observe, which components have exactly the same deviation, which deviations are reproducible, which trends can we measure?
5   *Who* causes the problem?
    Result: the initiator of the actual problem (so not the consequences that arise from the real cause).
    Who causes the problem, who is bothered by the consequences of this problem, who can solve this problem, who can contribute to a solution at the root of this problem, who has observed this problem before, whose problem is it exactly?

6   *How* does the problem manifest itself?
    Result: the expression of the problem.
    What does the problem look like exactly? How would you describe it? How does it become visible? What do the consequences of the problem look like?

During this first step, the scope of the deviation becomes visible. It also becomes clear what does and does not belong to the deviation. When these components of the deviation are clear, the deviation can be converted into a problem definition, with an improvement objective.

You do this by asking "Why?" five times. This clarifies the cause of the problem: why did the problem occur? Why did a deviation occur? Why did the deviation occur here? Why does the problem occur? Why did this happen? The why-question always arises from the answer to the previous question. In this way, you continuously go down one level.

In practice, these two methods are often mixed up and used simultaneously. For this reason, the funnel-tunnel model was developed, see figure 3.2. This model visualizes the questions in accordance with the 5Ws (What, When, Which, Who and Where) + H (How) that define the problem. The 5xW+H questions form the funnel. Asking "Why" five times, when the problem has been defined, forms the tunnel of this model. This is the (root) cause analysis. In this way, two different instruments together form one model that can contribute to clarifying and specifying a problem.

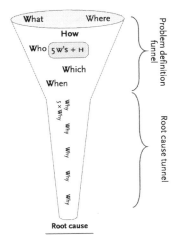

Figure 3.2 *Funnel-tunnel model*

Here follows an example of a made up example of the funnel-tunnel model. One day a operator in a coffee factory finds out that there is coffee on the floor next to the machine. He is about to clean up the coffee, when his team leader wonders what exactly happened here. The following discussion naturally does not take place with one person, in the same place, at the same time. The total run time to answer all questions is approximately one week, but if you were to put all questions down in sequence, the following conversation would take place:

What is the problem? *There is coffee on the floor.*

Where exactly is the coffee? *It's below the transport tube. That's the only spot.*

Since when has the coffee been there? *Since yesterday.*

What changes took place yesterday? *Yesterday revision took place at this part of the transportation system.*

When is the coffee detected for the first time? *Yesterday*

Who first saw the coffee? *The mechanic, this morning at 7:13 according to the report.*

How did he discover this? *During his regular inspection.*

Why was the coffee there? *Because the lid of the transport tube didn't function well.*

Why didn't the lid function well? *We don't know, but it is the same problem as last time.*

Why did the problem occur before? *Because this is a new lid from a different supplier.*

Why do we have a new lid from a different supplier? *Because the maintenance department can't order the other lid anymore.*

Why can the technical service no longer order the other lid? *Because the buying department made a choice to change suppliers.*

Why did the central buying department make a choice in suppliers? *Because they wish to save costs by reducing the number of suppliers.*

The root cause is cost-cutting which has been initiated by the central purchasing department: this leads to coffee on the work floor by a faulty valve.

Actual practice has shown that you can't simply answer these questions by improvising. Measurements have to be conducted to discover how often a problem occurs. Usually, more instruments have to be applied in the process of the funnel-tunnel model. With this, the model offers a simple but powerful visualization of problem solving.

3.3   Step 2 Collect measurable improvement data

When the definition of the problem is clear and an improvement objective has been formulated, the problem can be analyzed and structured more thoroughly. You can use analytical methods such as an Ishikawa diagram, graphs, trend lines, Pareto-overviews or a simpler brainstorming technique for this. Some methods focus primarily on uncovering performance related causes, others focus mainly on behavior related causes and yet others can uncover both types of causes.

In this section, we discuss a number of measurement and analytical techniques. Each method for collecting and presenting data has its own specific advantages. Both measurement techniques and analytical techniques will be discussed, because some techniques are applicable for both collecting information and analyzing information. The analytical techniques are also helpful in step 3.

Brainstorming

Brainstorming is a technique that is aimed at developing a large number of creative ideas. With a few simple rules, brainstorming can relatively easily elicit the most important root cause of not only the performance component (*what*), but also of the behavior component (*how*).

Brainstorming is a structured, delayed judgment, where all ideas are good in principle. The three most important starting points of a good brainstorm are:

1   All ideas are good and more is better: quantity above quality;
2   Use the ideas from one person for the new ideas of another: link and expand;
3   Don't categorize the ideas and don't apply classification: generate as many ideas as possible without filter.

This technique provides a good overview of the playing field in which the problem occurs. The goal of brainstorming is to generate all possible ideas about the root causes in order to create better insight into the scope, depth and width of the problem arises.

However, the disadvantage of brainstorming is that if you forget a theme, you usually won't remember it at all. You have a better chance of remembering when structurally viewing all possibilities with the *issue tree*.

Issue tree

The issue tree comes from the philosophy that when you divide a large, unclear problem into smaller sub-problems, you can eventually solve the big problem by solving the sub-problems. In the issue tree, a sub-question (level 2) that relates to the main topic is taken from the larger problem (level 1). Subsequently, sub-questions are derived from the questions that were formulated at level 2 (level 3). In this way, a tree of questions unfolds. Eventually, all questions have a connection to the topic. Usually, the main problem is first divided into a few sub-areas. For instance: how do we solve the liquidity problem? (Large indefinable problem). Subsequently, we name a number of sub-areas, such as customer, turnover, costs, credit and efficiency, that cause the problem. Afterwards, we can ask a number of questions about these sub-areas. For example, we can ask with credit: "How large is our supplier credit?" But immediately below, this following question follows: "What is our own average payment term and that of our customers?" In this way, we create a specific image of all questions we can answer to eventually solve the problem.

Cause-effect diagram

Cause-effect diagrams, also called Ishikawa diagrams or fishbone analysis, are specifically intended to record and investigate the causes of problems in a clear way. You can use these for both the performance and the behavior component.

The cause-effect diagram clearly visualizes the causes of the problem. You can use it to categorize all possible causes after a brainstorming session. It is also a good tool to apply when a multidisciplinary team needs to map the causes of a problem quickly and efficiently and according to a fixed pattern.

On a category-to-category basis, the cause-effect diagram looks at the creation of the problem at increasingly deeper levels. The five-times-why technique is an important tool when setting up a cause-effect diagram.

The five-times-why technique in combination with 5xW+H is applied to the funnel-tunnel model. Here, 5xW+H takes care of defining the problem and the five-times-why technique of the root cause analysis. It's not a thorough, but an accessible method that can be applied easily.

The categories used in the cause-effect diagram are dependent upon the organization. In product environments, the five Ms are often used:

1   Men (People);
2   Means (Resources);
3   Machine;
4   Methods;
5   Materials.

All possible causes are visually accommodated in one of the five categories and then divided down to the lowest level. Other Ms can also be added: management, measurements and even Mother Nature (environment) are other examples that are applied in practice. In the service sector, the eight Ps are often used:

1   People;
2   Product or service;
3   Price;
4   Promotion
5   Policy;
6   Processes;
7   Procedure;
8   Place.

There are a number of applications (for instance MS Visio or mind mapping) that contain fishbone templates that allow you to easily revise and store the diagrams digitally.

Pareto diagram or 80/20-rule

A Pareto diagram is a column diagram that displays data classes; for instance, data in relation to different types of errors is displayed in descending order of size from left to right. The Pareto diagram clearly shows which errors contribute most to the deviation. By means of a Pareto diagram, you can determine which problems or errors should be dealt with first. Another strength of the Pareto diagram is that the cause of the problem's duration or frequency is graphically displayed. Figure 3.3 shows this.

Often, making a Pareto diagram is seen as the final stage of the analysis while, in fact, the analysis starts with a good Pareto diagram: a Pareto analysis is nothing more than an overview of data.

A Pareto analysis provides surprisingly clear insights in a simple way. In most companies, 80% of the turnover is generated by 20% of the products and, at the Olympics, 80% of the medals are won by 20% of the countries.

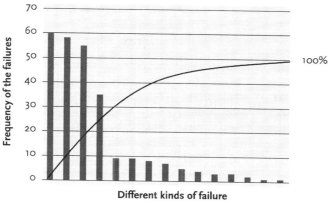

Figure 3.3 *Pareto diagram*

Histogram

A histogram is a column diagram that displays the frequency spread of per-formed observations or data obtained in any other way. The diagram portrays deviations with regard to the "standards". This makes it into a real analysis technique. A histogram groups the data into classes. Therefore, histograms are used to check certain processes. The data that has been collected and entered into the histogram can be related to both the performance and the behavior component.

Flowchart

A flowchart is a technique to schematically display a process. By making use of symbols for the various process aspects, you can describe the process flow in more detail. A flowchart visualizes the bottlenecks in a process. When identify-ing a problem, making a flowchart can provide many different points of view. The flowchart is suitable for behavioral data, but also for performance data. A value-stream map is an application of a flowchart.

Scatter plot

A scatter plot, also called a correlation diagram or scatter graph, graphically portrays the relationship between two types of data. For instance, this could be the relationship between the two causes of a problem, or the relationship between a cause and effect. This is a data-analysis diagram, because it provides visual information about the characteristics of the data. Scatter plots are used to perform correlation and regression tests. The goal of these tests is to analyze which specific variables bring about change in a product or process.

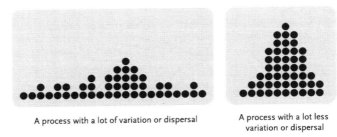

A process with a lot of variation or dispersal | A process with a lot less variation or dispersal

Figure 3.4 *Scatter plot that shows a process with a lot of variation in the process on the left, and a process with less variation on the right.*

Time-value map

With a time-value map, you show how time in a process is utilized. You make a time-value map by taking random indications of the activities of a role or person at various, predetermined times, in order to map which behavior adds value for the customer and which behavior subtracts value. These techniques can especially be used to map value-adding elements of behavior.

Deduction: what isn't it?

There are countless possibilities to categorize brainstorming lists. A highly effective method is the "is"/ "is not"-method. This method is applied to specifically determine which elements are part of the problem area and which elements are not part of the problem area. This technique can be applied to behavioral analysis, but also to performance analysis.

Observation

In structured observation, behavior is observed with a specific goal or focus. No standards are applied to the behavior; facts are merely registered. If necessary, these facts can later be subject to an analysis. This is not the interpretation phase. As soon as you start interpreting during the observations, the observation becomes unstructured.

During this phase, you can register a number of observations: frequency and duration of the perceived behavior. This can be verbal, but also non-verbal behavior. It is extremely important to remain as "value-free" as possible during observation, that is, without judgment.

Time series graph

A time series graph is intended to identify patterns in the data within a specific period of time. Subsequently, we can extract trends from these patterns. A time series graph of, for example, a safety, health and welfare service shows that absence through illness is lowest during the summer holidays.

ABC-analysis

The ABC-analysis maps why the behavior takes place and what the consequences of it are. A stands for antecedents, these are the stimuli that lead to behavior. B stands for Behavior, the behavior itself. And C stands for the Consequences of behavior. An ABC-analysis clarifies why the behavior occurs, without attaching a value judgment to this.

STARR

The behavioral interview is a method for analyzing behavior in more detail. Such an interview focuses on the actual behavior in a situation, not on the desired behavior. To clarify this, you can use STARR. STARR stands for Situation, Task, Action, Result and Reflection. The interviewee answers questions regarding the Situation (the context) in which the behavior took place, which Task (responsibility or role) he had in this, which Actions (what he did, thought of or delivered) he took, which Results (what did the action yield) he achieved with those actions and subsequently what the Reflection (to what extent has the result been achieved, but also what are the lessons of the process that took place) after achieving the result was.

Organizing improvement data in a structured way makes sure that the decisions are made on the basis of well-founded facts instead of on the basis of assumptions and opinions. An example of this is an improvement initiative that was taken by the commercial department of a brewery. They suspected that some representatives held many more commercial meetings than other representatives. By means of a scatter plot, the management of the brewery obtained insight into the performances of the sixty representatives of this company, with reference to the number of actual customer visits per week. The number of customer visits varied from -60% to +100% with regard to the average, while the performance, expressed in beer volume delivered to the locations visited by the representative, varied from -50% to +70%. The most often heard argument from the representatives who did not do enough visits: "But I mainly visit major customers." However, the scatter plot showed that the representatives with most visits also generated the largest total turnover. Standardizing the number of visits per week (performance) to at least eight prepared meetings (behavior) brought about an increase in turnover of 15% in the three years afterwards.

ORCE

ORCE stands for Observing, Registering, Classifying and Evaluating. This method is used to observe behavior in a structured way. First, the behavior is specifically observed, without attaching a value judgment to it. This increases objectivity. Subsequently, the observed behavior is recorded. Then, the behavior is classified and organized. Finally, the observed behavior is evaluated and compared to a standard. The behavioral auditing methodologies of performance behavior have been built up in accordance with this method. You can read more about this in chapter 6.

In addition to these methods, many other competency and behavior profiling measurements, questionnaires, 360 degree feedback methods, etc., exist that can help you in collecting improvement data.

 For more specific improvement tools: 'The complete book of continuous improvement tools' by Webers, Van Engelen, Luijben (2012)

3.4 Step 3 Analyze the data and get the subsequent improvement information

In search of the root causes of a problem, we often encounter a practical problem: in 99% of cases, not one specific root cause can be found; rather, the problem often has more underlying causes. This is one of the reasons for mapping the root causes and documenting them correctly, so all possible solutions are considered for all issues related to the problem.

During this third step, we attempt a diagnosis. We do this by answering the following two questions as specifically as possible:

1   What is the underlying cause behind the measured or observed cause?
2   Which pattern can we recognize in the discovered root causes?

A simple method to start this is the funnel-tunnel model (see page 94), which was also discussed in the description of the fishbone analysis on page 97.

It is important to find and test the analysis of the root causes statistically. However, it happens all too often that actions are based on a hypothesis about the root cause that is accepted as true without actually having been tested properly. The hypotheses you formulated during the analysis of the data can be tested with the help of "test values". A null hypothesis is formulated which has a specific presumption about the data set, and is compared to the alternative hypothesis by statistical testing. An example of a null hypothesis when investigating the possible root cause of the quality of cheese could be: "there is no relationship between the production temperature and the size of holes in cheese". The accompanying alternative hypothesis subsequently is: "there is a relationship between the production temperature and the size of holes in cheese". By testing hypotheses in this way it is possible to draw up conclusions that are based on facts instead of conclusions based on "feeling".

With data (pattern) analysis, you can analyze the improvement data to extrapolate the root causes. There are several statistical methods you can use to quickly identify common or unusual patterns. For each analysis the following is true: the more data you have to analyze, the larger the reliability of your analysis is, and therefore the more reliable the hypothesis or solutions you base on them.

A much-used statistical program to perform data-analyses is Minitab. With this program, simple statistical analyses can be visualized easily. In this way, the significance of a deviation or the spread in a process can be calculated.

3.5   Step 4 Map all possible solutions without ranking

In the production process of a famous cheese brand, the slightest temperature deviations in the process could lead to deviations in the cheeses. A deviating cheese has large holes, does not have the right shape, or the right color. It is obvious that these deviations are not allowed to occur, because these cheeses cannot be sold to the consumers. First, it seemed as though small temperature changes of a few tenths of degrees Celsius were not significant, but after a scatter plot and correlation diagram had been made with data taken over the course of a few months, a relationship between the deviations and the temperature in the process appeared. In this way, the process could be better controlled with the use of a correct analysis of the available data.

In this phase, all possible solutions are mapped. Many improvement teams skip this step and immediately go from the analysis phase to the choice for solutions. However, you can miss important solutions when skipping this step. Therefore, it is better to use the issue tree or brainstorming technique in this phase to generate all possible solutions, before moving on to the next phase and selecting the best one from all of these solutions.

3.6   Step 5 Choose the best solution(s): corrective and preventive actions

Now, it is time to split up all possible solutions into corrective and preventive actions, to choose the best solutions and place them in a priority list. When determining the actions, you can look at:

- The financial impact on both the costs and the gains (high or low, fast or slow);
- The risks of the solutions;
- The extent to which the solutions contribute to the strategic objectives of the organization (high or low contribution);
- The extent to which the solution can be implemented (difficult or easy).

PICK-diagram

There are various methods to select the best from all of the possible solutions. One of these is the PICK-diagram, which has four quadrants. PICK stands for Possible, Implement, Challenge and Kill. On the x-axis and y-axis, two variables are shown: the level of difficulty of implementation (simple, difficult) and the result (small, large). In this way, the following priorities become visible:

1 Perform first (Implement): large result and easy to implement;
2 Perform possibly (Possible): small result and easy to implement;
3 Challenge: large result and hard to implement;
4 Do not perform (Kill): small result and hard to implement.

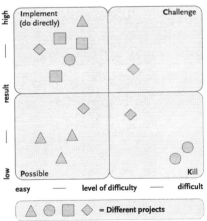

Figure 3.5 *PICK-diagram*

The actions in category one are also called quick fixes. These quick fixes are implemented parallel to step 6. The other corrective and preventive actions on the priority list are included in a detailed plan from step 6.

Generating solutions is usually obstructed by the image of the solution that seems most logical. This would be like trying to solve a murder when the suspect has already been arrested and only the evidence needs to be found. This happens sometimes with murder cases, where detectives work towards the suspect in custody. This is a good example of tunnel vision: the detectives are no longer open to alternatives and therefore cannot objectively determine what should be recorded on the basis of facts. Therefore, it is really important to first map all the solutions, whether good or bad, and only then (and not while generating the solutions) determine which is the best solution.

3.7   Step 6 Plan the improvement actions in detail

In daily practice, improvement actions are often implemented on the basis of insight. This leads to the problem that the improvement actions usually quickly recede to the background. In performance behavior, improvement actions are not implemented on the basis of insight but on planning. With this, we have a unique tool: we can measure the results of the plan. A good implementation plan contains:

- Objectives;
- Resources;
- Measurement points;
- Planning.

3.8   Step 7 Execute the improvement plan exactly as it was planned

The greatest enemy when implementing the plan as it has been planned is "progressive insight". And naturally it sometimes is necessary to adjust the plans: each implementation plan is implemented in a living context that changes daily. However, the experience is that most implementation plans are already altered when the ink on the paper is still wet. That is not the way in which we perform the plan in performance behavior. When so much time has been spent on analysis and planning, the plan itself deserves to be executed in the way in which it was invented.

3.9   Step 8 Measure the results of the improvement action

In this step, we measure the (interim) results of the actions. We do not only measure the performance gain of the plan, but also the behavior gain. The performance gain, or gain related to content, is the result the plan was intended for: reducing the deviation between actual and goal value. The behavior or process gain is the way in which the plan is performed and the deviations that occur in this.

3.10   Step 9 Confirm the result and secure it by adjusting the daily standard

When, after conducting measurements, the results match the objectives in the improvement plan, you can celebrate! Confirming the desired result is the most effective way to consolidate the result into behavior. Subsequently, it is important to actually include the improved standard in the daily standard. Just as at the level of safeguarding the standard, securing that the improved standard are deployed in the organization can be done with the Job Instructing program from Training Within Industry which was described in section 2.6.

3.11   Step 10 Steer based on deviations

If a deviation is measured in the result of the improvement plan, follow the "back to the problem"-analysis. Start with question 1. If you can answer this with yes, proceed to step 2 etcetera.

1   Have the results been measured correctly? If not: go back to step 8;
2   Has the improvement plan been performed exactly as planned? If not: go back to step 7;
3   Is the plan for the improvement action correct? If not: go back to step 6;
4   Have the corrective and preventive actions been named and performed correctly? If not: go back to step 5;
5   Have all possible solutions actually been mapped? If not: go back to step 4.
6   Has the analysis that was used to make the correct diagnosis been performed correctly? If not: go back to step 3;
7   Has all data been measured and have all measurements been performed correctly? If not: go back to step 2;
8   Has the improvement objective been defined correctly? If not: go back to step 1.

4

RENEW THE STANDARD: FIVE STEPS TO CREATE A BREAKTHROUGH

When the root cause of a problem is unknown, or is very complex with many variables and difficult to implement solutions, improving the standard becomes impossible. Instead, the standard has to be renewed. This chapter is about the steps that lead to a new standard. In practice, this means a project that has to lead to a stringent improvement: the renewal.

In this chapter, you will recognize a lot from existing project management. Based on practice experience, a model has been developed with these existing performance behavior methods. This model matches safeguarding and improving the standard. It places strong emphasis on securing the project performance that is expected in relation to the required project behavior. We zoom in on the infrastructure of the innovation project, but also on the aspects needed for the project management.

In innovation projects, program management is also often needed to maintain the cohesion between various projects. Program management is not part of performance behavior, but the existing methods for this can be used well in combination with performance behavior.

The standard for program management, Project Management Institute, (2006) Amazon

4.1   Control projects and solve problems

Existing project management methods have been refocused on controlling projects or solving problems. For example, the DMAIC-process, which is used within Six Sigma to Define, Measure, Analyze, Improve and Check process in a structured way, was developed to remove variability from the work process by removing defects – it was not designed to manage a project. And a project management structure, such as Prince2 and CCPM, was primarily meant to control projects, and not to solve problems.

When renewing the standard, we use a combination of both: defining the problem is an objective that is strongly based on data and analysis and this cannot be achieved through process improvement. It can only be achieved through renewal, while the form of execution can be approached in a project-like way.

As we discussed in the previous chapters, there are two roads that can lead to renewal of the standard:

1 Measurements show that, on a strategic level, a gap exists between the ideal situation and the current situation; a gap that cannot be bridged with a "normal" process improvement. A process renewal is needed to achieve the ideal situation.
2 During the improvement of the standard, we notice that the effect of the improvement intentions is insufficient to bridge the gap between the current value and the goal value. Then, the interventions are scaled from level 2 (improving standard) to level 3 (renewing standard) in the performance-behavior model.

When renewing the standard, the gap between the current situation and the desired situation is too large to bridge with an improvement step. The process of renewing the standard consists of five steps:

1 Define;
2 Measure;
3 Analyze;
4 Improve;
5 Control .

These five steps are the underlying process of the Six Sigma improvement method that is heavily based on statistical data and is defined as standard for the number of errors per produced amount. With 6 (sigma), the number of errors is no more than 3,4 errors per million produced units. With 4 (sigma), the number of errors is on 6200 per million possibilities, which is much higher. In that sense, the value of 6 is the symbol for striving for (near) perfection. This line of thought matches the lean philosophy of performance behavior: the goal value can be increased until the improvements result in the achievement of Six Sigma, or zero defects.

1 *Define*: determine objective and scope.
   The result of this step is that the innovative idea is converted into a business case with clear defined objectives, a clearly defined scope and calculations that justify the innovation.
2 *Measure*: collect all relevant data.
   The result of this step is the availability of plenty relevant and reliable process data for the next step. Furthermore baseline performance is determined in this step and the reliability of the measurement systems is determined.
3 *Analyze*: identify root causes.
   The result of this phase is the identification of root causes that are causing the deviation between the current performance and the desired performance.

4   *Improve*: identify and implement solutions
    The result of this phase is the selection of the best solution combined with
    an implementation plan for that solution.

5   *Control*: anchor and secure
    The result of this phase is that the renewed process is secured within the
    organization. It is now part of the standard and this standard is transferred
    to the "level of safeguarding the standard.

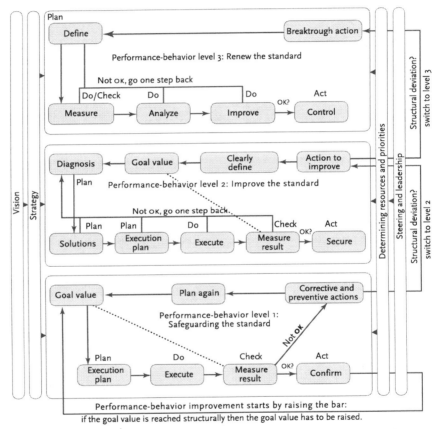

Figure 4.1   *The three performance-behavior levels including renewing the standard*

Pitfalls

It often happens in practice that the next phase in the DMAIC-cycle is started
before the previous step has been concluded. When you begin the preparation
activities for the next step, it is possible you will do all the work for nothing,

because technical or organizational changes can still occur in the previous step. Therefore, it is better to completely conclude each phase before starting the next.

4.2 Step 1 Define: determine objective and scope

During this phase specific problems are identified which could not be solved at the level of improving the standard. Subsequently these problems are clearly defined and a business case is created to let the sponsor of the project determine if it is desirable to start the innovation project.

The aim of this phase is to establish the project objective, to clearly define the project and to determine the scope. Furthermore it is determined which resources need to be deployed and what the exact result of the innovation project needs to be. The project team is composed and the project leader is appointed. That latter is specifically important, because in practice, the establisher of the business case is often automatically viewed as the driving force behind the project and therefore as project leader. However, a project leader needs different competencies and plays a different role; perhaps someone other than the establisher of the business case is much more suitable as project leader.

All of the issues mentioned above are formulated in a business case that also concretely contains the objective and the desired result (or deliverable) of the innovation project. This is backed up by calculations that justify the execution of the project.

The accuracy in planning or run time, in money or in resources has to be as high as possible at the end of this phase.

Three forces

Often there are three forces that underlie the realization of a project. These three forces can be used to assess the desirability of the realization of the project. The three forces are:

The power of the wishes of the customer from inside and outside the organization

When you weigh the power of the wishes of customers, the wishes of the external customer (the one who is prepared to pay for the added value to the service or product) take precedence over the wishes of other beneficiaries. In order to determine to what extent you can meet the customer's wishes, you can make use of Quality Function Deployment (QFD), a method to translate customer wishes and market demands into design demands. On the basis of QFD, you compose a matrix, which displays the weighed customer wishes, the strategic test of the customer wishes with an estimation of the efforts and a feasibility test.

The power of the strategic organization of the company

Whether or not the innovation contributes to the strategic objectives of the organization is also an important question. Since the innovation will have a long-term impact, it is important to perform this strategic test.

The power of the possibilities, limitations and the risks of the innovation

The third force field is the test of technological, organizational and therefore also behavioral possibilities and limitations of the innovation. Here, you also map when innovation is possible and which resources should be employed for this. Moreover, you make a thorough analysis of the possible risks of innovation. For this, you can conduct a brainstorming session with experts of specific sub-areas, but you can also use simple risk diagrams. An example of this is the following formula:

$$Risk = Chance \times Effect \times Response\ time$$

The three risk factors – chance, effect and response time – are displayed on a fixed scale (for instance 1 – 5) and on the basis that the risk is calculated per risk component or risk area: the specific component or area of which the risk is calculated. For example, the risk of organizing a barbecue lies in the weather, but also in the quality of the meat or the turn-up of the guests. These are various risk areas for which the risks can be calculated.

The Six Sigma technique FMEA is also used for this. FMEA stands for Failure Mode and Effect Analysis. The FMEA-technique ensures that taking precautions beforehand prevents possible failure in a process or product.

It is important that all involved parties are aware of what the most important result of this phase should be: the business case. This forms the starting point for the project and is the basis for safeguarding and steering by the commissioner.

Act only in the customer's interests. In the end the innovation project is all about increasing value for the customer. This value increase should be reflected in the business case.

Activities in the define phase

In the define phase there are three components of the innovation project that are described:

1 *Performance*
  Motivation (declaration of innovation), objective, (customer) expectations, project scope and definitions.
2 *Planning*
  Planning and activities, method of monitoring and measuring, agenda and milestones.
3 *Behavior*
  Roles, responsibilities, authorities, behavioral profiles of the team, team declaration and the critical success factors.

Together, these components form the basis of the business case that has to justify the innovation. Subsequently the statements about the improvement project are *verified* and *analyzed* before the business case will be defined in full detail.

1 Performance

○ *Declaration of innovation*
  In the declaration of innovation the most important motivation or justification for the innovation project is declared; the motivation for renewing the (sub-) process. In this declaration, a part of the expected results of the activities in the define phase are determined. The declaration of innovation, as part of the business case, names the following components:
  ‣ What is the background of this innovation and how big is the problem really?
  ‣ Why should this innovation be performed now?
  ‣ What are the consequences if we do not perform this innovation?
  ‣ How does this innovation relate to other organizational efforts we deliver at the moment?
○ *Objective declaration*
  Here, the project objective is described in accordance with the SMART-criteria, the scope is explained and the run time of the renewal is described. The phasing and the boundaries are also defined here. In this objective declaration, we name a number of components:
  ‣ Which deviations have we measured sufficiently to justify it as a reason for the innovation?
  ‣ Which specific added value will yield innovation: saving costs, turnover

increase, increase of customer satisfaction, volume increase, productivity increase, increase of employee satisfaction, cost price decrease, etc.
  ➤ In the context in which the innovation takes place, what exactly is the innovating component?
  ➤ How do we measure the success of this innovation?
  ➤ When is the innovation successful?
- *Project Scope*
  Here, the most important questions to ask to be able to determine the project scope are concerned with question about what the scope of the project is not. These are questions like: "What shouldn't we do" and "In what areas are we not going to venture ourselves?". This is a different starting point than most innovation projects have, which usually concentrate on the question: "What should we do?" By working the other way around you explicitly state which activities and areas do not belong to the project. This results in more focus on those activities and areas that do belong to the project.

2 Planning

- *Deliverable*
  Here, the project results are noted and the actual deliverable of the improve phase is described.
- *Resource*
  Here, the resources are noted qualitatively and quantitatively. The composition of the project team, roles and the team members with their behavioral profiles, competencies and authority are important here, as are other resources such as space. Also the budget, or the *capex* (*capital expenditures*, the costs for the development of durable production goods) for larger investments, is determined.
- *Calculation and substantiation of the yields of the innovation project*
  The contribution of the innovation project in terms of added value for the customer is calculated here. This step looks beyond the gains for the organization alone and includes the gains for the customers.

3 Behavior

Regarding behavior it is necessary to determine which specific actions of the project team have an effect on the success of the innovation project in the different areas of result. Subsequently, the frequency of the performance is aligned to the frequency of the behavior. Steering the behavior occurs at the same frequency as steering towards the performance. In this way, the behavior is secured in the performance steering system.

When composing a team it is relatively simple to increase the effectiveness of the team by making use of the behavioral profiles of the various team members. When we want convincing team members, we choose people with "dynamic" and "inspiring" factors in their behavioral profile. However, when we prefer more social and thorough team members, we choose people with more "social" and "correct" factors in their behavioral profile. Often, however, different types of behavior are needed in the different phases of the project. The defining phase requires more thoroughness and accuracy, whereas the improve phase requires someone who can influence, focus and even push where necessary.

When composing a team, it is wise to look at the behavioral profiles:

- *Dynamic*
  Team members with the "dynamic" profile factor prefer openness and directness. They focus on their goal and don't like details, because they prefer to focus on the main points. They like to discuss things and reach a consensus by negotiating.
- *Inspiring*
  Team members with the "inspiring" profile factor are focused on their team members. They talk a lot and sometimes have a tendency to digress from the objective of the project. They do not always discuss in a goal-oriented way and they like to reach decisions together with the team.
- *Social*
  Team members with the "social" profile factor are focused on personal relationships within the team. They are the stable factors within a team and are especially capable in their own area of expertise. They prefer to work systematically and don't like sudden change.
- *Correct*
  Team members with the "correct" profile factor are focused on detailed tasks. They are good at analyzing data and testing facts. They need clear substantiation and base their input on their own experiences.

Within a football team, you could see the "dynamic" and "inspiring" profile factors as attackers and the "social" and "correct" profile factors as defenders.

Verification, analyses and detailed defining

At this point all components (performance, planning and behavior) of the business case are described. To arrive at an accurate, reliable and detailed business case there three more steps needed:

1   Verify the data and information that used in the business case so far. This

concerns the validation and verification of the technical data, but also the organizational data. This step ensures that the correct data and information is used for the business case;

2 Analyze the data and information of the performance, planning and behavior components that was verified and validated in the previous step to determine the value of the outcomes for the innovation project.

3 Define the project in such detail and based on the outcomes of the analysis, that it is possible to continue to the next step in the DMAIC-cycle. This final step results in an elaborate and detailed business case that includes the following content:

- A concrete description of the objectives. The objectives should be carefully described both quantitatively and qualitatively;
- The scope of the project, including its boundaries;
- The requirements set for the project by the sponsor;
- An overview of the assumptions that cannot be immediately influenced, but do influence the project, such as *sales forecasts* or price index numbers;
- A list of the work to be done;
- A thorough description of the resources (personnel, materials, services, components, infrastructure) to be used. Here, thorough could relate to amounts, costs and (delivery) time;
- A description of the provisional work structure and the accompanying methods;
- A detailed planning of the activities that need to be performed in a fixed order;
- An overview of anticipated outsourcing, activities that will be performed by third parties for the project;
- An overview of all tools for checking and recording;
- The composition of the project team;
- The obligations related to both content and the obligations related to the process of the project group (and the project leader as chairman of the project team) and the sponsor of the project;
- The preconditions. In most cases, a precondition forms a limitation of the possibilities for a project. The preconditions are imposed externally and you cannot influence these. These are the requirements that the result of the project will eventually have to meet. An example of a precondition is a Water Authority tank that is used for a water purification process which emits gasses with sulfur (they smell) always has to be located in a reserved zone;
- The functional requirements. The functional requirements mention what the sponsor of the project wants the result of project to be or what he wants to achieve with the project. A functional requirement for the puri-

fication tank mentioned above is, for instance, the capacity of the purification installation;

- ▸ The operational requirements. The requirements that are set for the application or use of the result of the project and which the project needs to meet. An example of an operational requirement could be the accessibility of the purification installation;
- ▸ The design limitations. These are the limitations of the design within the framework of what is feasible within the execution of the project. An example of a design limitation is the height of a purification tank in relation to the horizon pollution in the reserved zone.

In the define phase there are several tools with which you can map the process or with which you can identify the waste of the process that needs renewal. Two are discussed here: the SIPOC-diagram, which is a Six Sigma instrument, and the *value-stream map*, which is a *lean*-tool.

SIPOC-diagram

The SIPOC-diagram is intended to generate a general process description. The letters stand for:

- ○ *Suppliers*
  Everyone, internal or external, who takes care of the supply of the raw materials, the semi-finished product or the information that is needed for the process at any given time.
- ○ *Input*
  The raw materials or the semi-finished product, but also, for instance, the information that is delivered.
- ○ *Process*
  All process steps that have to be performed to add value to the raw materials, the semi-finished products or the information, in order to give the product or service the form the customer wants to pay for.
- ○ *Output*
  The products or services that go to the internal and external customer.
- ○ *Customers*
  The next person (internal) in the process, or the customer who asked for the product or service (external).

The SIPOC-information is often displayed in so-called *swim lanes*, referred to as process schedules.

1 Supplier – 2 Input – 3 Process – 4 Output – 5 Customer

The process steps are subsequently placed in each of the lanes, to provide more insight into the total process from supplier to customer.

We could make the same overview at a micro level, where we also include the internal input, the internal process, the internal output and the internal customer. The way you make a SIPOC-diagram strongly depends on the level at which you wish to observe the innovation or the problem. Often, SIPOC-diagrams are only made on the basis of the physical process stream. With performance behavior, it is a challenge to apply the existing and tested models to both the performance component (the *what*) and the behavior component (the *how*) of the process.

Value-stream map

The SIPOC-diagram provides a visualization of the entire process; the value-stream map investigates the specific losses in the process in more detail. A value-stream map shows which components in the process add value and which components add costs to the result. Value-stream maps are based on process data and they are specifically intended to map value streams that contain losses (such as waiting times or storage) and to eventually eliminate those losses.

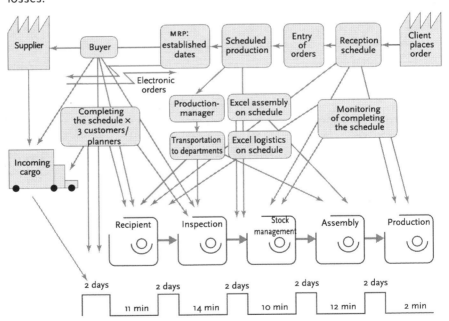

Figure 4.2 *Value-stream map*

Composition of the project group

Within innovation groups, and therefore within the project team, each project member has a specific role. These roles are written out in such a way that the performance contribution of each specific role is defined. When this definition is clear, the role can also be monitored at the same frequency as which this role delivers performances. Assigning the roles within a project team occurs on the basis of the following criteria:

- Behavior profile (see chapter 1);
- Competencies;
- Experience.

Importance of the define phase

In practice, many innovation projects exceed their projected run time and budget and they do not achieve the intended results. There are numerous examples of innovation projects that significantly exceed their budget and run time. Especially when the complexity of a project increases, less value can be attached to the estimations of both gains and costs. The reliability of the estimations in an innovation project is reversed proportional to the complexity of it.

The define phase should provide insight into the possible risks, chances, strengths and weaknesses of the innovation project. Too often, the risks and weaknesses are neglected in the first phases of the projects, which eventually lead to higher costs or a longer run time. Because of this, they pose a threat to the intended result of the innovation. These innovative, ambitious and revolutionary projects often do not go as planned because:

- The larger the project, the higher the budget, the more political forces are involved. This advocates for a division into controllable project components;
- The project manager falls prey to the optimism pitfall: the more ambitious a project is, the less the cognitive ability to make the expectations fit with the reality. This advocates for a thorough calculation on the basis of investigated facts;
- The more resources are used, the more delay they cause: more control, alignment and coordination is necessary and therefore the resources are less efficient. This aspect also advocates for a "cell approach" where small responsible teams address defined performance areas;
- The more time is needed, the greater the chance this project is delayed. The enthusiasm that prevailed at the beginning of the project slowly decreases, no matter how challenging the objectives are. On a project level, this also

advocates for high-frequency milestones where success is celebrated and can be shared, so behavioral success can be achieved each time. This provides renewed motivation and energy for the project every time, irrespective of the performance success.

Result of the define phase

The result of the define phase is a carefully defined, detailed and accurate business case that is presented to the sponsor of the project for approval. When the business case has been approved, the project can begin. It is also possible that the sponsor decides not to start the project. This could mean that the total project will not be carried out, but it might also mean a change of scope. However, when changes to the objectives are made, it is necessary to go through all stages of step 1 again, to be sure that the business case meets all specifications.

When the business case meets the demands of the sponsor and he grants his approval, the innovation project can begin.

4.3   Step 2 Measure: collect data

This phase is all about the collection and measurement of data. This can concern both technical data, but it can also concern organization data or experience facts that might contribute to the project. During this phase the critical inputs (Xs) and outputs (Ys) of the process are determined and subsequently a measurement plan is created to specify what data needs to be collected regarding the critical process inputs and outputs. Furthermore a measurement system analysis (MSA) will be conducted to determine the reliability of the data that will be collected.

Specify how much of the variation in the data is explained by the measurement system. This makes it possible to assess the variation caused by the process input factors in the analyze phase.

Activities during the measure phase

- Define the critical inputs and outputs of the process;
- Define the measurement plan;
- Test the measurement systems;
- Collect data;
- Determine baseline process performance.

Measurement plan

It is important that you know exactly what needs to be measured and analyzed before you start measuring or analyzing. Therefore, it is necessary to develop a solid measurement plan that contains an overview of the critical variables to be measured and analyzed. This overview has to be highly detailed, the unit has to be known per variable, a definition of the unit to be measured has to be given and there has to be a reason to measure these variables.

The reason for this is that data-analysis at large organizations is often very complicated due to the size of databases and due to the fact that randomly analyzing data costs unnecessary resources (time and money). You cascade from your project objectives and problem definition and determine what needs to be measured. Therefore, in the measurement phase, you mainly investigate what you will measure and analyze; the actual analysis takes place in the next phase, the analyze phase.

During the measurement phase the focus should not only lie on the 'hard', technical data, but attention should also be given to organization data and experience facts that can contribute to the innovation project. This type of data is often neglected, but can easily be retrieved from earlier project reports and meeting minutes.

The measurement plan is the backbone of the measure phase. As stated above it should specify exactly what data will be measured and how this data will be measured. The measurement plan should give answers to the following questions:

- What exactly is measured?
- When is this measured?
- Where is this measured?
- How frequently, for how long and how often is this measured?
- How is this measured?

After the completion of the measurement plan the project team can start the collection and measurement of the data. The collected data can provide new insight on which analysis can be done in the next step of the DMAIC-cycle: the analyze phase.

Project meetings

In this phase of the project, the project is just launched and often the team meets for the first time. Therefore, it is wise to determine how information should be handled and what project meetings with this group should look like in this phase.

Controlling the information during an innovation project is no easy activity. In innovation projects, most things go wrong in the information and communication structure. Misalignment and mismanagement of the expectations of the project leader and the project sponsor score high on the list of major project blunders. In a project structure, it is especially essential that each member receives the correct information in a timely fashion. When a clear system is lacking, time (and therefore money) is lost. It is therefore essential to set up an information system that guarantees that everyone receives the right information at the right time. In performance behavior, we use the PRSCI-system to this end. The letters PRSCI stand for Performing, Responsible, Supporting, Consulting and Informing. When using this system, the responsibility for each phase of the renewal project can easily be presented in a table.

An example of this is a manager of a department for continuous improvement. In the define phase, he is supportive, but in the measurement phase, he has to be consulted. In the improve phase, he is responsible. When you establish the right role in the right phase for every person involved, you ensure that the project group remains lean.

The information within and outside of the project group has to meet three criteria:

- Information has to be correct;
- Information has to be delivered at the right time;
- Information has to be delivered to the right person.

When information meets these three criteria, it is useful.

The project meetings that take place in many organizations are often ineffective and inefficient meetings instead of structured and performance-oriented meetings during which decisions are made and efforts are made to steer the project. By clearly defining the roles and establishing the information system and communication in a plan, you create a structure that stimulates the desired behavior. This structure may not guarantee an exchange of information within the team and between the individual members of the project team, but it will definitely encourage this.

Nowadays, video conferencing possibilities are used more often as an alternative for a physical project meeting. When you do opt for a physical meeting, you can pay attention to the following matters to guarantee a useful process for all project members:

- Preparation
  - Aligning agendas, times and rooms with fellow project members;
  - Choice for suitable place, room and time;
  - Choice for participants by phase (with PRSCI as tool);
  - Ensuring auditing of the most important roles within the project group;
  - Composing the agenda in a timely fashion;
  - Prioritizing the points on the agenda.
- Meeting itself
  - Starting at the agreed upon time;
  - Finishing on time;
  - Announcing the objectives;
  - Safeguarding time during the meeting and naming the remaining time;
  - Monitoring the roles of participants and speaking time;
  - Finishing at the planned time.
- After the meeting
  - Developing action and decision list and mailing it to the participant
  - Evaluating the meeting briefly in terms of process and content
  - Should feedback interviews be held with particular individual participants in response to the results of the auditing of behavior?

Result

The measure phase should result in the availability of plenty relevant and reliable process data, organizational data and experience facts that can be used for analysis in the next phase. Furthermore the baseline performance of the process is determined and the reliability of the measurement systems is determined.

4.4   Step 3 Analyze: identify root causes

In this phase the collected data from the measurement phase is analyzed to identify potential root causes for not achieving the determined goal value as determined in the define phase. The question that needs to be addressed during the analyze phase is "What is the cause of the deviation between the current performance and the goal performance?". To be able to make improvements it is necessary to first identify the causal factors.

Activities during the analyze phase

- Identify the gap between current performance and goal performance;
- Making graphical analyses of the data variances;
- Identify causal links in the patterns and the data variances. Here, you can answer the following questions:
  - What are the root causes of the variation in the data?
  - Which patterns can be discovered or measured in the data that is analyzed?
- List the identified root causes;
- Prioritize the root causes based on the impact on performance.

Tools and techniques that can be used during the analyze phase are:

- Value flow analysis to identify what steps in the process actually create value and what steps contain waste;
- Cause and Effect diagram to visualize the relationship between a root cause and its effect;
- Regression Analysis to test hypotheses about the root causes;
- ANOVA-analysis to analyze if the variance of the process is significant.

Result

At the end of the analyze phase it should be clear what root causes are causing the deviation between the current performance and the goal performance. Once the root cause is known, action can be taken in the improve phase to eliminate it.

4.5 Step 4 Improve: Identify and implement solutions

During the improve phase possible solutions to the root causes are identified and subsequently implemented. The work of all previous phases is integrated here. All efforts from the previous phases come together in the improve phase and the higher the quality of the previous phases was, the fewer failures and errors the improve phase will have.

In this phase, the project team needs members with creative and inventive characteristics. These are usually people with the "inspiring" or "correct" profile factors. Based on the identified root causes in combination with the demands from the business case that were formulated in the define phase, various solutions are developed. Subsequently, the best of these solutions are selected as a basis for the realization of the innovation project. Here, you can once again make use of the analytical methods described in chapter 3: Ishikawa diagrams, graphs, trend line, Pareto overviews, histograms, flowcharts, scatter plots and the brainstorm technique. The best solution is further developed in this phase.

If necessary, samples or prototypes are made and a pilot study is conducted in the service sector that tests the chosen solution in practice. The advantage of this is that you can demonstrate that the chosen solution meets the demands and wishes that were defined in the previous phase.

In the previous century, projects were generally designed in their entirety and then subsequently implemented. The speed of change has increased so much since 2000, that it is necessary to design solutions in smaller steps so the project can be carried out in smaller goal steps and new objectives and resources can be determined in case of altered circumstances.

Activities during the improve phase

- Identify solutions for the root causes;
- Choose the best solution that meets the requirements of the business case;
- Create a detailed implementation plan that includes all actions that need to take place to implement the chosen solution;
- Execute the solution according to the implementation plan;
- Safeguard the progress of the implementation in terms of quality, time and costs;
- Give support to the implementation team.

The PDCA-cycle for the improvement phase

After the implementation of the chosen solution it is important to check if the implemented solution had the desired effect. In essence the improve phase has its own PDCA-cycle in which:

- The implementation of the solution is planned in the implementation plan;
- The solution is implemented according to the implementation plan;
- The effect of the solution on the performance is checked by means of measurement;
- When the current performance no longer deviates from the goal performance the project can move on to the control phase;
- When the current performance still deviates from the goal performance it is necessary to take action.

When, after implementation, there still is a deviation between current performance and goal performance it is necessary to work back through the DMA-IC-cycle to identify where the root cause lies for not achieving the expected result. When this root cause is identified the PDCA-cycle can be followed again until the performance meets the goal performance and a deviation no longer occurs.

Result

This phase should result in the selection of the best solution combined with an implementation plan for that solution. The implementation of the solution is checked on result and should have resolved the deviation between the current performance and goal performance. During this phase it is important to stick to the plans, because when the implementation is not achieving the desired result it is possible to take action according to the PDCA-cycle. Finally the implementation should satisfy the results that were determined in the business case. Once this predetermined result is achieved, it is time to move to the next phase to ensure that the result is secured within the organization.

4.6   Step 5 Control: anchor and secure

The control phase is the phase in which the project is carried over to the performance behavior level "safeguarding the standard". During this step it is ensured that the renewed process becomes part of the standard. This is a vital step in the project, which makes it more than a project evaluation. It is a full-fledged step we use to embed both performance and behavior in the organization.
In this phase, the result is controlled, used and maintained by the organization. Since it is a renewal, this means an adjustment of processes, structures, and behavior and with that, also an adjustment of results. This is often a difficult task, since old patterns of behavior are often deeply ingrained and require attention to change. Therefore, it is a good idea to set up a separate embedding program, including objectives, planning, resources and processes. With a lot of major renewal projects, you should consider this phase as a separate project where you go through the same steps and phases as in a renewal project. Also at this level of renewing the standard the Job Instructing program, discussed in section 2.6, can be used to ensure that the renewed standard will be applied within the organization.

Activities in the control phase

- ○ Set up an follow-up program
- ○ Executing the follow-up program as it was set up.
- ○ If necessary, performing maintenance to the result of the project and to the tools belonging to the project.

Result

The execution goes according to plan and the renewed process is secured within the organization. Securing means that the renewed process is now part of the standard and that the process does not deviate from the predefined objectives.

Some project management methods consider the control phase as a continuous project. However, performance behavior shows that an innovation project is a temporary organization that is eventually embedded into the existing organization. After the level of renewing the standard, the project is again embedded in safeguarding the standard. Checking the new activities that result from renewing the standard takes place on the level of safeguarding the standard and not on the level of renewing the standard.

5

FROM CHANGE AS A PROJECT TO CONTINUOUS IMPROVEMENT

For most organizations, the implementation of performance behavior is a change in itself. That is the reason why a significant part of this book is dedicated to managing this change process. This chapter will hand you insights and techniques to develop your organization into a performance-behavior organization.

It may look like a contradiction: performance behavior strives for continuous and incremental improvement, but this is achieved by a (rigorous) change to the current way of working. We will discuss this in further detail in section 5.1. This chapter also discusses the various forces that play a role in change processes.

You can consider the performance-behavior model as a navigation system for implementing policies or strategy. When using a navigation system, you need the maps of the countries you drive through on the way to your destination; the performance-behavior model as route planner for change processes works the same way. By means of the performance-behavioral model, you determine what next step you need to arrive at your final destination from the current situation.

5.1   Why organizations need to be continuously changing

There are plenty of examples of organizations that did not adjust, or did not adjust quickly enough, to the demands of the future. The Dutch East India Company fell apart because the management could not respond to the English and French competition. A similar, but more recent, disaster hit the tire manufacturers Dunlop and Goodyear, who did not manage to copy the radial tires of Michelin in time and lost a major portion of the North-Atlantic market. The banks who thought the possibilities were endless during the credit crisis were deceived: due to the cobweb of reinsured papers without underlying value, the value of the prestigious Lehman Brothers – with a history that dates back to 1850 – decreased by 40% within one day, resulting in bankruptcy of the company within five days. Only in 2009 did the first fragile signs of recovery of the crisis become visible. The price for this wake-up call was unbelievably high: 2.000.000.000.000.000.000 dollars (estimation at the end of 2009).

These are all examples of organizations that did not change when it was necessary. But there are also examples of organizations that did anticipate change. Apple, Google, and of course the Berkshire Hathaway company are great examples of organizations that were aware of their market environment and adjusted to the changing conditions. When we look at Nokia as example of the biggest mobile phone company in the early days, who is now making 'the Microsoft Move' to keep up with its market competitors. Will it be on time?

Additionally, there are also organizations that want or have to change as a result of a takeover or merger. The bursting of the internet bubble after the millennium also brought about a wave of takeovers and dissolutions. This happened because, for the most part, management reacted too late to the changing circumstances, meaning that the level of ambition could not be realized.

Since the circumstances change with an increasingly higher frequency, it is necessary that companies employ a structured system that embeds continuous change, renewal and improvement in all processes within the organization.

The cycle of performance development has become faster. This has inevitable consequences for behavior development. The behavior that has led to a certain performance in a company in the last ten years might not be the same behavior that will lead to the same performance in the same company in the coming ten years.

We can summarize the need for change in four arguments.

Argument 1: The continuously and increasingly faster changing environment

Organizations have to work more efficiently, cheaper, more sustainably, faster and better. Not only customers demand these conditions, but also the government contributes to this with stricter laws and regulations, as well as stakeholders, the market and one's own employees who also demand continuous improvement and adjustment. After all, the world around us is constantly moving and this will not stop after the first improvement. And when an organization stops improving, the changes will still occur at the competing firms. This means that stagnation is decline: this has never been as clearly visible and noticeable as in this 21st century.

Compare this to a professional swimmer who swims a world record. After the match, he goes home and celebrates, but the next morning, he reports at the pool again. And then? The bar is raised a little again to provide stretch in the objective: a deviation between the current value and the goal value has been created again, and the journey of development begins already the day after the world record.

Additionally, in this age of information, you do not merely have to deal with local competition; nowadays there is worldwide competition in nearly each type of organization. A few centuries ago, we only had to fear the competition in our own street; last century, we had national competition and now even global competition. The age of global hyper competition has begun: an age of enormous competition in which the combined forces of globalization, new technologies, interconnectivity, economical liberalization, an increasingly large gap between rich and poor (and especially the increase of rich consumers), a shortage of fossil fuel, a rapidly deteriorating environment and a shortage of highly-educated employees make the lives of organizations more difficult than ever before.

Moreover, the fast growth of economies in Asia has radical consequences for the competitive position of the established markets and the global market. Therefore, it also has consequences for the way in which organizational processes have to be shaped. Even during the Credit crisis, there was a growth of over 3% for the Asian region in 2011. This was still a major decrease of growth compared to the years before, but it was still growth. Of the 1,3 billion inhabitants of China, only 300 million live according to the western standard. Asia is a market with growth opportunities for the established markets but it is also a competitive threat of unprecedented proportions that force us to improve and renew.

Argument 2: The law of the decreasing lead

Organizations are only prepared to change when there is an immediate need to do so. When business is good, organizations trust that the future will be the same. However, the world continues to develop. There will come a time when the law of decreasing lead will make sure that your organization has to implement a radical change in order to once again meet the wishes of the environment. Waiting for this to happen is highly reactive. It is better for you organization to actively work on change. After all, becoming the best is a challenge, remaining the best requires discipline and constant will-power to improve.

Jan Romein gives an illustrative example of the law of the decreasing lead in his book *The dialectic of progress*. At the beginning of the 19th century, London was one of the first major cities that changed from candle light to gas lighting for city lighting, at a time when it was advantageous to opt for gas as an energy source. A short period after London implemented gas lighting; a newer, cheaper and safer energy source for city lighting was discovered: Electricity. At that moment, the new city lighting in London still worked well, but had become outdated immediately due to this development. Other cities switched from candlelight to electrical city lighting, whereas London continued to use the expensive, maintenance intensive gas lanterns that have not been written off yet until the 20th century.

Argument 3: From unique situation to daily practice

By means of continuous change, you prevent yourself from suddenly becoming threatened and forced into rigorous change. When an organization hasn't been through a change trajectory for a long time, they have a good chance of being in a "sleep state" or vacuum. This is a situation in which employees perform their activities comfortably, but in which their work method is not critically scrutinized in order to investigate whether this work method is still the best. In case of an external threat (see argument 1), an organization will have to undergo radical change. The more radical the change, the more resistance this will bring. By continuously critically scrutinizing your own organization, it is possible to gradually implement radical changes. The advantage of this style of change is that the employees are less strained. After all, implementing improvements is already part of the daily processes of the organization. Therefore, change is in the very genes of the organization.

Argument 4: Development has a positive character

When you do not change until the change is absolutely crucial, this creates (too much) pressure. This extra pressure can result in a failure to implement the change. This possible failure in turn puts extra pressure on the employees, which increases the chance the change actually fails. This is the ultimate self-fulfilling prophecy. The basis of development lies in the philosophy "We can always improve". Not survival, but optimization should be at the basis of change. This requires a different mentality: not change as a reaction to a problem, but instead, we should anticipate situations that could occur and critically observe the on-going processes in the organization. Do not individually protect what we have now, but attack with the entire team to improve.

 Adaptability is the main core quality of organizations in the 21st century.

In this, we differ greatly from Asia in terms of mentality and behavior. Since Asia has more collectivism in human behavior, employees in Asia focus more on performing "together" in regard to executing concepts such as 5S. When the instruction is to perform cleaning activities together with your team, no one in Asia would doubt that the entire team would actually participate. In Europe, we would sooner have a look at the division of tasks and "Who will do what?" instead of looking at how this job could be done together. Because of this, many European organizations miss the core of the improvement philosophies that were developed in Japan. For these companies that tried to adopt the philosophy, the philosophy became a trick. You do not implement a philosophy with a major change, but with incremental, yet clearly defined, measurable steps. Only then will the "trick" become part of the shared values of an organization.

These arguments, however, do not advocate that organizations should continuously change for the sake of change. They do imply that organizations should continuously investigate whether they can improve. You are never finished; look at the swimmer who creates stretch again, the day after his world record. Organizations are never finished either and will always have to create stretch. When an organization can reach this stage of improvement, there is not only change, there is development as well.

5.2   Resistance to change

Change endangers our safety, as was clarified in chapter 1. We develop resistance to change, because we wish to protect the safety we have built up in the situation as it is now. This is not merely true for people, but also for the sum of the individual behavior: the organizational behavior. The behavior of an organization and the structures that were built within this organization protect "the old" and keep "the new" at bay. We will only tread these new paths when we know they will lead somewhere useful. Otherwise, we will not take this road.

Field study: what's in it for me?

Figure 5.1 is a schematic display of our brain containing an imaginary pathway. In a simplified way, this pathway portrays a route we take daily in our mind. It is a think-route that determines our behavior. In reality, there are millions of routes you go through each day within your mind, but in order to simplify this example, we will stick to one. This route is so often taken that other pathways, that are not used, are slowly broken down until they are no longer accessible, because the pathway that used to exist has disappeared completely.

You could translate the route you take in those millions of situations a day into a literal route: the road you take from home to work each day. This is also a route that will become increasingly natural and after a while, you will get used to it. You know how long the route takes, with and without traffic, and you know what you can expect and what the surroundings look like in the different seasons. This example is highly suitable to serve as a practice test to show how people make choices in the self-evident daily routes they take in their mind. This tells us something about people's motivation to display other behavior with a different result.

What does this study teach us? When we experience there is something in it for us, we are prepared to surrender the old safety since the new safety gives us something better or different.

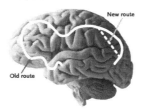

Figure 5.1 *Route through the brain*

In our fieldwork we did two years of testing with a group of varying composition and of varying size. We drew a figure (such as 5.1) on a flip-chart and we picked a random person in the group, who drove to work by car. We explained to him the meaning of the picture and checked whether he could imagine that this new 'way' was also applicable to his route from his work to his home. Then we started our testing in the presence of all colleagues. Usually the tension was running high as everyone wondered where this strange story went.

Imagine that we, as an alternative to this route, have discovered a new route that is shorter (or better, prettier, faster). Would you consider using this route? Our research shows that the vast majority of people say no (about 95%)in advance. While they knew (they had just been told) that the route would be shorter (or better, prettier, faster).More people said no when they were in a group, also when the group members did not use the same route. It seemed as though they tried to protect what they had built up with the group. When we talked to these people alone, approximately 30% of them were willing to change their route in advance.

We asked the selected person to virtually drive the route with us and visualize it. The route consisted, as you can see in figure 5.1, of t a part of "the old road" and later of "the new road". We started "driving" and asked the person how he sat in the car and if he had a navigation system. The person told us that he was usually relaxed and leaned back in the car: usually listening to music, sometimes making a phone call, the navigation system was turned off and all people were relaxed in the car. This was the case until the moment we arrived at the new part of the road. Previously they said that, in reality, they would never take this road, but that they would try it now, in thought.

We saw that the person literally sat up straight now. And then we asked: "And how do you feel now, what do you see, what are you doing?" Nearly all people said they had to sit up straight, because they wanted to be able to see exactly where they were driving. Some turned down their music, so they could focus better. Others wanted to switch on the navigation system so it could show them the way. The resistance was clearly noticeable. Some said: "This road cannot possible be shorter". But we told them: "And now that you have arrived at your destination, ten minutes earlier than usual, how do you feel now, what do you think, what do you do?" Everyone, hundred percent of the people gave the reaction: " If only I had known this sooner!", "I won't take the old road again!", and there were many other similar responses.

However, this study also teaches us that merely the message of change does not suffice to move people, even though it clearly promises improvement. After all, people have built up years of experience with their own pathways that have been (according to their own standard) successful. Why would they change? Sometimes, you need a little push from someone else to experience what a change could yield for you. Without that push, you probably would not have experienced it.

 'What got you here, won't get you there.' Marshall Goldsmith

The example also illustrates that social pressure contributes to the rejection of innovations, even if they have been proven to be successful. This has also been researched in the tobacco industry. Employees in this industry, who do not smoke, because they know that it has been scientifically proven that smoking causes cancer, usually do not address the smoking behavior of colleagues who do smoke. We conform to the behavior that the majority displays, even when we know better.

Insecurity and self-worth

What happens in the minds of the employees when we enter into the performance-behavior change process? When we learn about what they might think, we have a chance to help the employees in your organization.

The psychologist Abraham Maslow gives us a few starting points in his hierarchy of needs, in which he explains that basic needs, such as the certainty of food, a roof over your head and safety, first have to be fulfilled before there is room for (personal) development. It is a good model to explain why we return to the controllable, lower level of needs at moments when our securities are threatened by change. As you read in chapter 1, our schemas provide security. We know what we can expect and display behavior that matches these expectations. When changes in our environment occur, especially when these changes require different behavior from us, most people experience this as a threat. When we look at this from the perspective of the behavioral profiles from chapter 1, we see that people with specific profile factors find this more difficult than others. For instance, people with a strong social profile factor in their behavior profile generally have more difficulty with this than people with a strong dynamic component in their behavior profile.

When a change is effectuated (becomes reality in the eyes of the person that considered the change as a possible threat), we ask ourselves questions, both consciously and subconsciously, about our safety (What is the influence of this change on my role and work?), appreciation (What does this mean to my status and influence?), securities (What does this mean for the future?) and values (Who am I and what do I want?).

We implicitly compare the answers to these questions to our sense of self-worth: we compare them to our inner frame of reference, which is built up from numerous situations we have experienced before, and that provides us with information about ourselves and our environment. Our self-worth is the self-appreciation that makes us feel good about ourselves. For healthy people, this self-appreciation is slightly more positive than what is realistically justified, because in this way we are stimulated to try again in case of failure. If we were to have a purely realistic idea of ourselves, in practice, this would not lead to a new attempt and this, in turn, would drastically diminish our chance of survival. Depressed people often do have a more realistic, or even a negative idea of themselves. This group often does not take enough action and has a tendency to throw in the towel, which causes them to become stuck in the negative spiral they entered due to the illness.

Our self-worth has two foundations. The first is an internal foundation, where we evaluate ourselves on the basis of our own values and standards. However, most people start with the external appreciation from other people and let their own evaluation depend on the appreciation others give them. Our sense of self-worth is dependent upon the image we have of ourselves and the image that others have of us.

The value we attach to the appreciation of others depends on the value we attach to the person who appraises us. The appreciation from a person we think highly of has a greater impact on us than the appreciation of someone we see as insignificant. When one of our parents appraises us (assuming that we value our parents highly) this will have a large impact, whereas the appreciation from someone who just happens to pass by will have less impact on us. This also strongly depends on our behavioral profile. People who score high on "inspiring", will focus their compass more on other people rather than on themselves, whereas people who are especially "correct", will follow their own compass.

Each change that will occur has impact on the securities we have regarding the appreciation we receive and give ourselves. This is person and profile dependent. Changes give, as was previously mentioned, rise to questions such as:

○ What is the influence on the work I do? Now and in the future?

- What influence does this change have on my value for the company?
- Does this change have possible consequences for my job?

Most questions people ask about the threat of the appreciation they receive arise from threats and not from opportunities. In this phase of insecurity, employees will start asking questions to create certainties. In this way, each possible contradiction or dishonesty in the message is an exponentially increasing factor for the sense of insecurity. Each employee will subsequently try to ascertain his own securities as much as possible. Over the years, practice shows over and over again that organizations that are capable of communicating about changes in an open and clear manner are more successful than organizations that try to conceal or manipulate information.

Handle resistance

Expressions of resistance in case of changes are mainly expressions of fear; the fear that the safe environment an employee learned to work in (read: survive in) is turned upside down. Examples of such resistance in case of change and therefore also in case of the change into performance behavior can be:

- Is it necessary that we start this change now?
- Why do we have to do this now?
- I don't think this will ever work for us.
- Why is this happening now in our organization or on our department?
- We have so much to do already; this is just too much.
- We have never been told we weren't doing a good job.
- We're doing a good job, right?
- That will never yield enough.
- We have done something similar in the past, but it didn't work then either.
- In our type of organization, this won't work.
- I would approach this change completely different.
- I am convinced this won't work.

How do we handle resistance? What can we do to counter it? There are a lot of methods to implement change. You can read more about a number of these below:

- *Power-pressure method*
  This is a change method where change is forced from a position of power. This is the most direct method that seems to be effective to bring about behavioral change. The organization structure, with its hierarchical relationships and the possibility to employ sanctions and rewards, makes such an

approach obvious. In practice, however, the effectiveness is disappointing. This method often only leads to behavioral change for the duration of the pressure. Moreover, people with high speed behavior – these are the people with the "dynamic" or "inspiring" profile factors - will often experience this type of change as impeding, to which they will only display more resistance. This approach will work well with people with the profile factor "social" or "correct" for a brief time, but to achieve result with this method it is important that results are quickly achieved and that everyone experiences the benefit of the change.

- *Normative-reductive method*
  Behavioral change is pursued via the group the individual is part of. Here, the existing   standards are reduced. The downside of this is that the change takes a relatively long time, but this form of change does have the largest impact in the long term.
- *Rational-empirical method*
  This method strives for behavioral change by giving people rational information in order to bring about change in the group. The idea is that human beings are rational creatures and that their behavior will change when they understand that this is necessary, desirable or better. In practice, this only appears to work when the advantage is clear or when the employee actually has a rational behavior profile. This only applies to people with the factors "dynamic" or 'correct" in their behavior profile. If the change contradicts deeper convictions of the employees, this method is much less effective (Bennis, Benne & Chin, 1970).

In practice, a combination of change methods proves to work best, depending on the behavioral profiles of the people involved. When executing performance behavior, you should convey the message and the "what" of the change according to the power-pressure method. After all, no discussion about setting the standard exists. It is understandable that not everyone will like this, but it will happen this way. Subsequently, it is important to take people into the new situation. Visit a company that already uses performance behavior, or show what 5S means in practice. "Feeling, smelling, tasting and experiencing" is the motto, so that everyone can acquire his or her own images. Then, the rational-empirical method can be used: substantiate with facts and show numbers that underline the effect of performance behavior. Subsequently, everyone will actually start working on the implementation. The standards are established and that is the moment input can be delivered: how are we going to shape the content of the standards? Finally, the normative-reductive method is employed. In daily practice, there will be steered on the basis of deviations in performance and deviations in behavior. Furthermore, prevailing resistance will be analyzed, and communication is employed that addresses the various profile factors.

Law of resistance

Sometimes, when a manager is trying to break through resistance, this can instead result in even more resistance. Then, he actually creates resistance by supervising too strictly and not being flexible enough. When the manager is no longer able to switch back from a heavily result-oriented style of supervising to a more relationship-oriented style of supervising, the "law of resistance" occurs. This law means that, in a situation with a lot of support already, acceptance decreases when an overly strict style of supervision is applied. Subsequently, the manager feels he has to compensate with an even stronger style, which only results in even lower acceptance. Providing space and responsibility for the employee is a solution, but the manager should have sufficient style flexibility for this. Chapter 7 will discuss the supervising styles within performance behavior in further detail.

Important factors in breaking through resistance in supervising are: interest (gain), help (facilitation), involvement (ownership), level of supervision (pressure) that is needed, and timing (momentum). Supervision and momentum are both related to breaking through the resistance level.

The resistance mass of the change group is:

$$\frac{\text{Group size x old behavior x interest in keeping old behavior}}{\text{Group size x new behavior x interest in developing new behavior x involvement}}$$

This mass can be influenced by:

- Confirming and stimulating new, desired behavior;
- Addressing people's old, undesired behavior and slowing this down;
- Bringing down the context and structure in which the old behavior takes place;
- Changing the composition of the group;
- Changing the group size;
- Building context and structures in which new behavior can take place;
- Training, helping and stimulating people and applying structure to the new behavior;
- Addressing the present potential;
- Increasing the (self-)interest;

● Increasing (the sense of) involvement by letting people participate in the "how" of the change.

5.3   Changing in phases

Resistance, unwillingness, complaints, protest, hindering and objections are all words that are related to "not wanting". These are things the management can experience when starting the performance-behavior implementation process. However, the resistance does not arise from unwillingness to change, but from unwillingness to be changed. The responses that arise from resistance differ greatly per person. Perception creates reality.

During the implementation of performance behavior, employees go through various phases of coping with change. The time an individual spends in a certain phase differs significantly per person. Usually, people do go through all phases, but sometimes a phase takes up such a short time it seems as though it has been skipped completely.

Changing phase 1: Let it blow over

In this first phase, the employee does not yet pay much attention to the change. He hopes it will blow over, because it makes him feel insecure since he is not completely sure what the new plans and the changes will mean for him. This uncertainty arises from the fact that he is confronted with a change he perhaps did not see coming. Therefore, the change (no matter how small this might appear to someone else) is a potential threat for the existence of his job. Acknowledge and accept the employee as he is and give him space, within the framework of change.

Changing phase 2: Denial

In the denial phase, the employee looks for arguments. Usually, people search for arguments against the change. In this phase, people question everything and everyone and they produce arguments that have nothing to do with the change itself, but that do give the employee in denial the idea he understands ("I already know why they desire this change, the managers want to earn more!"). From this, cynicism and sarcasm emerge and this can lead to a tense atmosphere on the work floor. Talk about the resistance, but clearly indicate what the objective is. Let the employee think along by including him in thinking about what he needs to achieve this objective.

Changing phase 3: Anger

When denial becomes pointless and the employee sees there is no way back, he will display an answer in this phase. In fact, the employee means: "I don't want this!" All emotions will be employed in order to reinforce this feeling. Give the employee the space to express these emotions (within reasonable boundaries). Often, he will not yet see the result of the changes and consequently it is logical he resists the change. Therefore, ask questions to uncover the real root causes of the resistance.

Changing phase 4: Finding compromises

In this phase, the employee negotiates in order to influence the changes. The first objective is often still to boycott or delay the change by negotiating. Later in this phase, the employee, seeking compromise, will look for elements that will benefit him. Explain the plans. Acceptance is important and influence is vital for the success of performance behavior, but once the plans have been made, there is little room to negotiate all facets of these changes with all those involved again.

Changing phase 5: Defeat

In this phase, the employee is no longer angry and he understands that further resistance does not offer a solution. It will simply happen. He does not yet support it, but he accepts it as the situation. In this phase, his behavior becomes passive and, eventually, it might even lead to stress when the employee is not capable of considering the change from his own circle of influence. It is important in this phase to clearly facilitate the employee and train specific behavior. In this phase, the emphasis lies on the aspect of "not being able to" and not so much on "not wanting to".

Changing phase 6: Asking questions

When the employee is capable of making the step from defeat to his own circle of influence, one of the first signals of this revival will be that he will start asking how-questions. A how-question is always a sign of recovery, because apparently the "what" has already been accepted and is (partly) known. In this phase, answer the questions and stimulate the employee to experiment and discuss his experiences.

Changing phase 7: Cooperating

In this phase, the employee has accepted the change. His use of language shows this because he uses "we" a lot, and the how-questions have made way for suggestions and often also for (sub) results. In this phase, it is important to show results specifically related to the behavior of the employee as soon as possible. Seeing that "other behavior" can be linked to a "better result" is the best motivation to bring about lasting change. This is the beginning of continuous improvement.

5.4 Success factors for change

All too often organizations focus primarily on the shape of the change process instead of on the content and the process itself. For instance, the discussion concerning who is allowed to be included in thinking and discussing about certain matters is often considered more important than the possible risks at each step of the change process. With every necessary change step, such as the implementation of performance behavior, various success factors can be observed that provide the right direction and speed for the change.

Necessity, strategy, structure, system, capacity and success – these are the six success factors that can influence the speed and direction the change is realized with. By means of these six forces, we can establish what the current situation is, what strategy needs to be defined, what the desired direction of the organization is and how the organization wants to get there. Moreover, the six forces help in executing the change trajectory, because they indicate which strings need to be pulled in order to successfully implement the change. These six success factors play a role in each change trajectory.

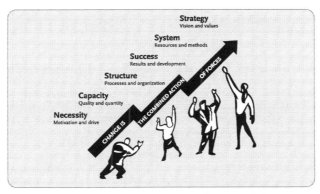

Figure 5.2 *The six success factors for change into a performance-behavior organization.*

Success factor 1: Necessity creates movement

Without necessity, no movement occurs. Only when management, supervisors and employees have accepted that change is necessary, they are prepared to change. After all, when people do not feel the necessity to do something that costs extra energy, they will not put in extra effort. The necessity has to be known to everyone, has to be felt by everyone. Furthermore, people will not only have to be sent into a new direction, they will also have to be helped to develop new securities in this changing environment.

In order to disseminate the necessity, you need a motivator and energy. The organization has to be charged and the present energy has to be clustered again. Often, a lot of energy is present in an organization, but it is spent on the wrong things. The organization needs pullers who go for it, who propagate the necessity and can also ignite the spark in others. Change cannot occur without these pullers, pillars, solicitors or others that are like-minded. They provide support within the organization. These people need to be placed in crucial positions in the organization; not merely in the management, but also in middle management and staff departments. Otherwise, you never achieve sufficient support.

Feeling the necessity is one of the forces needed to bring about growth and change within the organization. In performance behavior, it is necessary that this stimulus is constantly given. The question that may arise here is: "What do you mean, stimulate? Each employee always wants to improve, right?" Naturally, few people will be against better customer service or a more efficient company policy when it betters them. And "better" could also mean that their daily work process becomes smarter or easier. Usually, this also means that the employees have to perform new or different activities. In case of change, the following question is at the core of the matter: "Are both the employees and the management prepared to invest? And does it provide benefits for the employee who has to invest in terms of time or education?"

These questions arise when the consequences of the change for the organization and the way in which these work are considered. This means that a step has to be made away from an organization in which everyone tries to achieve a good performance in his own way to an organization in which people work in accordance with the agreed standards, methods and shared skills.

This means that the managers and supervisors have their work cut out for them: they have to take a difficult road of cooperation with other departments, they are addressed by colleagues and employees about their support to the program, they have to address employees about keeping agreements. Because of this, it often happens that the given "yes" in favor of change loses to the emotional energy after some time. By making results visible on all performance behavior levels and by also showing that the changed behavior yields results on an individual level, you bring about a faster and better development and at the same time you are securing the new behavior.

Objectives are set higher when making the change towards a performance behavior organization. In order to achieve these performance behavior objectives – and grow with them – resources have to be made available. These resources can be both quantitative (for example financial, extra capacity) and qualitative (for example increasing knowledge and skills by means of training).

How can you ensure that the management of the organization contributes to creating the need for the implementation of performance behavior? This is a difficult point. In the beginning of the change trajectory, the involvement of management is requested without them knowing exactly what this will mean. The most important method to create and retain support for the trajectory is by means of ownership. Ownership stands for the motivation to achieve a specific objective, without an immediate external stimulus (for instance financial). An owner knows what he works for. In order to create ownership, you can give (a selection of) the employees involved the possibility to contribute to the improvement actions and hence the possibility to influence these actions. This makes employees owners of their own process of change. Therefore, the development to give people the capacity to change is central to the change trajectory, rather than the change itself.

An example of creating ownership with management and supervisors is that you actively involve them in the "how", as soon as the performance-behavior change is known. It will also be necessary to analyze the specific gaps in performance in more detail and to develop possible solutions and actions together with experts. In practice, these think tanks are called direction teams. The management can participate in a number of these direction teams, from which a specific part of the performance-behavior implementation ownership arises since managers and supervisors will not merely feel responsibility (because they can steer the sub-process of change "themselves"), but will also experience the result of the change (because they make shared partial results visible within their own direction team).

To make the employee feel he is an owner of the change, you need pullers with persuasiveness. They have to explain to the employees why a certain strategy leads to a certain result and that this also results in an improvement in their own situation. Pullers can be found in key positions in the organization; this does not specifically refer to the actual function but can also refer to the social position within the organization.

Eventually, the feeling of necessity does not arise automatically. In order to create necessity, it is important to also arrange the structure, systems and capacities within the organization in such a way that this supports the strategy needed to achieve the desired situation. Increasing necessity is not merely influenced by increasing ownership, but also by sufficient focus on the other success factors for change that are described in this chapter.

Necessity and commitment

Commitment stands for obligation passion and engagement. No other word fits with performance behavior as well as this word does. The performance-behavior combination that is enclosed in the word has a measurable and controllable performance component, namely "entering into a binding agreement", and also contains the enthusiasm and energy of the behavioral component, namely "being involved in the company".

Employees' commitment, and with that the organization's commitment to change, determines the success of the change trajectory to a large extent. Feeling the need for change in the entire organization can be achieved in two ways: intrinsically and extrinsically.

The characteristic of *intrinsic necessity* is that the employee feels the change is necessary. The employee realizes what the benefit is for both the organization and for himself. An example of an intrinsic necessity is that an employee sees that the world around him is changing and that the organization has to change as well, since the competition will otherwise steal the market share.

Extrinsic necessity (or *imposed necessity*) is characterized by external stimuli (sanctions, financial bonus, promotion). Here, the employee does not need to feel the importance of achieving the objective itself, but he has little choice and will therefore adapt to the new situation. The motivation for change does not arise from a lasting stimulus; in other words: the employee does not change for the benefit of the organization, but because he has to. Because of this, he does not consider it to be advantageous for him. An example of externally imposed necessity is money as sole motivator for an unmotivated employee. This employee only focuses on performing exactly in accordance with the standard. This means that he will not work any harder than the performance indicators prescribes (for instance, the number of product checks, number of complaints dealt with per hour). A painful practice example of extrinsic necessity is that

Wall Street bankers primarily align their performance to their bonus during the Credit crisis and not to the consequences of their behavior, while they were perfectly aware of the risks of reinsurance.

Intrinsic necessity is eventually more effective than imposed necessity. In case of an imposed necessity, merely the conditions set to achieve the result are met and they will not give the matter any further thought. Employees' own initiative diminishes greatly. Therefore, using methods to stimulate intrinsic necessity is more efficient, as was also explained in the three methods to overcome resistance in the beginning of this chapter.

Yet, you can also make use of extrinsic necessity in performance-behavior. Here, timing plays a crucial role: in a change trajectory like this, where a change of behavior is needed, you will have to make use of the momentum: the right time provides the flywheel effect. In the vision of performance behavior, this is not a matter of "pushing" or "pulling", but of "pushing" and "pulling" at the right time. Sometimes, an employee needs to be "pushed" past a barrier by his supervisor and at other times during the performance-behavior implementation, the same employee will have to be "pulled" forward so he learns to recognize the advantages for himself and subsequently, intrinsic motivation will arise (not automatically).

It is possible to assess the degree to which the necessity to change towards a performance behavior organization is felt within the organization by answering the following questions:

- To what extent do the key players feel the necessity to change?
- What place does performance behavior have on the priority list of the key players?
- Do the key players know what the consequences are of not implementing performance behavior?
- To what extent do the key players feel themselves owner of the problems that arise during this change program?
- To what extent is there energy present within the company to develop engagement to the program?

Success factor 2: Strategy and objective provide direction

Researchers continue to discover more about the actual motivators of people. Research conducted on mice shows us that both giving a positive elementary stimulus (such as food) and punishment (for instance an electric shock as pain stimulus) can perfectly condition the mouse to display the desired behavior.

Such stimuli can also be applied in the change trajectory. We call these push-elements. These push-elements push the employee into the right direction. He has no choice; he simply has to do it. Examples of push-elements are steering and accountability moments, reporting structures, objectives and control processes.

Pull-elements also exist within the implementation of performance behavior. One of the strongest pull-elements is that the leader sets the right example of the desired behavior. The behavior in the organization is not merely influenced by the role models, but also by the people who identify with the role. This works positively, but also negatively. When a supervisor in a company expresses his opinion about a customer who has not contacted them in months in a haughty way, this leads the employees to worry less about the customer. The hypothesis is that if you were to put up a sign saying, "the customer is king" in this company, this message would completely miss its goal when the supervisor displays this kind of behavior.

> The manager who shows not enough discipline at meetings will eventually cause the lack of discipline in following the safety procedures in the workplace. One centimeter of deviation at the top is a meter on the work floor.

In order to generate pull, it is necessary to completely clarify the objectives. However, the danger of this is that different employees will translate the objective to their daily job in a different way. The long-term objective has to be translated into performance and behavior objectives for the short term. Moreover, "the story" behind the objectives has to be clear: what purpose do they serve? In this way, employees can place the performance-behavior objectives for the short term within the context of the long term objectives.

Someone who is especially capable of placing the long term objectives into a story and translating these to the individual who has to contribute to this objective is the U.S president Barack Obama. He wrote the following speech on September 20 2006, before he was elected president.

(...) We must strive for an agreement with "The Big Three" car manufacturers, our government spent no less than 6,7 billion dollars on the health care costs of their retired personnel. In exchange, these companies should invest money in more economical cars. However, in addition to increasing the economical standard, it is time to replace oil as America's fuel completely. (...) This means that important steps have to be taken to create a national infrastructure for bio-fuel.

A number of cars on the road already have the flexible fuel tank needed to drive on E85, a cheaper, cleaner mix of 85% ethanol and 15% gasoline. But many millions of cars do not yet have these tanks. It is time for the car manufacturers to install these tanks in each car they make, and it is time for the government to cover these costs, which are a mere 100 dollars per car. We also have to make sure that each car the government buys is a hybrid.

It is also time to make sure that more E85-gas stations are made available for the consumer. Currently, only 681 of the 170.000 gas stations in America offer E85-pumps. This is unacceptable. Each American has to be offered the choice for E85 at each gas station. And oil companies should stop thwarting this and instead have to participate in the success of this. If the major oil companies were to spend 1% of their profit of the first quarter of this year on E85-pumps, over seven thousand gas stations could be equipped with these pumps.

Finally, we should reduce the investment risk in retrievable fuel by granting guarantees for loans and venture capital to the entrepreneurs with the best plans for the development and sale of bio-fuels. And we must create a market for retrievable fuel by raising the standard for retrievable fuel and we must create an alternative diesel standard that makes it possible to mix 250 billion liters of retrievable fuel with oil in this country each year.

In the days and months after 9/11, Americans waited for a call to serve a goal higher than themselves. Just like their parents or grandparents of the Greatest Generation, they were prepared to serve and defend their country – not just in the war, but also at home.

This is our chance to serve. For decades, we have heard one president after the other advocate for energy-independence in this country, but all those decades we fell short.

Now is the time to bring ourselves to order. We mustn't wait until the fuel once again costs 3 dollars a gallon. And we should no longer accept headlines about a dying car-industry or a terrorist plan to use oil as a weapon against the U.S. We must act and we must act now.

This is the last part of Obama's speech, which illustrates an aspect of telling the story behind the objective. Obama is highly skilled in telling stories: he masters the switch from macro images to micro images like no other. When he speaks of 250 billion liters of retrievable fuel, the average American has some trouble fitting this into their frame of reference. However, it is an important macro image, used to sketch a greater whole. From those 250 billion liters, he switches to "We must call ourselves to order before our gas costs 3 dollars per gallon again", after which he continues with "We need to act and we need to act now". With this, he eventually reaches the American on micro level within his own frame of reference, from a substantiated macro necessity. That is the power of telling the story behind the objective.

Board, managers and employees will only accept the need for change when they understand what will change for them. Change is an individual choice employees make when they see that the change leads somewhere. This does not mean a clearly defined end objective always needs to be present. Yet, the direction of the change needs to be clear in order to know when you are "on the right track"; this requires a translation from the "abstract" strategy to (measurable) performance indicators on an organizational level, departmental level and individual level. Additionally, the strategy is translated into goal values, competencies and behavioral criteria, which shape the "soft" guidelines of the organization.

It is possible to assess the degree in which the vision and values of the change program are clear to the key players and to assess if they understand the vision and values of the change program towards a performance behavior organization. This can be done by answering the following questions:

- Is the strategy of the change program clearly formulated in a written plan?
- Do the key players know the vision of the change program?
- Are the key players familiar with the performance behavior context and its principles (awareness)?
- Is the vision translated towards a concrete implementation plan with objectives, planning and resources?
- Are the key players role models in carrying out the values and the necessity of the program?
- How big is the difference between the existing values in the organizations and the values that are formulated in the performance behavior program?

Success factor 3: Capacities create achievability

In order to determine what the capacity of an organization is, we look at qualitative and quantitative capacity. Qualitative capacities are, for instance, intelligence, competencies or behavior profiles of employees. Quantitative capacity is the extent to which the organization possesses the present qualities. Here, you can think of the number of people, but also of the capacity of individuals. The entire capacity of an organization together forms the organization capacity: the ability the organization has to change. This indicates the amount of the capacity we have available to achieve our performance.

It is important to align the current capacities of the organization to the capacities needed to achieve the established objectives.

Quality

Change usually hurts. After all, people have cooperated with each other (or not) in a specific way for years and that "suddenly" has to change, due to which their only certainties – in the form of old familiar ingrained patterns and behavior – ceases to exist. This irrevocably leads to insecurity; people will need time to build up understanding and respect for each other. When people are given this time, a faster and more effective collaboration will be the eventual result. Additionally, people should regain faith in their capability to handle the work; that the required competencies (knowledge, skills and attitude) are handed to them by means of education, training and supervision. People only want to participate in the change when they believe they can handle it.

Since continuous improvement of your organization is a story without an end, it is necessary to align the ability to improve to the necessities for the continuous improvement activities. Often, organizations only think of competency-oriented education, but the employees also have to be stimulated to exchange innovative solutions with each other. Create preconditions to feed the improvements by increasing the improvement capacity.

However, capacity is not merely individual ability. A good team has synergy and achieves more than the sum of all individual capacities.

> If a football team consists of only attackers, the team gets so many goals against due to the lack of defenders, and can never win.
>
> If a football team consists of only defenders, the team will never score the goals it needs to win.

Invest in collaboration skills and respect the individual differences. This will make the team stronger. A pattern analysis of the qualities of the individuals and the teams provides more insight into the availability of the qualities of the organization and the existing potential. In most organizations, this information is not or hardly available. However, it should always be immediately available, just like performance-information.

Quantity

The availability of the right resources might also play a critical role in the change process on the way to performance behavior. When the organization has too many flexible (temporary) employees, the investment in knowledge might not be as worthwhile, since the knowledge will not remain restricted to the organization. What is the number of full-time employees/part-time employees/direct employees/indirect employees/temporary employees/overtime in your organization at the moment? Is this in line with the best organization in the branch? What is the staff turnover within your organization? Do you know why? Setting up a pattern analysis on the basis of this data provides insight into the availability of the capacity of the organization. Ensure an optimal alignment between the various capacities, otherwise this can delay the processes.

Determining the required capacity

The description of an employee's function contains his place in the organization (function environment, organization department, function name or number), activities (tasks, authorities, responsibilities), knowledge and skills. This can be used to determine what required knowledge and skills will change for an employee, given the new strategy and the accompanying desired situation. The role description contains, more specific than the function description, the information about the (most important) roles the employee fulfils. There is also a relationship between the roles of people and the capacity demand within an organization: which specific qualities do we quantitatively need to achieve the result within the department/organization?

It is possible to assess the degree in which there is capacity (both qualitative and quantitative) available within the organization to implement the change program towards a performance behavior organization. This can be done by answering the following questions:

- What is the level of competence of the program manager?
- How much experience does the program manager have with the implementation of change programs?
- What is the level of competence of the team that implements the program?
- How much experience does the team have with the implementation of change programs?
- To what extent are the resources available as planned in the implementation plan?
- Is action taken when planned resources turn out to be insufficient for implementation?

Success factor 4: Structures provoke

Organizational structure has to be shaped in such a way that this does not hinder the desired performance-behavior changes, but supports these. For instance, a culture of result responsibility does not fulfill its purpose in an organization with a lot of hierarchical layers. Collaboration between departments does not arise easily when each department forms an island. The structure of an organization also establishes who has which tasks, responsibilities and authorities on each level within the organization. The value of a good structure that fits the organization can be illustrated by using the metaphor of a maze. Figure 5.3 and 5.4 depict two mazes; one without structure, one with structure. The maze without structure that is showed in figure 5.3 is unable to steer the person effectively and efficiently through the maze. On the other hand the structure in the maze in figure 5.4 provides a mean to steer the person to reach his goal in an efficient way; to find his way out of the maze as quickly as possible.

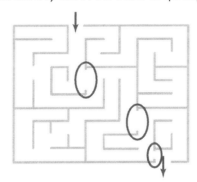

Figure 5.3   *A maze without structure lacks ability to steer*

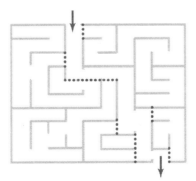

Figure 5.4   *A maze with structure is able to steer towards the goal*

Many experts have investigated the importance of organizational structure for the (change) process and with emphasis on which structure is the best fit for the organization. That the structure influences the organization process is well known.

With the help of structure:

- Activities are divided across people by using tasks and functions;
- Functions are grouped in departments;
- The way in which mutual alignment takes place is established;
- Activities are coordinated in line with the organization objectives;
- Roles and functions with accompanying authorities and responsibilities are established;
- Communication possibilities are determined, through which employees can hand over information to each other.

In short, organization structure is the way in which the activities of the organization have been divided into tasks and functions, responsibilities and authorities.

The organizational structure is essential to determine the necessary underlying structures within the organization: formal and informal structures, meeting structures, communication structures, team structures, appraisal structures, work meeting structures.

Each organizational structure consists of three different sub-structures: the organic structure, the functional structure and the personnel structure. It is important to align these three sub-structures in order to create an optimal collaboration between the various components. The organizational chart describes the shape of the hierarchical and functional organizational structure within an organization. This could be departments, but also business units or teams. The functional structure presents all functions (in hierarchical order) that exist within the organization. The functions included in this together shape the so-called job matrix of the organization. Each function has a function description. With regard to the personnel structure it is the question about demand that is key. Which behavior and how much of this behavior do we need to bring about the desired performance within the organization or department?

The question now is what the right organizational structure is in light of the desired situation and the strategy that has been determined in order to reach the desired situation. According to Mintzberg (1983), four factors are important:

1   *Age and size*

Depending on the age and size of the organization, the need for differentiation and formalization of the activities increases. As the size of the department increases, more staff and help services are needed to support the management.

2 *Technical system*

The more the work is performed by machines, the more the work can be standardized and formalized. Bureaucratization and decentralization of tasks are common consequences in this process.

3 *Environment*

The more dynamic the environment is, the more flexible (organic) the organization structure has to be in order to meet the changing needs and to adapt to the changing environment in which the organization operates. Additionally, the more complex and diverse the environment is, the stronger the decentralization (with various product or market-oriented departments) has to be in order to meet all different wishes.

4 *Power*

The most powerful external (stakeholders, customers) and internal parties (work council, staff departments, group leaders) have most influence on the choice for organizational structure. When the largest power lies with the top management of the organization, there is a tendency to centralize decisions and responsibilities. When the middle management and the supporting service wield most power, decentralization arises.

These four factors influence the decision-making processes and the reaction speed: the lower the responsibilities and authorities lie within the organization, the faster decisions can be made. When we place this within the change of the organization in a continuously improving performance-behavior organization, it is crucial that the organizational structure offers support when implementing change. After all, structures provoke: structures describe who has which responsibilities and authorities in what function.

The performance-behavior model clearly distinguishes between the three different management levels within the organization: monitoring, steering and action level. Each management level has its own responsibilities.

Monitoring level: the top management

This level is responsible for the long-term course of performance behavior. The cycles of forming strategies generally become shorter; the trend is that the strategy is outlined in an increasingly higher frequency and that the strategic adjustments are more incremental. This has consequences for the performance-behavior strategy and matches the philosophy of performance behavior. After all, the small but goal-oriented steps that are continuously made to give the organization maximum control over the improvements are at the core of performance behavior.

> At this moment, in organizations the contrast between the sustainability objectives and the temporary presence of each employee is too big.

The top management takes decisions regarding the vision on change. This concerns determining the strategy and creating the conditions to achieve the desired situation. These decisions have an effect on the entire organization and therefore have to be taken at the highest level. The top management makes decisions about the division and alignment of resources, safeguarding the improvement objectives, assigning authority and constantly communicating about the big organizational objective. Organizational decisions in the field of systems and capacities correlate with this; in other words: the consequences for the amount of material and personnel resources needed to be able to produce.

The middle management is accountable to the top management with regard to the progress and results and the top management steers on deviations of the plan that is executed by the middle managers.

Steering level: the middle management

The core task for this management level is to steer the performance-behavior activities in the organization. The supervisors in the middle management supervise the operational supervisors. The members of this steering level:

- Translate the plans of the monitoring level into an activity plan within the department;
- Provide the people and resources to perform the plans;
- Supervise the activities;
- Check whether the execution of activities goes according to plan;
- Steer the activities if necessary;
- Are accountable for the progress of the improvements to the top management.

In most cases, the middle management consists of the heads of department. However, depending on the size of the organization, the middle management can also directly supervise the executers. In this situation – the operational steering level – we talk about chefs, department managers, unit leaders or first-line managers. In addition to the activities mentioned above, these people take care of the immediate supervision of the performance.

The frameworks for functions and the accompanying responsibilities and authorities within the organization are fixed within the structure.

Action level: the operational management

The core task for this management level is the supervision of the execution of the performance-behavior activities. The supervisors on this operational level supervise the performance of the employee's within the department. The supervisors of this operation level:

- Perform the plans of the steering level;
- Translate the plan into concrete activities;
- Align people and resources optimally;
- Supervise the executed activities;
- Check whether the execution of activities goes according to plan;
- Steer the activities if necessary;
- Are accountable for the progress of the improvements to the middle management.

In most cases, the operational level consists of foremen, team leaders or group leaders. However, depending on the size of the organization, the operational level can also participate directly in the group of performing employees. In addition to the activities mentioned above, these people perform part of the work.

It is possible to assess the degree in which the structures (both process structures, as organizational structures) within the organization facilitate (or hinder) the change efforts towards a performance behavior organization. This can be assessed by answering the following questions:

- Is the organization capable to identify the correct deviations and to subsequently set the right priorities based on these deviations?
- Are the processes defined with which is steered on deviations?
- Are these defined processes communicated to all involved stakeholders?
- Do the key players conform to the new, desired structure?
- To what extent are the project structure and organization formulated and communicated?
- Are the key players available and reachable for organization and support?
- How big is the decisiveness of the organization?

Success factor 5: Enforcing systems

We can employ all existing, but also new systems in order to reinforce the intended change into the desired performance-behavior organization. In this way, for example, information systems can be used to inform employees. Check systems, reward systems and quality care systems can lead to more motivation and a higher effort. Monitoring and evaluating the development of employees is made possible by appraisal systems.

Systems also exist to make the work easier; the system is a resource, not an objective. The advantages of systems are numerous. Systems save time, offer structure, provide access to current information for everyone, streamline the processes within the organization, prevent double information, offer access to information always and everywhere, and they can be integrated with each other due to which knowledge multiplication occurs. Most organizations emphasize the use of new or more systems and little attention is paid to (the costs for) the maintenance of existing systems and eliminating systems where they are redundant.

Many systems are used in organizations: SAP, personnel information systems, hour registration systems, CRM-systems (Customer Relationship Management), financial systems, but also the agenda and e-mail on the Blackberry or iPhone are systems some organizations employ. The goal of each system – and information systems in particular – is to acquire, divide, use, distribute and evaluate data. In other words: systems take care of the processing and the availability of the requested information so the organization can deliver the planned results.

Usefulness, employability and flexibility are paramount in the change trajectory to the desired performance-behavior strategy.

It is possible to assess the degree in which current systems are available and usable to support the change program towards a performance behavior organization. This can be assessed by answering the following questions:

- Is it possible to collect facts to get a clear and true image of the current state of the organization?
- Are the right systems in place to be able to determine deviations at the right level in the organization?
- Are the resources that are used for the change program used in the right way?
- Are the methods that are available in the organization used in the right way?

(problem solving methods, assessment methods)

- Is the behavioral auditing system used in the right way?

Success factor 6: Success makes us believe

Employees and managers should see and experience that changing behavior leads to better results. From top manager to cleaner: to retain the motivation for change, everyone wants to see what the results of his efforts are. Successes and knowledge about successful improvements should therefore be shared. This is not only true when the final objective has been achieved; interim successes also have to be celebrated.

It is possible to assess the degree in which success is visible and shared in the organization by answering the following questions:

- Is the progression of the change program followed by the organization and made clear visually?
- Is progress of the change program shared within the company?
- To what extent is desired behavior stimulated by the supervisors (at each level)?
- To what extent are behavioral-PDCA applied at the right frequency and via feedback loops?

The six success factors show that actually changing people's behavior is not merely a question of developing competencies by means of training, which is usually done in practice. Particularly the combination of these success factors in the organizational atmosphere results in growth and change.

5.5 A continuous improvement culture

The change towards a performance behavior organization that strives for continuous improvement is inevitably accompanied by a cultural change. We describe culture as the sum of the behavior of all individual employees that is embedded in the formal and informal structures and systems in an organization. These formal and informal structures and systems give meaning to this behavior. Culture is expressed by the behavior that the employees display, it is expressed by the norms, values and convictions that prevail in the organization.

Often, "culture programs" are used when it is deemed necessary to change the company culture. With this approach, the change of culture becomes an objective in itself. However, within the performance behavior approach, cultural change is neither an objective, nor a means. It is the result of the change towards the performance behavior organization and is an indicator of the progress of the implementation of performance behavior.

In a performance behavior culture everybody is aware of the link between performance and behavior that exists on each level in the organization. The employees are aware of the performance that they delivered and the performance they yet have to deliver. Because they know which performance needs to be delivered, they know exactly what they have to do to perform their job well and with which indicators they can monitor their performance.

The degree of discipline within a performance behavior culture is high, which means that all activities are performed in a structured way. Meetings, for example, are highly structured. The same subjects are discussed in the same order and everybody uses the same terms to discuss performance. If any problems arise these problems are addressed structurally by solving them correctively and preventively. No hesitant language is used and everybody knows his role, and what is expected from this role.

At all levels in the organization, from work floor to board room, people take ownership for their own performances and account for these performances. A 'shame culture' prevails over a 'blame culture' which makes sure that people think ahead at each level and that problems are solved at that level instead of passed on to the next person. Subsequently the employees at the level that solved the problem account for the solution by explaining it to the level supervising them. Trust in judgment of others over the performance of oneself is critically important here. That is why transparency in performance and behavior is a critical precondition to be able to account for performances. Furthermore feedback on ones performance is accepted and used to improve performance.

In a performance behavior culture the teams are formed in such a way that the behavioral DISC profiles complement each other and do not hinder the teamwork. Furthermore, leadership is used to facilitate and coach, but also to steer on the performance that needs to be reached. This means that the leaders need to steer on objectives that are clear for everybody and that they train and coach the employees to reach these goals. More about performance behavior leadership can be found in chapter 7.

To sum up, the performance behavior culture strives towards concrete objectives that are achieved by working with standards and routines in a disciplined way. Performances are accounted for at each level and any deviations on the objectives are investigated critically at the level at which the deviation occurs. Subsequently these deviations are handled in a structured way and eventually solved. By working in this way, deviations are solved and the objectives can be stretched to achieve continuous improvement.

5.6   Lean as point of reference for continuous improvement

Up until now, this chapter mainly focused on the change trajectory of an organization into a performance-behavior organization, because this is a change trajectory in itself in most cases. In order to make the step from improvement (as process step) to continuous improvement (as continuous process) it is important to first clarify what lean exactly is and why the starting points of the lean-method contain good suggestions for the implementation of performance behavior within the possible improvements. Subsequently, other methods for continuous improvement will also be discussed, such as Six Sigma and World Class Manufacturing.

The most important reason the starting points of lean fit well within performance behavior is that it can be applied widely: at the office, in production, in technical departments, etc.

The principles of what is now called lean have existed since the beginning of the mass production of goods. Ford wanted to make a tailored car for everyone, as long as it was a black Ford. The assembly line he built for his factories was the first production system based on the strong standardization of parts and tools. Ford did not invent the philosophy of standardization himself, but based it on the principles of Taylor's Scientific Management. Ford's lessons were subsequently developed by Taiichi Ohno. He started at Toyota as an employee and eventually became a manager. He refined Ford's starting points and in the fifties he laid the basis for the Toyota Production System. At first, the system was meant to reduce waste (muda in lean-terms), but Ohno soon turned it into a project in which he attempted to achieve his factory's "ideal" state by eliminating all activities that did not add value. In the eighties, more manufacturers in the United States started with methods to improve productivity, because the economy began to shrink. In the nineties, researchers from the Massachusetts Institute of Technology introduced the term lean manufacturing in the book 'The machine that changed the world'. In this book, the Toyota Production System was explained. Since then, we have used the term lean as generic term for a concept that primarily stands for adding value-creating activities for the customer and banning activities that add costs for the customer.

> Within lean methodology performance behavior perceives improvements from two perspectives: the macro perspective, which focuses on improving the value chain, and the micro perspective, which focuses on eliminating waste in the process.

The following six principles form the basis of lean. They provide insight into value from the customer's perspective:

1 Solve my problem completely;
2 Don't waste my time;
3 Deliver exactly what I want;
4 Deliver value where I desire this;
5 Deliver value when I desire this;
6 Reduce the number of decisions I have to make to solve my problems.

The power of lean lies in the focus on the total experience, reasoned from the perspective of the (final) customer. The principles that are employed are based on eliminating waste. How easily (or difficult) can customers find, install, use, maintain, actualize and/or recycle the product or the service? The customer does not only look at the service or product itself, but involves the total time and effort of a solution in his evaluation.

In the ideal situation, lean creates process streams in the organization that only add value to the product for the customer. This happens in five basic steps:

1 Determine the value of each product;
2 Identify the value stream per product;
3 Ensure that the value stream occurs without interruptions;
4 Let the customer obtain value from the product;
5 Strive for perfection.

The *lean*-method offers an incremental approach for this; that is: in small steps. We also call this approach *continuous improvement*. This also has a connection to performance behavior. After all, you cannot make grass grow faster by pulling it; developing other behavior takes time. Small, but clearly measurable steps with a concrete and defined objective are needed for this. This might be a process objective (less process steps) or a design objective (leaving out components while the functionality remains the same) or a material objective (using fewer materials). What all these objectives have in common is that they are based on what the customer deems necessary, what he is willing to pay for it. Many instruments are available for this, such as Kaizen (a daily improvement activity), Poka-Yoka (foolproof system design) and the earlier discussed *value-stream mapping*. However, in essence, the tools are not the most important aspect; applying the philosophy in detail in order to consider each form of added cost as waste and eliminate this waste step by step is more important.

In most organizations, this requires a rigorously different behavior culture and that can be difficult: the original *lean*-concept originates from Asia, where people focus more on the collective than western cultures do. The instruments that are applied were designed with a collective culture as the natural starting point. When we blindly translate the philosophies and instruments to western cultures, we will encounter serious bottlenecks in practice. That is the reason many *lean*-change trajectories are incomplete or fail prematurely; it only rarely occurs that a department or organization is completely *lean*.

When the translation of behavior is not aligned with the company culture, the concept becomes a piece of equipment that might be very useful, but one we do not (yet) know the added value of. This is like falling for a beautiful kitchen tool that is demonstrated on the market: it grates, cuts and scrapes everything and the price is right. But once at home, it doesn't work nearly as well as it did at the market. After two, three attempts, the device is put in a drawer and after a year it is sold at a yard sale.

The lean principle is meant to eliminate all losses that occur in the value chain.

> We rarely invest enough money, time and effort to do it right the first time, but there is usually money and time to do it over.

In the original lean-concept, the loss of quality and the loss of quantity are strongly emphasized. Sometimes, the loss of talent or the loss of competencies is added to this, but usually the lean literature discusses these seven categories:

1 Loss from motion;
2 Loss from waiting;
3 Loss from over-processing;
4 Loss from overproduction;
5 Loss from inventory;
6 Loss from transport;
7 Loss from rework.

These seven losses cost the organization resources, but do not add value to the product; they add costs. Let's look at these seven losses in more detail and consider their relationship with behavior. There are three categories: quantity loss, quality loss and human loss. The behavioral aspects within *lean* are especially important in fighting human loss.

1 Quantity loss

This includes stock, movement of a product or raw material - and for instance the transfer of files to be signed - and overproduction.

> *Quantity loss: loss of process time*
>
> At a U.S. bank, the intake for tenders for car insurance was performed via the internet. The potential customer had to go through 6 pages with 9 questions each. Each page was provided with a status bar that visualized the status of the customer in the total intake process.
>
> A behavioral analysis on the basis of site visits of potential clients showed that 5% of the clients didn't proceed after the first page. On the fourth page, even 60% of the potential customers left. Eventually no more than 4% of the potential clients got an actual tender. The board wanted to increase this percentage, because this would drastically reduce the number of tenders requested by telephone, which would lead to a significant reduction in costs.
>
> The original tender trajectory contained questions that originated from departments: there were questions related to content that evaluated whether the customer was eligible for insurance on the basis of his car with certain characteristics, financial questions that evaluated whether the customer had sufficient money to pay the car insurance, questions that had to ensure that the customer was not on a black list of other insurance companies and even questions from the marketing department concerning fire and theft insurances and continuous travel insurance. Each department believed his questions added value to the process of tender approval. During a meeting with all department managers involved, the direction gave a clear objective: the visit-tender conversion had to be increased from 4% to 15%. People were selected from each department to form an improvement group that made a structured analysis reasoned from the needs of the customer. This improvement group reduced the number of questions from 54 to 16 on 3 pages. The conversion immediately rose to 18%. So the turnover increased as a result of the significant reduction in process time.

2 Quality loss

This includes both a quality level that is too low and a quality level that is too high (over-processing). When the quality level is too high, more resources than necessary are used to make the product or provide the service.

3 Human loss

This includes, among other things, losses that are caused by the way in which people work (loss of efficiency), the structures and the systems that bring about the result of the work, but these are also losses that are caused by lacking competencies or an attitude that does not match the values of the company. Moreover, this includes people waiting during a process and unnecessary movement of people to get their things or parts for the benefit of the process. Finally, this includes intelligence and personality. On the one hand, this has to do with the fact that when people leave an organization, value-carriers, competencies and behavior also leave the organization. On the other hand, human loss is also the lack of intellect, personality, competencies or attitude needed to correctly perform a certain part of the process. When the human capacity is not in line with the established objectives, your organization has insufficient capacity to achieve the desired performance.

To actually improve these losses, an improvement strategy that is primarily driven by the difference between the current values and goal values is needed. At the performance indicator level (low frequency, large impact), the improvement trigger is the difference between the current state of the organization and the future, or desired, state of the organization. At a lower level, the action indicator level (high frequency, low impact), the improvement trigger is the difference between the current performance value and the goal performance value. The system is the same; the level and the reach (short versus long term) are different.

Chapter 6 will discuss the human losses in more detail.

5.7   The development of the improvement strategy: from potential to performance

Your organization does not grow into a continuously improving performance-behavior organization automatically. You need a plan that provides information about the current situation of your organization and about where you would like to go. With this, you can consider which specific losses you can eliminate within your organization. You can also look at the difference between your own performances and the performances of your best competitor. In the previous section, we discussed the various types of losses. An analysis of these losses can help you to determine the areas within your own organization where possible losses occur. The outcomes of this analysis can subsequently form the basis of your improvement strategy in which you outline how you will utilize the existing capacity within your organization and what your time frame is in which to do this.

In order to develop the improvement strategy and to actually utilize the potential of your organization, it is necessary to measure the capacity of your organization. This organizational capacity indicates the boundaries within which the organization can develop within a specific time frame. In order to measure the organizational capacity, you have to establish what the ideal situation of your organization can be. In lean, this is called the *ideal state*.

Establishing the *ideal state* is the first step in mapping the organizational capacity. You quantify the vision of the company in a strategic document by defining a number of important performance indicators. The performances indicated are directly linked to the resulting bill of the organization. A correct breakdown of performance indicators is also needed. This breakdown shows how the most important performance indicators are related to the lower performance indicators and steering and action indicators. To secure a correct breakdown you can look at the various performance indicator levels: which indicator is steered on at which level? And is the frequency with which the performance occurs equal to the frequency with which the behavior is displayed that achieves the performance. You will have to answer these questions during the quantification of the vision.

The second step is making a snapshot of the current state of the organization. You determine what the values of the performance indicators are right now, where the greatest opportunities lie, what the strengths of the organizations are and which capacity exists in the organization. Subsequently, you can determine the organization's capacity with the following formula:

> Capacity = Ability, measured in a quantitative and qualitative level,
> over a limited period.

The next step is determining what the organization's potential is to unused capacity. This unused capacity is only being tapped at the moment the organization is in stretch. When, for instance, a manager has never been coached, what could his possible development be when he is coached? When the 'bar' is raised at a certain level, the manager will come into stretch. This stretch gives him pull to develop. This gives the following formula to determine the future state:

> *Current state* ⊕ *capacity* ⊕ *stretch* = *future state*
> (this is the capacity that can be developed)

The *ideal state* is the ideal situation of the organization. This is usually not equal to the future state of the organization. In a continuously improving performance-behavior organization, the ideal state of the organization is always "unreachably" far ahead. Because each time we achieve the *future state*, the *ideal state* has moved so far ahead that we determine a *new future state* to work towards.

It is possible to influence the future state by adjusting the objectives or the run time. It is also possible to develop the capacity of the organization. In most organizational development trajectories, the latter will be the most obvious option to implement the improvement strategy. The potential of the organization is not determined on the total level, but each hindering process indicator determines the boundaries of the organization's capacity. Therefore, it is important to conduct analyses on the action level, steering level and monitoring level and not merely compare the monitoring performance indicators to those of the competition to determine the potential.

The strategic process of capacity via development to performance emphasizes a clear focus on what is important for your organization and gives a clear definition of the responsibility for result and behavior. This can be visualized in the following steps:

1-Ideal situation ◗ 2-Current situation ◗ 3-Capacity ◗ 4-Potential ◗ 5-Desired situation ◗ 6-Stretchlevel ◗ 7-Plan

Managing the daily activities is aimed at improving and checking the KPIs in order to achieve the desired results.

Once established, this strategic cycle will be repeated on a yearly basis. The progress made in achieving objectives is discussed during periodic evaluations. During these evaluations, action plans can be adjusted if necessary. This evaluation process stimulates the communication between departments and will become a way of life for the management team. In this way it is possible to steer on deviations between current values and goal values, which forms the backbone of the development of the organization. In performance behavior this is divided in performance goal values and behavior goal values which makes it possible to steer both on performance and to steer on the behavior that is needed to bring about performance.

To subsequently be able to link the organizational objectives on the monitoring level with the objectives on the steering level and finally to connect these with the objectives at the action level, we need to unravel the steps from mission to individual performance.

Steering level	Definition	Example
Mission	The reason we do this	Getting in shape
Vision	The way we want to achieve our mission	Exercising – running
Objective	The formulated SMART-action we need to realize our vision	Running a marathon
Strategy	The way we think we will achieve our goals	Running 30 kilometers every week
Execution	Executing the sub-activities in the strategy	Monday 8, Wednesday 5 and Sunday 17 kilometers
Measurement	Measuring the results of our actions and if necessary adjusting the actions on the basis of the results	Measuring heart rate (no more than 153 beats a minute) and speed (average 12 kilometers per hour)
Securing	Securing actions by celebrating successes and capturing the process	Displaying medals, preserving training schemes and repeating measurements with a lower frequency
Improving	Raising the bar a bit higher as first improvement step	Next year: 10 minutes faster

Table 5.1 *Marathon running breakdown*

The right set of performance indicators is:

- Top-down consistent: there is a correct coherence between the monitoring, steering and action level;
- Horizontally aligned: there is a mutual connection between the objectives of the various company departments or between the related company processes.

After the desired situation has been mapped, the following question needs to be asked: "Does the current situation match with the desired situation we envision as an organization?" When this question is posed, the organization works on determining the strategy. Strategy is:

- The road to bridge the difference between the *current* and *desired* situation;
- A systematically developed future vision of the organization for the coming three to five year
- Determining the direction within the organization;
- Indicating what the organization wants to do, wants to achieve;
- A large number of measures that concern the various forces within an organization;
- Also the choice of what the organization won't do.

When determining the strategy, it is necessary to prioritize and to make choices that are connected to these priorities.

The improvement strategy consists of a mission and a vision and describes the identity of the organization. The mission and vision answer the question "Why does this organization exist?" and provide a shared view of the future that describes the ambitions and core values. When formulating the strategy, limiting and refining are keywords to clearly define the frameworks of the organization. The strategy should include those aspects that are essential to the success and viability of the organization, for example:

- Short run times;
- High level of expertise;
- Timely delivery of products or services;
- High degree of capacity utilization and productivity;
- High involvement of employees.

Strategy is not an objective in itself; it is a resource, a route map, to achieve the desired result.

In order to achieve maximum performance, it is not merely necessary to fight the losses, but also to display the right behavior and the right leadership at the right time. In the following chapters, we will further discuss the specific behavioral components and leadership styles needed for performance behavior.

6

CONTINUOUS BEHAVIOR DEVELOPMENT

In this chapter, you can read what *performance behavior* versus *waste behavior* is. You will also read how you can apply performance behavior in a continuous improvement structure. The chapter explains the differences in types of behavior needed to create a performance-behavior culture. The need for clear roles, to be able to link the desired behavior to the performance, is also explained in more detail. We again make a link between the roles and the behavior profile factors.

6.1   From waste behavior to performance behavior

The opposite of performance behavior is waste behavior. We could also call this *loss behavior*. In any case, this is behavior that does not add value to the process; behavior the customer is not prepared to pay for. All behavior within an organization should serve the production process so it contributes to the service or product the customer is prepared to pay for.

The various loss categories were discussed in chapter 5. The most important of these categories is, from the point of view of performance behavior, the category "human loss". These are losses related to behavior. Performance behavior eliminates these losses within a secured PDCA-system.

In this section, we will discuss how you can convert the eight types of human loss into a well-functioning performance-behavior system so that we move away from waste behavior and move towards performance behavior.

Leadership loss

Leadership loss is the loss that arises through the incorrect use of leadership. The leadership does not add value for the customer, but instead harms this. Leadership loss can arise as a result of excessive steering (*push*-leadership) or as a result of too little steering (*pull*-leadership). Excessive steering is a management style that is too strict (over-*push*) and too little steering is a management style that is too weak (under-*pull*).

Push-leadership means that the leader acts as an authority and pushes the employees into a certain direction. The opposite of *push*-leadership is *pull*-leadership. In *pull*-leadership, the leader is proactive and ready to help. He does not push his employees, but "pulls" them with him in the right direction.

When the organization is safeguarding the standard and is determining and implementing the standards, *push*-leadership can be useful. When the actual improvement initiatives come from the employees themselves (which is the eventual goal), the *pull*-leader is the one who can achieve the best results with his team. We will discuss the performance-behavior leadership in further detail in chapter 7.

Comfort loss

Comfort loss means that loss arises because the employees feel too comfortable. This happens when capacity and goal are balanced (see the goal-resource model, figure 1.8 on page 35). Then, the employee delivers the requested performance without being challenged by a higher goal – there is no stretch. In practice, only few employees have the natural urge for continuous improvement. For this reason, the goal always has to be set higher so the employees remain challenged by the stretch they feel. In this way, the organization remains in a situation of stretch, which ensures the presence of a continuous improvement trigger, because the bar has been raised a little higher again.

Communication loss

Communication loss is loss that arises through misunderstandings in communication. Therefore, it is important to *seal* the communication. When communication is sealed, the sender of the message knows that the recipient has received the message in the way the sender intended, because the recipient loops the message back. This feedback is called a *"seal*-signal".

An example of sealed communication is the standard procedure at McDonald's for the preparation of the hamburgers. The frozen hamburgers have to be grilled for 39 seconds. When the right number of hamburgers has been placed on the grill, the employee who grills the hamburgers signals to his colleague who toasts the bread that the right amount of bread can be toasted. The sandwich employee confirms the number of sandwiches to his grill colleague, so the communication is completely sealed. Due to this, the grilled hamburgers and the toasted bread are finished at exactly the same time and in the right amount and they can be joined without loss.

Discipline loss

Discipline loss is the loss that arises when discipline in the organization is lacking. Discipline is the way in which someone is capable of keeping agreements. When we talk about organization discipline, we talk about the way in which the organization is capable of keeping agreements that were made on the organizational level. This could be about being on time for a meeting, or the way protocols are followed. In a performance-behavior organization, the daily, nearly self-evident standards are well arranged – such organizations have a strong organizational discipline. We can look at organizational discipline on a macro level and micro level. Organizational discipline on a macro level is, for instance, cost leadership and product leadership. In what way are we capable of controlling our costs in a disciplined way or how do we remain leading in the market regarding our differentiating capacity of products or services? The micro level is concerned with following the agreed-upon standards in the organization.

Goal loss

Goal loss arises when the goals are not clear enough, as a result of which employees do not know exactly what is expected of them. In a performance-behavior organization, all employees know what the specific goal values are on their own level and steer on deviations of which the measurement is aligned with the frequency in which the performance behavior comes about. Naturally, these deviations from the goal can only be discovered when the goal is clear. A performance-behavior organization has a secured system to detect deviations.

Involvement loss

Involvement loss is loss that arises because people do not feel responsible. They do not feel they can influence (parts of) their work within their own area of responsibility, but view it as the responsibility of others. As a result, they will show less care for their job(area). This contrasts with the role people have to fulfill in continuous improvement processes. In a performance-behavior organization, everyone feels as if he is the owner of the part of the process he can influence. In this case we speak of psychological ownership that results in desired actions. For this type of ownership it is not necessary to be the extrinsic (legal or financial) owner of the part of the process.

Solution loss

Solution loss arises when an organization immediately starts fighting the symptoms in case of deviations. In a performance-behavior organization, the root cause of the problem is sought, rather than taking quick actions that only solve the consequences of the problem ("quick fix"). Only when the root cause is known can the best solution be chosen and only then will the action receive an owner and a deadline.

Alignment loss

A system – as is also the case for performance behavior – is only optimally utilized when all components are aligned optimally. When this is not the case, alignment loss occurs. In a performance-behavior organization, the result of the performance and the behavior that brings about this performance are steered at the same frequency in a closed and secured system. The steering and accountability system, the facilitation and auditing, but also improvement groups (at the level of improving the standard), materials, tools and leadership are all components that can individually add value. But their real value will only show when they are applied together at the right level in a closed and secured performance-behavior system.

Waste behavior

The losses described above consist of various loss factors. Some factors are well observable. Other factors are more concealed and therefore harder to perceive. For example, whether someone has sufficient capacities to perform a certain task is not always visible, even though this is strongly dependent upon a person's profile: people with the extravert profile factors "dynamic" and "inspiring" have behavior factors that are better visible than people with the profile factor "social" and "correct".

Examples of loss factors and therefore of waste behavior are:

- Being late for a meeting
- Attending meetings unprepared
- Not providing feedback to undesired behavior and therefore tolerating it implicitly
- Having insufficient knowledge of what happens on the work floor
- Provoking conflicts
- Being emotional
- Misleading
- Not sharing information on purpose
- Forcing decisions
- Giving preferential treatments
- Breaking promises
- Quick fixes
- Confusing employees by not answering questions or only answering part of them
- Inflicting fear
- Not listening well
- Not keeping agreements
- Obeying blindly
- Only focusing on department objectives
- Sowing confusion
- Being unreliable
- Not responding rapidly to customers' signals
- Gossiping
- Sarcasm
- Responding slowly to performance deviations
- Being prejudiced
- Acting irrationally
- Ignoring results of satisfaction studies
- Narcissism
- Acting out of self interest
- Subjectivity
- Rewarding on the basis of assumptions instead of on the basis of observations and facts
- Scoring for yourself
- Egocentrism or even egoism
- Cynicism
- Being solution-oriented
- Nitpicking
- Have a double agenda
- Barriers due to self-imposed limitations
- Skewed work-private life balance
- First urgent, than important
- Viewing the management as responsible

This is merely a small selection. The core of this list is that we want to be able to distinguish between functional, value-adding and dysfunctional, loss-adding behavior. Naturally, the opposite of waste behavior is performance behavior.

Examples of this are:

Goal-orientation	Listening
Detail-orientation	Sincerity
Preventing problems	Trust
Modesty	Objectivity
Patience	Wisdom
Working between and with people	Honesty
Self-awareness	Long-term fixes opposed to 'quick-fixes'
Taking small steps	Pride
Compassion	Calmness
Good work-private life balance	Rationality
Self-reflection	Everyone helps
Openness	Taking a stand
Rather scoring as a team than scoring on one's own	Result-orientation
Generosity	First important, than urgent
Respect	Taking responsibility

6.2   Competencies, roles and behavioral patterns

With regard to performance behavior, attitude, but also competencies and knowledge are the most important building blocks to fulfill a function. Within a function, however, we can often distinguish between various roles. Each specific role requires different behaviors or competencies. In performance behavior, we therefore specifically consider the role that has to be fulfilled and the required behavior for this role rather than the function itself. Let's look at the most important building blocks that influence performance behavior in more detail.

Competencies

A competency is the capacity to effectively perform in a certain task situation or in a certain problem situation. A competency contains integrated knowledge, insight, skills and attitudes that allow someone to deliver effective, high-quality performances, aimed at a specific role. These performances are visible in concrete actions and they are linked to a specific context.

According to Sluijs and Hoekstra (1999), a competency consists of two elements, namely expertise and behavioral repertoire. Expertise is having the knowledge, experience and insight available that are required or useful given the fixed characteristics of a problem or task. Behavioral repertoire is having the behavior, attention and emotion available that is required or useful given the changing context in which a task has to be performed.

These definitions emphasize the difference between fixed and variable characteristics of a task situation. However, what is missing in the descriptions of a competency is the influence of the environment. After all, the context in which competencies are used influences the extent to and intensity in which they are applied. Moreover, the capability of the employee is important, but applying that capability in practice is even more important. After all, the capabilities of a Porsche are useless when you only use it to go grocery shopping down the street.

When we also include context, the formula for applying a competency is:

$$\text{Competency application} = (\text{knowledge skills}) \otimes (\text{behavior repertoire} \otimes \text{behavior context})$$

Tasks and problems have a number of characteristics that remain the same, but when performing tasks, you will also have to handle changing and unexpected circumstances that can influence the result. You can more or less estimate these circumstances to subsequently adapt to these adequately. The basis for estimating the unexpected circumstances is not so much your expertise, but mainly the behavioral repertoire you have built up. This repertoire is influenced by your behavior profile, temperament and experience.

Knowing that you should not get angry when something does not go quite as planned is knowledge, but your actual response to the moment itself is determined by your behavioral repertoire and the behavioral context. This is especially true for emotions. You usually only apply your knowledge and expertise afterwards, when the fight or flight hormone in your body has already done its job.

Applied competency contains expertise, behavioral repertoire and behavioral context and is indispensable for effective performance. Having expertise means knowing how it works. Having behavioral repertoire means being able to do what is effective in a certain situation. And behavioral context is the context in which the competency and attitude together can evolve to the right capability.

Roles

There are various elements that influence the behavioral repertoire. One of these elements is the behavioral profile (see chapter 1). This behavioral profile has a connection to the roles people can fulfill.

The behavioral profile consists of the profile factors that make up someone's personality. In chapter 4, we discussed the four profile factors that determine the personality: dynamic, inspiring, social and correct. People have at least one and no more than three profile factors. The combinations of these profile factors provide thousands of personality types that are all different. In chapter 1, we already discussed that someone's behavioral profile is relatively fixed. The profile can develop within a certain range, but measurements over a period of five years reveal that the profile remains relatively stable, if no drastic changes occur in the environment that might influence the behavioral profile and the role someone fulfills. From the age of seventeen, when puberty is finished, our personality hardly changes anymore.

The most important characteristics of personality and the accompanying profile were explained in chapter 1. Now, it is time to look at a few different types of roles employees can fulfill in more detail.

We can distinguish the following three types of roles on the basis of the employee's contribution to the goal values in the organization:

1   *Task roles*
    Task roles contribute to achieving the performance goals. Each function can
    be divided into roles on the basis of the various tasks someone in a specific
    role fulfills. When someone enters data all day, this person probably fulfills
    one role in his position: typist. The competencies needed for this do not
    change because he only has a singular role in this position; a role is linked
    to a specific task area within this position. It is different for the head of de-
    partment of a nursing home, for instance. Within his position, he has multi-
    ple roles: he fulfills the role of nurse when he has immediate contact with
    client and patient. Additionally, he fulfills the role of manager when he has a
    work meeting with one of his employees. The competencies needed to ade-
    quately fulfill both roles are completely different, despite the fact that they do
    occur within the same function. A role indicates what is needed in terms of
    competencies to perform a certain task. With this, a role is much more spe-
    cific than a function is.

> In assessing the performance of employees the effectiveness will be greater by
> assessing in a high frequency at role level than by assessing in a low frequency
> on job level.

2   *Relational roles*
    Relational roles contribute to the creation of relationships that can in turn
    contribute to the organizational objectives, the maintenance of contacts,
    the alignment of information but it can also contribute to solving problems
    between people. Also, a relational role to create support or show interest-
    contributes to achieving the objectives. For example, the head of the nursing
    home does not only fulfill two task roles, that of nurse and of manager; he
    also fulfills interpersonal roles. Showing interest when one of his employees
    has private problems is part of the interpersonal roles of the head of the
    department. Because the head of department shows interest, the employee
    feels appreciated through which the head of department indirectly contrib-
    utes to achieving the organizational objectives; after all, involved people add
    more value than people who do not feel connected to the organization they
    work for.

3   *Individual roles*
    When we assume that everyone displays behavior to fulfill his personal needs
    and not (merely) to achieve the objectives of the organization, everyone also
    fulfills his own individual roles. The individual roles are primarily aimed at
    the individual who fulfills this role and are not aimed at another person or
    on the task. These roles are also aimed at achieving the personal goals and
    not the organizational objectives. In this respect, they do not always directly

add value to the performance of the organization, but it is possible that they add indirect value, for instance because they provide stability within a team. For example, it may occur that someone is concerned with a colleague's fate and therefore spends a lot a time listening to his problems. As a result, the colleague is still productive instead of being ill at home. The behavior may not seem to add value, but, in fact, it does.

The various roles, task roles, relational roles and individual roles, are driven by someone's behavioral profile. "Dynamic" and "correct" are more task-oriented profile factors and "inspiring" and "social" are the more relationship-oriented profile factors. Different roles fit with different combinations of profile factors.

Role	Profile factors (in order of importance)
Advisor	Inspiring-social
Lawyer	Social-inspiring-correct
Mediator	Correct-inspiring-social
Contemplator	Correct-dynamic-social
Director	Inspiring-correct-social
Compromiser	Social-correct
Consultant	Inspiring-correct
Conductor	Dynamic-inspiring-correct
Go-Getter	Social-dynamic
Expert by experience	Social
Inspirer	Social-inspiring
Leader	Dynamic-inspiring
Motivator	Inspiring-social-dynamic
Entrepreneur	Dynamic

Role	Profile factors (in order of importance)
Researcher	Social-dynamic-correct
Convincer	Inspiring
Perfectionist	Correct-social
Barrister	Inspiring-dynamic
Counselor	Correct-inspiring
Film Director	Dynamic-inspiring-social
Specialist	Correct
Criminal lawyer	Social-correct-inspiring
Challenger	Dynamic-correct
Craftsman	Correct-social-inspiring
Changer	Inspiring-dynamic-social
Chairman	Inspiring-social-correct

Roles during performance behavior meetings

In the performance behavior concept, meetings are crucial to be able to account for, and steer on performance and behavior. To ensure effective and efficient meetings it is necessary to have a clear division of roles with matching role descriptions. In the performance behavior meetings we distinguish between four different roles: chairman, vice chairman/note taker, participant and facilitator.

Chairman

The chairman is responsible for the meeting. He has to assure that the meeting will run smoothly, and that the meeting is effective and efficient. This means he is involved in assessing priorities, directing discussions and setting the agenda.

During the meeting the chairman has to:

- Ensure the agenda of the meeting is followed;
- Set the right priorities regarding discussions that are held;
- Ensure that discussion is based on facts, not opinions;
- Ensure that discussion do not go into detail unless necessary
- Ensure that the rules of the meeting are followed;
- Ensure that actions are noted down according to the SMART criteria;
- Address participants that display undesired behavior (e.g. being late, unprepared etc.).

Vice chairman/ note taker

The vice chairman/ note taker is partly responsible for the meeting. He has to assist the chairman when the chairman does not act on the moments he has to act. During the meeting he has to:

- Formulate the actions (according to SMART criteria) on the action board;
- Safeguard that actions are formulated according to the SMART criteria;
- Ensure that discussion take place based on facts;
- Ensure that the agenda is followed;
- Ensure that the rules of the meeting are followed;
- Address participants that display undesired behavior (e.g. being late, unprepared etc.)

Participant

The participants of the meeting are responsible for the content of the meeting. They account for the performances of their responsibility area and all participants together are jointly responsible for the result of the meeting. During the meeting a participant has to:

- Be prepared for the meeting (in conformance with the rules for the meeting);
- Account for the progression of current actions that he is responsible for;
- Make sure that actions are formulated where necessary;
- Seek cross functional collaboration with other participants where necessary;
- Stick to the rules that are established for the meeting.

Facilitator

The facilitator is responsible for the development of the quality of the meeting.

The facilitator has to improve the quality of the steer and accountability meeting. During the meeting the facilitator has to:

- Ensure that the right discussions are held (the right priorities and no detailed discussion);
- Safeguard that all participants fulfill their role in the right way;
- Facilitate the use of the PDCA-cycle for current actions;
- Measure the quality of the meeting in an audit;
- Stick to the rules that are established for the meeting.

The role of the facilitator is not limited to the meeting only. The facilitator also fulfills his role before and after the meeting. We will elaborate on this in chapter 7.

Behavioral patterns

To get an idea of the person's development in his role, more information about his behavior is needed. This information should not be a snapshot, but a "film". We call this film, which shows behavior over a longer time period, a *behavioral pattern*. The behavioral patterns provide information about the variations, patterns and specific behavioral elements over a longer period of time, and this provides the opportunity to formulate hypotheses about future behavior and to test these with the person concerned. In order to uncover the behavioral patterns, you can perform behavior audits.

A behavior audit of web-developer Sarah shows that she consistently does not fill in the root cause of a problem on the performance board, but instead fills in the solution she chose. Sarah's own analysis of this finding is that she tries to solve the problem instead of first attempting to determine the cause of the problem. We can also go deeper and try to uncover the root patterns of the behavior. Why does Sarah focus on the solutions rather than on first mapping the cause? An interview with Sarah reveals that she's not quite sure how to look for the cause. Moreover, she often thinks that she knows how to solve the problems on the basis of her experience. However, measurements indicate that the same deviations occur over and over again, which shows that the root causes are not solved. There is a discrepancy between her perception and the facts on the basis of the measurements. When analyzing Sarah's behavioral pattern in more detail, we discover that she enjoys solving problems immediately because her colleagues express their admiration for her swift actions, without realizing that Sarah merely fights the symptoms and not the real problems. Her colleagues' stimulation and confirmation of this undesired behavior ensured that the undesired behavior continued, even though Sarah encounters the same kind of problems that she "solved" in the past.

Ingrained behavior is easy, it is familiar and you are usually good at it (in that one familiar way), it costs little energy and it often occurs subconsciously. People nearly always do what they do because they were good at it from the start; in other words, it was "easy" for them from the start. New behavior is difficult, unfamiliar, uncertain, it occurs consciously and it therefore costs a lot of time and energy. This new and different behavior is often something someone was not very good at to begin with, due to which it is often more difficult to learn. Allowing new behavior to become ingrained takes a lot of time and therefore a lot of energy and this is often not a good choice in the short term, but in the long term it can be a very advantageous strategy. However, due to the natural need humans have to deal with urgent matters first, it is always difficult to continue to prioritize correctly and to opt for the most important activities (the activities that add value to the performance) instead of for the urgent activities (the activities that can only be done right now). Therefore, it is important to consciously focus on this.

6.3   The pitfall of the wrong priorities in performance behavior

When determining and implementing a new system, such as performance behavior, it is crucial to determine what is important and what is urgent. But how can we determine what is important and what is urgent? And what is the difference? To answer these questions within the framework of strategy determination, we first have to give a short introduction in the terminology in order to outline how the continuous choice between urgent and important matters influences daily life as well. Urgency is connected to living in the illusion of the day; immediately responding to what you encounter. A few examples: the phone rings, you have to answer. Someone knocks; you have to open the door. Someone says: "I need this now." "Can you come right now?" "You are late for your appointment."

Some people get used to the rush of adrenaline that is released when solving urgent matters to such an extent that they become dependent upon that feeling of excitement or energy. We also call this an *addiction to urgency*. What does urgency feel like? Stress? Agitation? Tension? Exhaustion? This is definitely the case when the feeling of urgency lasts longer. However, urgency can also be stimulating. It gives a sense of usefulness, of success. The sense of self-worth is reinforced. For this reason, people often address urgent matters first when a problem occurs, so they can feel satisfied at the end of the day; after all, they have done a lot of work. Urgency yields instant results and instant gratification – a temporary feeling of happiness. And when dealing with less important matters, the longing for urgency is often so strong that people are attracted to everything that could be urgent, even if this is simply to have something to do.

Being busy is also a status symbol in the current society: when an employee is busy, he feels important. When the employee is not busy, he finds this difficult to admit. Although the busy activities do not always actually add value to the performance, they do bring about a sense of tranquility, of safety and also a sense of self-worth and popularity, and therefore they give satisfaction. They form a good excuse to not always take into account the really important activities because an important assignment does not always need to be performed immediately. An urgent task, on the other hand, requires immediate action. The temporary attraction of these tasks seems irresistible and consumes all energy.

Urgency is opposed to importance. These are all activities that directly add value to achieving the objectives the employee is responsible for on that level are of importance.

The ratio between urgent and important is essential for performance behavior. Figure 6.1 is a decision matrix on the basis of importance and urgency.

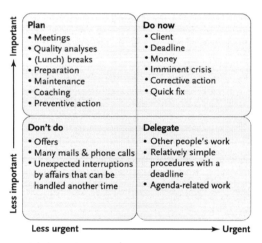

Figure 6.1 *Decision matrix importance and urgency*

Activities that have to be performed can be divided into the following four categories:

Do now

The quadrant at the top right represents matters that are both urgent and important. These are the most clearly defined tasks, which have a direct relationship with the customer, with safety, with costs or turnover. An example of an urgent and important task is listening to a dissatisfied client or fixing a machine that has to produce the product. Time needs to be spent on matters that are both urgent and important; otherwise, failure is inevitable. Nevertheless, you should realize that many important but non-urgent matters will eventually become urgent when putting them off or when planning is lacking. Therefore, you should also keep a close eye on the top left quadrant: *Plan*. Planning the activities and actions in this quadrant well can prevent that these matters become urgent as well. This makes a good spread of the activities possible and prevents undesired peaks.

Plan

The top left quadrant contains activities that are important, but less urgent. This is the quality-quadrant, where the long-term planning is made. This includes anticipating problems, but also increasing skills through study or training and the preparation for an important meeting.

The more time we spend in this quadrant, the larger our ability to actually perform all activities that have to be done. When this quadrant is ignored, this increases and feeds the top right quadrant through which stress, wear and tear and deep crisis arise. Investing in the plan-quadrant reduces the top right quadrant. After all, planning, preparation and prevention ensure that fewer matters become urgent.

Delegate

Delegating is moving (part of) the tasks or activities to employees or colleagues. In doing so, the responsibility for the task or activities remains with the owner, but the authority is transferred to another person. Sometimes, management books refer to "delegating responsibilities". However, in practice this is usually not possible. Responsibility is part of a position or role and cannot simply be detached from it. The responsibility therefore remains with the person who delegates, but the work itself moves.

The lower right quadrant contains activities that are urgent but not important. This is the quadrant of deception (and also of temptation). The pressure of urgency creates the illusion of importance. Yet the real activities in this quadrant are only important to someone else, if they are important at all. Numerous pho7.8ne calls, e-mails, meetings and unexpected visitors are included in this category. A lot of time is spent on this quadrant in an attempt to meet the priorities and expectations of others. This while the employee himself actually believes he is active in the top right quadrant.

Don't do

The lower left quadrant contains activities that are not urgent and not import-ant. This is the waste- quadrant. No time should be spent on this quadrant. You busy yourself with it unnecessarily: gossiping with colleagues, private Internet use, etcetera.

It is important to make choices in a change trajectory. After all, not all actions that are required to arrive at the desired situation from the current situation can take place at the same time. Differentiating between urgent and important mat-ters is therefore essential, because important matters contribute to the result immediately.

This directly demonstrates the effectiveness of the change to employees. After all, success makes us believe, as the six forces showed. Therefore, it is essential to work on important matters instead of on urgent matters. However, when we opt for urgency, we do not add sufficient value to activities that contribute directly to the objectives that were set.

When determining the strategy, it is not merely important to distinguish be-tween urgent and important matters. You also need to look at the impact of the plans that lead to the desired situation; not only the level of importance determines the choice of strategy, the speed and impact of the plans also are a determining factor. The right assessment between quick results and the size of the impact has to be made. On the one hand, successes can be celebrated quickly (high speed), while at the same time, attention has to be paid to the aspects with a large(r) impact. With the help of these elements, you can make a balanced consideration between adding value with important tasks and han-dling the pressure of urgent tasks.

6.4   Continuous development of behavior

In chapter two, we discussed the steering and accountability model. In this model, the objectives on the action, steering and monitoring level were linked to specific behavioral criteria needed to achieve the objectives on each level.

On the monitoring level, decisions take place with a high impact and a low frequency. On the action level, decisions take place with a high execution fre-quency, but with a low impact. In order to achieve continuous performance de-velopment, a system has to be established within the organization that follows deviations of both behavior and performance and that steers on these devia-tions in the same frequency as the behavior and the performances are delivered.

This means that both specific performance objectives and specific behavioral objectives have to be determined. The current values of both performance and behavior are measured and compared to the goal values that were derived from the objectives. When the current value of the behavior or performance deviates from the goal value, corrective and preventive actions are determined to ensure that the goal value will be achieved.

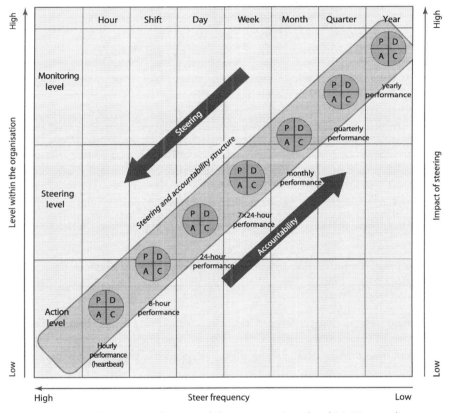

Figure 6.2 *Secured steering and accountability moments in a closed PDCA-cascading top-down and bottom-up*

The cycle that is used to steer on the performance deviations on the basis of the behavior deviations is the PRSS-PDCA-model. The continuous steering on behavior, aligned with the performance frequency, brings about the development towards the desired performance behavior. We call this the behavioral-development loop. The higher the frequency of the performance-behavior cycle is, the higher the frequency of the measurement of the performance and behavior needs to be. And the lower the frequency of the performance-behavior cycle, the lower the frequency of the measurement of the performance and behavior needs to be.

Steering on behavior deviations at the right frequency brings about continuous development. This occurs in the same way as performances are steered in the PRSS-PDCA-cycle (figure 2.6 on page 85).

This continuous behavior-development loop brings about a structured and steady development of the employee, which is directly measurable by means of performance and behavior values. In this way, the culture of the organization is developed into a performance-behavior culture step by step.

The culture of an organization is the sum of the behavior of all employees within the organization, embedded in formal and informal structures and systems that give this behavior meaning within the organization. The experience, the behavioral profile, and the level of development of each employee are important to the culture of the organization. These elements play a role in the development of the employees themselves and therefore also in the development of the organization. This development has three levels:

1 *Operate*
   The operating level is the level on which the employee starts to develop his competencies and attitude to fulfill his role in the right way, so it adds maximum value to achieving the desired performance. In the "operating" stage, the employee needs instructions in the area of knowledge and skills on the one hand. On the other hand he also needs to be steered in the field of attitude. The behavior in the operating stage is reactive. An organization at the operational level is reactive, and aimed at survival. No common objective exists yet and values are not yet shared. Everyone fights for his own piece and tries to protect himself. The organization is a collection of separate parts that do not yet form a whole. The management style is *push*-oriented. Improvement activities are not yet possible, because the basis, safeguarding the standard, is not yet in order. When the organization remains in this stage for too long, this eventually leads to loss, because the organization does not develop at all, while the competition does

2 *Control*
   The controlling level is the level at which the employee control their competency, but not yet master the complete repertoire and not yet within each context. Moreover, the employee can solve problems, but not before they occur: he is confronted with the problem when it occurs. The behavior in this

phase is responsive and both *push-* and *pull*-leadership are applied.

The organization on the controlling level is aimed at objectives that contribute to the medium term. Coordination is still necessary, but within teams, improvement initiatives are already taken because the common objective becomes increasingly clear. These improvements occur primarily on the performance level and not on the behavioral level. Desired behavior is stimulated and less strict steering is needed because employees' acceptance is higher. In this controlling phase, the organizational objective and the performance are strongly determinant and the focus already lies on behavior more than it did on the operating level, but not yet as much as on the directing level

3   *Direct*

The directing level is the level in which the employee masters the complete repertoire of competencies and also knows how to employ these within each context. This means that he, in this phase, can also recognize problems before they actually occur; the behavior in the directing stage is proactive.

Here, the organization is in a state where activities are planned from a vision aimed at the future. In this phase, employees know what specific behavior leads to which performance and how they can continuously improve this to direct the organization towards the common objective. Behavior in this phase is completely integrated within the performance. In this phase, employees demonstrate a large extent of ownership.

Performance-behavior leadership is completely applied in this phase. *Push* hardly occurs. The system is running and therefore, people no longer experience the formal procedures and protocols as irksome, but as part of the system that allows space. Due to this, new energy is released to work on continuous performance and behavioral improvement.

Figure 6.3 shows this development.

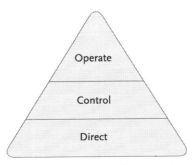

Figure 6.3 *Levels of development of employees and organization*

6.5   Behavioral profile-oriented development

Performance behavior stands for a rigorously different appraisal model than is currently used in 99% of the companies. The behavioral audits occur with a much higher frequency and are role-oriented. Therefore, it is important to develop in a role specific (what role does someone fulfill at a certain moment in the organization) and profile specific (which profile factors does someone have) way. However, this does not mean that individual learning replaces collective learning, but it does mean that individual development is the foundation of the learning organization. The most common form of learning within performance behavior is learning through experience. From the high-frequency audits, employees receive immediate feedback on their behavior, at the moment the behavior occurs. They can apply the new behavior directly within their own work context and frame of reference.

Interesting studies about feedback have appeared in the last few years that explain the similarities between training animals and coaching people.

> Imagine: after having been away for three hours, you come home and your dog greets you enthusiastically. He is happy to see you and wags his tail. Then you discover that he peed in the living room. And this while you took him to training each Tuesday evening for a year to teach him to pee outside twice a day. You decide to confront the dog with his behavior and smack him on the nose, so he feels he should never do this.

You will probably feel the same way we do: this isn't right. The signal "This is unacceptable behavior" does not reach the dog. The correction took place much later than the behavior. The dog now relates the smack to the current behavior, wagging his tail while greeting his master, and is confused. But why do most companies and managers believe this will work for people? Although people are capable of clarifying their behavior verbally, and therefore of placing it in a different time perspective, it is much more effective to give feedback about behavior (positive or negative) as quickly as possible after the displayed behavior.

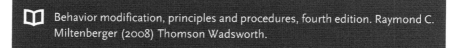

> 📖   Behavior modification, principles and procedures, fourth edition. Raymond C. Miltenberger (2008) Thomson Wadsworth.

The result of studies conducted on the work floor of organizations are clear: on the one hand, the high-frequency behavioral audits of performance behavior allow to steer the behavior in the short term and on the other hand, it analyses the patterns of behavior for long-term development, which allows you to train or facilitate employees specifically for areas where performance deviations occur.

On the one hand, performance behavior steers behavior by means of corrective interventions in the short term and on the other hand, the long-term patterns are analyzed, the root causes are mapped, solutions are figured out and preventive actions are taken. In this way, the deviations in behavior are steered and developed with the same frequency as the deviations in performance: this is typical of performance behavior!

You can read more about auditing behavior in chapter 7.

The most important learning process in the short-term patterns is "do/experience ▶ check/steer". This is the corrective behavioral steering route. During evaluations of behavior and interventions, gained experience regarding behavior is developed in small steps.

The long-term patterns also have to be analyzed. This allows you to observe on a deeper level and to steer in a more systematic way. This route is equal to that in the PRSS-PDCA-model (figure 2.5 on page 79) in performance development. We call this the preventive behavioral steering route.

When developing behavior, Kolb's learning cycle is continuously used. In this cycle, Kolb describes four learning styles in which active is opposite to reflective and abstract is opposite to concrete. On the basis of someone's preference, you can determine the "learning starting point" that works best. Everyone eventually goes through the four steps, but the starting point may be different for everyone. The four phases of Kolb are:

1   Do and feel: *the accommodator*
    By acting, you create a concrete experience.
    "What am I doing
2   Feel and watch: *the diverger*
    By observing actions and thinking about this observation, you discover (root) causes.
    "What did I do and what did not meet the goal value? How do I see that situation now?"
3   Watch and think: *the assimilator*
    By converting the experiences from the observation and reflection into experience rules, models and assumptions, you can discover correlations and patterns. You can also test hypotheses and generalize insights.

"Which correlations and patterns do I observe? To which insights does this lead?"

4   Do and think: *the converger*

By trying out new insights in practice, you can experience what behavior leads to what performance and what does not work (yet). On the basis of this, you can determine actions that lead to new performance behavior.

"What behaviors will I integrate and in which time period do I want to achieve this?"

Everyone learns in a different way and the behavioral profile plays a primary role in the choice for a learning style. The behavioral profile determines which style you are comfortable with. For example, someone might prefer a more personal approach in which everything is first explained before he will practice this new behavior in his own work environment. Someone else might prefer to first try it themselves and only then look into the theoretical framework he can place the new behavior in. Let's look more closely at the various profiles and their development preference. It is important to bear in mind that people cannot simply be placed in one of the four profiles; most people will have a combination of multiple profile factors. More knowledge of the four profile factors provides insight into the way the combinations of profile factors influence people's behavior. This leads to a more focused development, and therefore more effective performance behavior.

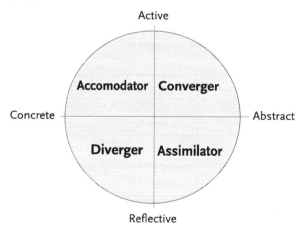

Figure 6.4 *Kolb's learning styles*

Dynamic

Someone with the profile factor "dynamic" prefers to try out in practice whether new ideas, techniques and theories are effective to achieve his objective or solve his problem. He does not want to debate endlessly; he wants to act. Since he is heavily goal-oriented, the method is less important: as long as the resources contribute to his objective. If not, he chooses a different method.

The learning question of someone with the profile factor "dynamic" usually begins with "What...?"

Inspiring

Someone with the profile factor "inspiring" has the tendency to try his learning experiences immediately. Since this inspiring person is enthusiastic about everything that is new, he usually acts first before he thinks about the consequences of his actions. However, he has a short attention span, which means he quickly shifts his attention to other new things. He is easily distracted due to his wide interests. He is averse to details, rules and procedures and wants to be liked.

The learning question of an "inspiring" person usually starts with "Who...?"

Social

Someone with the profile factor "social" likes to look at new ideas and models from various points of view. He strives for a stable situation, and will not quickly try new things unless he is truly convinced that this is better. But he usually only knows what the benefit of new things is when he has tried them and therefore, this person has a tendency to go around in circles. He likes to analyze and delays in drawing conclusions about the analysis as long as possible, because this means he needs to do something with it. His stable behavior means that he will safeguard and protect his current behavior as much as possible.

The learning question of someone with profile factor "social" usually starts with "How...?"

Correct

Someone with the profile factor "correct" will attempt to find coherence in his observations and draw logical conclusions from these. He enjoys analyzing, as does the "social" factor, but subsequently continues with logical and consistent steps. He appreciates structure and due to his perfectionism, he sometimes needs a lot of time before acting. The learning question of "correct" person usually starts with "Why...?"

Figure 6.5 shows how Kolb's learning styles and the behavioral profiles come together in one model.

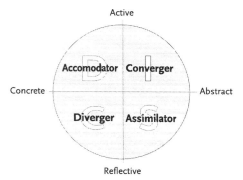

Figure 6.5 *Learning styles in combination with behavioral profiles*

6.6   Continuous behavior development leads to performance

In this chapter so far we have been discussing many behavioral topics, however the real question remains: "Is there evidence that continuous improvement of behavior results in improved performance?" The answer is yes. Over the years we have been implementing performance behavior at many different clients. At these clients we worked on improvements in behavior to eventually improve the performance. To be able to back the performance behavior methodology with more 'hard' evidence we also started some statistical analysis of the development of performance in relation to the development of behavior. At most clients the same pattern showed up again: A strong correlation between behavior and performance and a strong regression in which performance depends on behavior.

Figure 6.6 shows one of these statistical analyses at a client. In the graph both performance (Overall Equipment Efficiency – OEE) and the audit results of all the steering and accountability meetings are plotted. The graph starts at P05, which was the moment the implementation of performance behavior started. This graph together with the corresponding correlation and regression analysis provides the evidence that the development of performance is influenced by the development of behavior.

The more extensive tables of the correlation and regression analysis can be found in the Appendix on page 255.

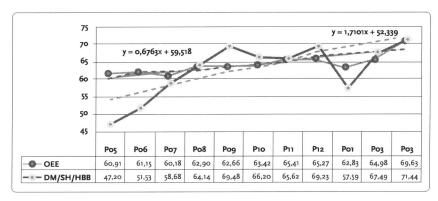

	Po5	Po6	Po7	Po8	Po9	P10	P11	P12	Po1	Po3	Po3
OEE	60,91	61,15	60,18	62,90	62,66	63,42	65,41	65,27	62,83	64,98	69,63
DM/SH/HBB	47,20	51,53	58,68	64,14	69,48	66,20	65,62	69,23	57,59	67,49	71,44

Correlation Analyses	SA Total
OEE	0,745 0,009

Regression Analyses	SA Total
OEE	46,4 + 0,280 0,000 / 0,009 R=Sq(adj) = 50,5%

Figure 6.6 *There is a proven relationship between development of behavior and performance*

In the next chapter we will elaborate on 'how' behavior can be developed by explaining the concepts of auditing and facilitating in section 7.7 and 7.8 respectively.

7

PERFORMANCE BEHAVIOR CHANGE MANAGEMENT AND LEADERSHIP

In chapter 5 it was emphasized that it is necessary for organizations to improve continuously. The chapter described issues as resistance and the different phases people go through to cope with change and concluded with the success factors that are needed to enable change towards a performance behavior organization. This chapter will describe the different steps that can be used to arrive at a performance behavior organization while it makes the connection to how to manage this change process from a performance behavior perspective. Meanwhile the role of leadership in this process is highlighted.

7.1 Towards a performance behavior organization in 8 steps

A performance behavior organization is characterized by its drive to continuously improve. However, to arrive at this state in which the organization is capable to improve continuously it is necessary to change the organization in such a way that continuous improvement is made possible.

The change process towards a performance behavior organization can be described according to the eight-steps that were described by the famous change expert John Kotter in 1995. This eight-step approach to change overlaps with the success factors to change that were described in section <5.4>. It provides a pathway to how change towards a performance behavior organization can be brought about.

The eight steps of the change process are:

1 Establish a sense of urgency;
2 Create the guiding coalition;
3 Develop a change vision;
4 Communicate the vision for buy-in;
5 Empower broad-based action;
6 Generate Short-term wins;
7 Never let up;
8 Incorporate changes into culture.

 Leading Change, John P. Kotter (2012) Harvard Business School Press

Step 1: Establish a sense of urgency

Creating a sense of urgency for change is essential to start the change process. The challenge is to let everyone in the organization realize there is a necessity to change towards a performance behavior organization. This was also covered in Section 5.4.

Step 2: Create the guiding coalition

When the sense of urgency is created and everybody in the organization realizes that it is necessary to change towards a performance behavior organization it is time to put together a team with enough power to lead the change. To enable the change it is important that this team has the right composition, has high levels of trust and that the team has a shared objective. Kotter argues that an effective guiding coalition has four qualities that should be present in the team:

- *Position Power*: It is vital to have enough key players from within the organization on board to ensure that the people that are left out cannot hinder the process.
- *Expertise*: The team should have expertise in all areas that are relevant in decision making, so that informed decisions can be made.
- *Credibility*: The group should have respect within the organization so that the decisions and actions of the team are taken seriously by other employees
- *Leadership*: The group should have proven leaders that can inspire others and can drive the change.

Step 3: Develop a change vision

The purpose of a clear change vision is to inspire people to take action towards the new situation. Furthermore the vision guides the action to ensure that the right actions are taken towards the future state of the organization. To make sure that the vision will be accepted and supported by the organization it needs to be easily explainable in a way that it intuitively makes sense to the people in the organization. In his book Kotter describes that an effective vision has six key characteristics:

- *Imaginable:* It conveys a clear picture of what the future will look like.
- *Desirable*: It appeals to the long-term interest of the different stakeholders of the organization.
- *Feasible*: It describes objectives that are realistic and can be achieved.
- *Focused*: The vision is clear enough to provide guidance in decision making.
- *Flexible*: It allows alterations when conditions change during the implementation of the vision.

○ *Communicable*: It is easy to communicate the vision to the organization and can be explained quickly.

Step 4: Communicate the vision for buy-in

This step makes sure that as many people as possible understand and accept the vision. To make an effective change the vision needs to be communicated intensively. A memo announcing the change or a single speech by the CEO is far from enough to make sure that the vision is understood and accepted. It needs to be communicated anywhere and everywhere. Kotter describes four factors that are important to keep in mind when communicating the vision. It should be:

○ *Simple*: The vision should contain no technical language or jargon.
○ *Vivid*: Metaphors, analogies and examples will make the vision vivid.
○ *Repeatable*: Everyone should be able to spread the vision to anyone.
○ *Invitational*: The vision should allow interaction

Step 5: Empower broad-based action

This step is concerned with removing as many barriers as possible to enable people to do their best work. This step relates to structures that are in place within the organization. The right structures provoke the right behavior, so it is important to assess these structures and to establish the right structures that facilitate the change. This was discussed in the subsection 'Success factor 4 structures provoke' in Section 5.4.

Step 6: Generate Short-term wins

Short-term successes are crucial to the success of long-term change initiatives. The realization of short-term success often is hard, but every little success should be used to emphasize the achievements so far. This makes everybody that is involved in the change process believe in the change initiative and keeps the spirits high. Therefore the achieved successes should be made visible and must be related to the change initiative. This will boost the morale and motivation of everybody involved.

Step 7: Never let up

In many change initiatives victory is declared too soon and the change initiative is seen as finished. The consequences of this can be very big. When victory is declared too soon and the focus shifts this can mean that critical momentum will be lost. As a consequence the new behaviors and practices are not retained and people fall back in their old patterns of behavior. Once this happens it is very difficult to gain enough momentum for the change initiative again.

Instead of declaring victory it is important to continue the change initiative. In this step it is important to add more projects to the change to drive the change deeper into the organization. Additional people are brought in to help anchor the new practices and behavior so that it grounds in the organizational culture.

Step 8: Incorporate changes into culture

Anchoring of the new practices and behavior into the organizational culture is the final step of the change process. This step ensures that the change is sustained. This step is extremely difficult since culture is composed of norms of behavior and shared values. These social forces are very strong and this makes changing them difficult. Kotter argues that because change is extremely difficult to ingrain into the culture this step should come last. He provides some general rules to keep in mind when attempting to change the culture:

- Cultural change comes last, not first;
- You must be able to prove that the new way is superior to the old;
- The success must be visible and well communicated;
- You will lose some people in the process;
- You must reinforce new norms and values with incentives and rewards – including promotions;
- Reinforce the culture with every new employee.

The different components of performance behavior during the change process

The 8-step change process provides a pathway to change towards a performance behavior organization. However this process has to be managed carefully to arrive at a performance behavior organization that is able to improve continuously. In chapter 1 we described the performance behavior model that distinguishes between the importance of the performance component and the importance of the behavior component. During the execution of the change process this model comes into play again. During the change process it is critically important to carefully manage both components of the performance behavior model properly and to ensure that both components receive equal attention.

The nature of the components differ from each other: the performance component is also described as the 'hard' side, that deals with 'measurement and rationality', while the behavior component is considered to be the more 'soft' side that deals with 'people and the organization'.

The performance component contains all the rational and visible processes at both organizational level and individual level. It is concerned with functions, authority, behavior, structure, work processes and output. An important part of the performance component is the DMAIC cycle that was described in chapter 4 to enable improvement.

At the other end, the behavior component is concerned with behavior and the way in which behavior can be influenced. It is about the prevailing patterns within the organization that prevent change from happening. The behavior component focuses more on perception, expectations and motivation of individuals, as well as on the culture, dynamics and commitment within the organization.

While a separation between the performance component and the behavior component is given in this book, the separation between the two sides is not always that clear cut. A lot of elements belong to both sides. An example of this 'gray' area is behavior: the right structure provokes the desired behavior. But if the desired behavior is not displayed within this structure, it is not necessarily the structure that is faulty. It could also be due to the attitude of the person who is not displaying the desired behavior. Another example is a new standard that is implemented because it is proven to be the best way to work. However, it becomes clear that the employees do not work according to the new standard, because they don't accept it. These examples illustrate that it is vital to consider both the performance side, as well as the behavior side during the change process. Leadership plays an important and facilitating role in managing these two components during the change process towards a performance behavior organization.

7.2 The meaning of change from different points of view

In this book we have been using the DISC methodology to indicate that people have different behavioral profiles with different preferences of behavior. This makes that people with different behavioral profiles react different to change. A person with, for example, a predominantly correct profile will be much more reluctant to change than for example a person with a predominantly dynamic profile, who wants to act fast.

An assessment of people in the organization, based on their DISC profile, can provide valuable insights that can facilitate the management of change. However, DISC is not the only way in which preferences towards change can be assessed. In their book 'Learning to change', change experts de Caluwé and Vermaak identify five different 'change prints' that each have a different color. Each 'change print' indicates how people, depending on their personal preference, approach change. Just as a DISC assessment, an assessment of the people in the organization based on colors of de Caluwé can provide insights which can facilitate the change process. It can provide help in choosing the approach to change and enables people to communicate about change more easily because people now recognize different preferences regarding the approach to change.

In this section the understanding of de Caluwé and Vermaak in regard to the different colors will be explained and a connection to the DISC methodology will be made.

1   *Yellow change print*
The yellow change print assumes that people will change their point of view, as long as their own interest is taken into account or when they can be convinced to accept certain ideas. Combining ideas, combining different points of view and forming coalitions or power blocks are methods that are used in the 'yellow style approach'. Change is seen as a power game or as a negotiation exercise aimed at feasible solutions. This way of thinking fits smoothly into change processes where complex goals or effects must be achieved and in which many people or parties are involved in mutually interdependent ways.

2   *Blue change print*
The blue change print assumes that people will change when a clearly specified result and process are determined in advance. All steps are planned into the last details. In this approach the change is carried out in a programmed and structured way that is determined in advance. Insights do not change with every step that is taken. Project management is a good example of a blue print approach. It is a favored approach in change processes where the result and the path can be well defined and predicted in advance.

3   *Red change print*
The red change print assumes that people accomplish their change journey by being stimulated. In this way, employees are being inspired and seduced to get them to perform the desired action. Red print viewing assumes that people and organizations will change if the right human (development, resource) tools are deployed and used correctly. This is more the reward/penalty style of motivating people.

4   *Green change print*
The green change print assumes that people have to make the change journey themselves by learning and developing. Learning and changing are more or less the same words from the green print point of view. This approach provides a good fit between what individuals want and what the organization needs.

5 *White change print*

The white change print assumes that people will change autonomously. Where there is energy, things change. Complexity is regarded as enriching the nature of things, not as disruptive chaos. White print viewing assumes that failure is the inevitable result when we think we can manage change directly. This approach is favored when change is not really needed and there is a lot of history and experience in the organization.

The different change print colors provide a means to assess the preferences people in the organization have towards change and thus can help in determining the change approach that the organization should adopt. Besides the preferences of the people within the organization it is also necessary to determine what is needed for the company.

	Typology	Examples of interventions		
	Pitfall	Individual	Group	Organization
Yellow	Politics, power, win-win situation, negotiation, reaching agreement	Personal commitment statement	Confrontation-meetings	Improve labor quality
	There is not always a mutual interest (lose-lose situation)	Outplacement	Third party strategy	Strategic alliances
		Protégéconstructions	Top level structure	Collective labor agreement negotiations
Blue	Manage, plan, control, clear results	Management by objectives	Working in projects	Strategic management
	No attention for irrational aspects, hurry, impatience	Working Hygienic	Archive	Business process redesign
		Working with an agenda	Decision making	Screening, Auditing
Red	Motivate, involved, feeling of 'we', punish and reward	Career development	Social activities	Reward within organizations
	Lack of tangible results	Recruitment	Teamroles	Mobility and diversity
		Task enrichment / task expansion	Management by speech	Triple ladder
Green	Become aware, learn, exchange, get to know each other	Coaching	Teambuilding	Open systems planning
	Unwillingness / inability to learn, too much reflection, no tangible results	Intensive 'clinic'	Gaming	Parallel learning structures
		Feedback interview	Intervision	Quality circles
White	Evolution from chaos, natural path, energy, creativity	T-group	Self steering teams	Seek-conferences
	Ideologizing, steering oneself, meaningless boasting	Personal growth	Openspace meetings	Rituals and mystique
		Networking	Explicit mental models	Rocking the boat

Figure 7.1 *The art of colors of change. From: 'Learning to change', Caluwé and Vermaak (2003) Sage publications, London*

All change approaches of the colors differ because of differences in goals, the different interests and the different support and negotiating tactics that are used by each approach. In choosing the appropriate change approach it is also important to consider the urgency of change. When the sense of urgency of change is high within the organization, a more push/top down approach of change management will be preferred. When the sense of urgency for change is lower, a more developing style and bottom up/pull approach is preferable. The relationship between the colors of de Caluwé, the urgency for change, and the adopted leadership style is illustrated in figure 7.2.

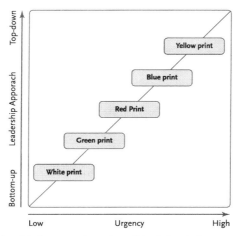

Figure 7.2 *The relationship between the colors of de Caluwé, the urgency for change, and the adopted leadership style*

Figure 7.2 provides insights in some practical issues that relate to how the different approaches could be used. In the paragraph that follows next a more practical and slightly more detailed description of the different change approaches is provided.

The yellow approach

The yellow approach of change is especially useful when results or output are difficult to predict. The creation of an area of negotiation in which the involved parties are represented is difficult. It is important to agree on the process level (the rules of the game) so you can concentrate on the content (playing the game). The yellow approach defines the outcomes in advance, with the end result in mind. This approach is about forming coalitions to reach the goal. The results can be measured by changes in opinions, developments in environment, positions of key players and agreements made between parties.

The blue approach

The blue approach of change is very useful when the change process is clear and obvious. It is feasible to rationally determine all 'change steps' and to predict when the change will be completed. The subject of the change and its object are often different people or entities. The results can be measured by proper and integrated phasing of the process. Roles and responsibilities are clearly defined.

The red approach

The red approach of change is a more emotional way to look at a change process. People will change as a result of the deployment and adequate usage of different HRM tools such as rewards, appraisals, structures, (out)placements and job changes or promotions. It has a fast and human oriented view that is focused on the development of people so that the organization can get the best out of its people. The red approach takes time. There is a large role for the facilitator to take the lead into the change process in which the management is in the lead. Questions that are typical for people with the preference for the red approach are: 'Who benefits from the change?' and 'Who is the owner of the change program?' The results can be measured by the fit between the goals of the organization and the goals of the people.

The green approach

The green approach of change is related to the action learning theories: you can't force a person to learn, so try to influence the process of learning and unlearning. The management is not very directive in this green type of change style, because they are the facilitators/trainers who have an important role in development. Furthermore management is in the lead. Thinking and doing are coupled in this style, but not as sequential as it is as in the blue print change approach. The results can be measured by means of the learning ability of individuals and groups. The motivation to learn and the openness between them to reflect are important indicators.

The white approach

The white approach of change is actually no approach at all. At least, not a management approach. Planning is irrelevant, and resistance is part of the concept. Nothing is managed and the process is the change in itself. The results can be measured by the degree of self organization of people who manage their own journey.

The categorization of change approaches or preferences into different colors provides means to create awareness surrounding the preferences to change of different people in the organization. This relates very much to the DISC methodology that discusses the different behavioral preferences people have. In this sense, DISC and the colors of the Caluwé can complement each other to be able to manage the change process. That is why we create a link between the different behavioral profiles of DISC and the different colors of de Caluwé. We can see, for example, that the Social behavioral profile of DISC is very close to the red approach of change in which the emphasis is on the people that will make the change possible. The other linkages between DISC and the colors of the Caluwé are listed below and are depicted in figure 7.3.

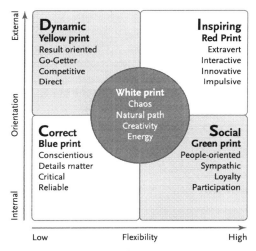

Figure 7.3 *The different behavioral profiles of DISC linked to the colors of de Caluwé*

- Yellow print: Dynamic (D)
- Blue print: Correct style (C)
- Red print: Inspiring style (I)
- Green print: Social style (S)
- White print: Not any particular behavioral style that drives the change.

7.3 Performance Behavior and Leadership

Leadership in an organization steers all forces that influence change. The leaders of the organization chair the steering and accountability moments and monitor and steer the behavior to ensure that the desired behavior is developed. It is clear that leadership plays a crucial role within the performance-behavior system. However, when we wish to determine what the success factors are for steering performance behavior, we will have to unravel leadership and consider each element of leadership from various points of view.

"But isn't performance behavior a Taylor-like way of drilling people to perform specific behavior?" This question was asked by a senior manager from England during a discussion about the leadership style needed to maximize performance behavior. It is somewhat strange that a strict accountability for results and the way in which is steered on the deviations are often considered the same as steering on result only. The way in which Taylor steered, during the beginning of the last century, was primarily aimed at work processes to improve productivity. Performance behavior adopts a rather different approach that is primarily aimed at the results and the behavior that is needed to achieve these results. Within this framework, employees are given maximum space to think about and interpret their work. It is true that the depth and detail of these objectives needs to be developed thoroughly at both the performance and behavior level, but especially with "safeguarding the standard", leadership plays an important role. And on the level of "improving the standard", the leaders will need to develop a leadership style that moves from push to pull more and more.

The development of the way in which leaders steer when implementing the performance-behavior system is portrayed in figure 7.4.

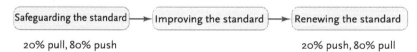

20% pull, 80% push   20% push, 80% pull

Figure 7.4 *The development of the way in which leaders steer during implementation of performance behavior*

This means that the leader needs to employ a different style at the level of safeguarding the standard than at the level of improving the standard. A high level of style flexibility is demanded of the leader. He needs to be able to flexibly switch between different influencing styles.

The steering cycle of the strategic layer has been accelerated drastically, because the speed of the market has increased considerably. In the past, the impact of a new CEO on a company was relatively low, but because the frequency of strategy adjustment has increased significantly, the consequences of such a change are much larger. Therefore, a leader's impact on the organization also has to be larger (otherwise he won't be able to make any changes) and consequently, changes within the organization follow each other up more quickly.

Organizational flexibility is one of the most important aspects of present-day leadership. The leader is on the frontline much more. In the past, the leader possessed a lot of knowledge with regard to content and he ensured that his people converted this knowledge into work. At the end of the previous century, a transformation of leadership style occurred; the leader became a true manager. He no longer had to be knowledgeable with regard to content; as long as he managed the process and achieved results, he was a good manager. This proved a useful strategy when the frequency of change is low. When a manager's decision is effective for ten years within an organization that hardly changes, it is possible to apply this style of distant leadership. But when the frequency of change is increasingly higher (and we have established earlier that it is imperative to develop, and therefore change, continuously), the leader will have to support (facilitate) and supervise more, because different knowledge and skills are required in each phase of change. Moreover, two matters are crucially different than they were twenty or thirty years ago:

1   The knowledge level of employees and their access to "instant knowledge" via the Internet have increased.
2   The communicative skills of people are much more developed.

Therefore, there is a great need to translate the vision and direction of the organization into performance, steering and action indicators for all layers within the organization more quickly. In this sense change management grows towards continuous improvement management more and more since the changes succeed each other so quickly that it is actually a continuous change trajectory. Moreover, more communication is needed to include people in these changes since they have more verbal skills due to the worldwide access to knowledge. Furthermore, higher demands are set for the behavior of new talent. The higher speed of the changes that occur around us influences the competencies of strategic, tactical and operational management.

Performance-behavior leadership is aimed at arriving at a state in which the organization is able to continuously improve the performance and the behavior that brings about high performances in this demanding, ever-changing time in which communication plays an important role. As discussed at the start of this chapter, performance and behavior are the two components that are vital to the change process, and leadership plays a vital role in managing these two components. The two components form the two axes of the performance-behavior leadership model.

The performance component of performance-behavior leadership is aimed at the following four subareas:

1   Performance objectives;
2   Root causes of performance deviations;
3   Continuous improvement;
4   Integrated processes.

The behavioral component of performance-behavior leadership is aimed at the following four subareas:

1   Behavior objectives;
2   Root patterns of behavior deviations;
3   Continuous development of behavior;
4   Integrated cooperation culture.

Steering on performances and on the development of behavior to achieve these performances is the most important aspect of performance-behavior leadership. Let's look at the competencies and behavioral criteria needed for performance-behavior leadership per subarea.

The performance component of performance-behavior leadership

Focused on performance objectives

The first subarea of the performance-behavior leadership model forms the foundation of leadership. Performance-behavior leadership is aimed at performance objectives. To be able to focus on this, certain preconditions have to be met. This means that a structured breakdown of the objectives into monitoring, steering and action goals needs to be performed; there have to be performance boards at each level and it is critically important to steer on standards — and these are merely a few elements of the preconditions that form the foundation. When this foundation is lacking, it is very difficult to put performance-behavior leadership into practice. After all, when objectives and performances are not visualized, on what elements will be steered on then? And when no standards are applied, what is considered a deviation and what is "normal"? Without standards there is no improvement possible.

A leader focused on performance objectives:

○ Focuses on deviations on the right level;
○ Sets SMART-goals;
○ Steers on standards;
○ Works according to fixed structures;
○ Steers consistently and consequently

- Asks questions and follow-up questions;
- Helps employees to define objectives;
- Gives performance feedback to individual employees.

Focused on root causes of performance deviations

The second subarea of performance-behavior leadership is a deeper analysis of root causes. The objective is that the problem is eventually solved permanently. The performance-behavior leader does not merely want to fight the symptoms but wants to tackle the real root cause. As illustrated earlier in our example: the performance-behavior leader wants to put out the fire, but he also wants to make a plan to catch the pyromaniac.

A leader who focuses on root causes:

- Utilizes the structure of the PRSS-PDCA-model to define the deviation and the improvement objective;
- Follows the structure of the funnel-tunnel model to arrive at a solution;
- Does not merely come up with a corrective solution, but continues until a preventive solution is formulated;
- Helps employees to find root causes;
- Steers on the matters mentioned above during steering and accountability moments.

Focused on continuous improvement

The most important characteristic of the third subarea of performance-behavior leadership is that the leader carries out the continuous improvement philosophy. This philosophy, which is strongly related to lean, is aimed at eliminating losses and creating value. This occurs on a micro level during, for instance, the steering and accountability moments, but also on a macro level when determining the new ideal state. The improvement focus can also be found in stretching the organization or department by adjusting the goal to the ever-changing circumstances. After all, increasing the goal value is the first step on the road to improvement. The continuous improvements in the value stream are aimed at adding value for the customer and reducing losses that add costs for the customer.

A leader who focuses on continuous improvement:

- Helps employees to find simple and cheap improvement possibilities;
- Creates stretch for employees over and over again;
- Focuses on improvement within his own work process.

Focused on integrated processes

The fourth subarea of performance-behavior leadership is the focus on processes that transcend one's own department and that add value or loss for the customer. This leadership aspect also concerns sharing best practices with other departments and colleagues. In this way, an excellent department eventually leads to an excellent organization.

A leader who focuses on integrated processes:

- Actively involves all other colleagues in improvement possibilities;
- Actively shares best practices with colleagues;
- Looks beyond his own department within the value stream.

The behavior component of performance-behavior leadership

Focused on behavior objectives

In the past, when labor was primarily performed by hand, it was possible to enforce performance, because the productivity and output of an employee were highly visible. But knowledge is a different matter; it is much more difficult to observe whether or not someone applies his knowledge. Employees determine to what extent, and how they utilize their knowledge themselves. You cannot enforce this; it requires trust. Trust cannot be bought and can definitely not be enforced. Trust can only be given and received. When a performance-behavior leader wishes to receive trust from his people, he will need to create clarity about the behavior needed to achieve the desired performances (the behavioral objectives). This automatically requires leadership that discourages undesired behavior. Within the behavioral objectives framework, the employee gets the space to practice his own style and identity. The employee can use his own style and identity in his operations, as long as his style or identity has no effect on the results. A great example can be found at the Toyota factories where it is even possible to use different standards, but only after it has been measured and proven that these standards yield the same results.

A leader who focuses on behavior objectives:

- Sets the example of applying performance behavior;
- Knows the organization's values and vision and can explain this vision in a way that everyone can understand;
- Sets individual behavioral objectives, aligned with the performance frequency.

Focused on the root patterns of behavior deviations

The second subarea in the behavior component of performance-behavior leadership is aimed at analyzing the root patterns of deviating behavior. We also refer to this deviating behavior as *waste behavior*, which is discovered via a root cause analysis on the behavioral level where the leader uses the PRSS-PDCA-model.

On the basis of a performance-behavior auditing, analyses are made over a longer period of time, which have to reveal deviating behavior. Consequently, specific interventions and solutions can be named to fight waste. You can read more about performance-behavior auditing in section .

A leader who focuses on root patterns of behavior deviations:

- Has knowledge of interpersonal processes so he can recognize behavior and steer if necessary;
- Does not merely respond to incidental behavioral deviations with a corrective action, but also looks for patterns in waste behavior;
- Looks for root patterns within his own department or organization, also in a benchmark comparison with other organizations;
- Focuses on solving (self-)imposed obstacles in behavior.

Focused on continuous development

On the basis of the analysis of the root patterns, a plan for continuous behavioral development is established, where a closed PRSS-PDCA-cycle of behavior is followed in a frequency aligned with the frequency of performance. So on boardroom level there is (or should be) high impact, low frequent behavior, while on the shop floor there is low impact, high frequent behavior to achieve results. The 'bar of ambition' is raised a little each time, so the employee experiences stretch and behavioral development occurs.

A leader who focuses on continuous development of behavior:

- Does not merely help employees in defining their own specific points for development, but also aids in the practical application of these;
- Actively searches for waste behavior and stimulates performance behavior;
- Does not merely name corrective actions to develop behavior, but also names preventive actions to secure behavior within the organization.

Focused on an integrated cooperation culture

Organizational behavior is the sum of all individual behaviors plus the context in which this behavior occurs. In this leadership subarea the leader does not only look at the individual patterns, but also at the interconnected patterns within and outside the organization or department. This leadership area also concerns sharing specific examples of behavior or successful behavioral interventions with other departments or colleagues, because eventually the success of the customer depends on the success of the behavior that occurs within the entire value stream within the organization. The performance-behavior leader achieves this by maintaining direct contact with the frontline and by observing steering and accountability moments on other departments or within other organizations.

A leader who focuses on an integrated cooperation culture:

- Actively shares examples of behavior and interventions with colleagues;
- Looks beyond the behavior in his own department in the value stream;
- Actively involves all other colleagues in the development of and focus on behavior in his own department.
- Actively trains and coaches teams to arrive at collective teams with collective leadership (see section 7.6).

7.4 Behavioral profiles and leadership: the performance-behavior leader

Each organization expects the impossible of a leader. "Unfortunately", leaders are also just people with limitations; they are not perfect. And that is probably for the best: no one can be good at everything; that would lead to a loss of focus and power. Someone who is an expert in one specific area is usually better at it than someone with a wider development.

In figure 7.5, the behavioral profile of a performance-behavior leader is compared to the leadership model from the previous section.

This model shows that a leader with both "dynamic" and "inspiring" in his profile resembles a performance-behavior leader most. These two profile factors lie at the two ends of the performance-(dynamic) and behavior spectrum (inspiring). However, the figure also clearly shows that the performance-behavior leader needs support from colleagues with "social" or "correct". As is shown in figure 7.5, these two profile factors lie in the middle of the performance-behavior leadership model. This shows that they support the way in which behavior and performance are steered: the dynamic profile factor is supported by the profile factor "correct", and the profile factor "inspiring" is supported by the profile factor "social".

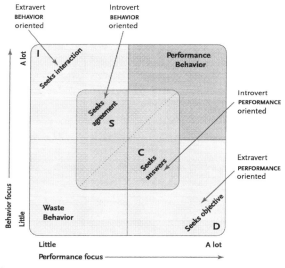

Figure 7.5 *Performance-behavior leadership in relation to the behavioral profiles*

Can a leader with a social profile never be a performance-behavior leader? Of course he can, but this leader will need help or guidance on several fronts or will otherwise need to be compensated by others, to eventually be able to practice performance-behavior leadership. In this book, we discuss natural leaders and less about the possibilities individuals need to develop performance-behavior leadership.

Would you like to know if you're a performance-behavior leader? You can find out in ten minutes via www.profile4free.com.

In this section, you can read what the typical leadership characteristics are per behavioral profile factor. The leadership types assume one profile factor, but please note: as we mentioned before, most people have two or sometimes even three profile factors. The factor with the highest value has the largest influence on behavior, but someone with multiple profile factors will also display characteristics of other leadership types. Furthermore, the behavior displayed by someone with multiple profile factors is also situation-dependent. A dynamic leader is not really team-oriented, whereas an inspiring leader is. Someone who has both "dynamic" and "inspiring" in his profile is able to work well alone or in a team, depending on the situation.

Please see chapter 1 for a specific description of the ways in which you can place various leaders within the behavioral profile system.

The dynamic leader

Basic description

The dynamic leader is extravert, rational, goal-oriented, dominant, assertive and action-oriented. Leaders with a dynamic profile factor have a natural tendency to assume a leadership role. They can take decisions and assertively express their opinion. They are rational and always want to win with regard to performance. The more clearly defined the objective is, the more goal-oriented the dynamic leader will work towards it. He has a powerful and goal-oriented personality, and is a real leader, even when he does not have a supervising position. The dynamic leader has a direct communication style. He often does not give others the opportunity to finish their sentences and takes charge of a conversation. He is impatient and restless; he listens selectively and can appear somewhat blunt and bossy. He mainly asks what-questions. The dynamic leader is not really a team player, because he tends to get ahead of himself. Sometimes, he can be impulsive, impatient and he has a tendency to overestimate himself.

Continuous development of the dynamic leader

The dynamic leader thinks in large steps. He pursues concrete objectives, so he works in a goal-oriented way. He does not want to use matters that do not contribute to his goal. This makes him an efficient leader, but sometimes development can be difficult because he strongly pursues his own objectives (read: interest). When people elaborate on topics that do not immediately contribute to his objectives, the dynamic leader loses interest. When matters do directly contribute to his objectives, he can handle details perfectly well, but these details do have to be placed within the framework of those objectives.

Motivating the dynamic leader

The dynamic leader needs space in the way in which he achieves his performance. Naturally, you can give him suggestions, but leave the decision to him. He has a naturally dislike of people who also wish to take charge: other dynamic leaders. Consequently, a dynamic leader has some difficulty in motivating other dynamic leaders.

Correcting the performance of the dynamic leader

The dynamic leader wishes to achieve results and has a rational outlook on the world. He wants to know what exactly the goal is that he needs to reach and what the current situation is. The dynamic leader prefers clarity: tell him exactly what you expect of him and do not beat about the bush.

> Performance behavior leaders achieve performance by leading people the way in which they would like to be led, can be led and should be led.

The inspiring leader

Basic description

The inspiring leader is extravert, influential, emotional, creative, friendly, and convincing and he enthuses people. He appreciates interaction with others. Leaders with this profile factor in their profile enjoy telling their story. The inspiring leader likes to be at the centre of attention, he likes to inspire. He motivates and enjoys teamwork. With regard to performance, the inspiring leader is sometimes too relationship-oriented and does not focus on the result as much. However, he excels at explaining the necessity of a change to people; he is affable, knows how to win people over. The inspiring leader is persuasive, enthusiastic and positive. He is full of self-confidence, helpful and charming.

Continuous development of the inspiring leader

This leader, who is influence-, relationship- and interaction-oriented, wants to be liked and it is possible that he might agree to something but not do what he says. Making SMART-agreements in a development trajectory is essential for this leader. This leader is the archetype "do-experience", so you should first let him feel what you mean and subsequently link back to what he understood.

If you do not specify the made agreements, this leader has already returned to his work place in the daily practice before he actually understood what should be done.

Motivating the inspiring leader

The inspiring leader is people-oriented. He likes a story: story telling is his thing and he can convince and inspire people. He is motivated by people who are thoughtful. He does not focus on the major things, but on the smaller things in small steps. In this regard, this leader fits in the continuous improvement patterns of performance behavior.

Correcting the performance of the inspiring leader

Inspiring leaders do not like to be rejected. They especially experience rejection when they feel they have been ridiculed in front of other colleagues. Correct the inspiring leader in such a way that loss of face is not an issue. Make the point of correction concrete and always ask the inspiring leader whether he understands it and how he thinks about it. Always speak from a mutual interest.

The social leader

Basic description

The social leader is an introverted, emotional, sincere and friendly leader who is easy-going and relaxed. A number of these characteristics do not especially fit with performance-behavior leadership, but these are characteristics that can support the dynamic and inspiring leader. The social leader is modest and usually takes a position in the background. He supports others and is prepared to help others or listen when they need someone to talk to. The social leader appreciates close and long-term relationships. Others see him as patient and caring. With regard to results, he is good at preparing for change while taking other people into consideration. The social leader has a hesitant communication style. He listens patiently and carefully and asks practical questions. He is a kind and modest interaction partner and mainly asks how-questions. Moreover, within performance behavior, he safeguards the standards and, in combination with a dynamic leader, he is perfectly capable of safeguarding and maintaining this standard. The social leader is not someone who will create stretch for himself: he needs someone to stretch him. Removing him from his comfort zone makes him more productive.

Continuous development of the social leader

The social leader opposes change. He fights for the status quo, safety and security and does not like rash, sudden changes. Just like the inspiring leader, this leader is also people-oriented; he likes to interact with people. He is also heavily practice-oriented. However, he is more thorough than the inspiring leader, so it is wise to divide the development trajectory into more clearly defined parts for the social leaders.

Motivating the social leader

The social leader strives for securities, where he is motivated by his earlier experiences. After all, this provides security. The social leader will also feel needed and therefore feel comfortable when he can support and facilitate his team.

Correcting the performance of the social leader

Social leaders need specific feedback, and since they often take feedback personally, we advise you to give feedback as objectively and value-free as possible. Never judge the social leader, but describe the situation and explain what the deviation between the desired situation and the current situation is.

The correct leader

Basic description

The correct leader is an introverted, rational, critical, correct and conscientious leader who prefers to avoid conflict. The correct leader is careful and reserved. He exposes himself less than leaders with other profile factors. Other people will often think: where do I stand with this person? Once (new) appointments have been made, he will do everything to safeguard these. The correct leader has a distant, factual and diplomatic communication style. He mainly asks why-questions that are highly detailed and related to content. He chooses his words carefully. He is an expert specialist, since he needs knowledge and acts on the basis of this knowledge. The correct leader is analytical and only makes a decision when he has carefully considered all information.

Continuous behavioral development of the correct leader

The correct leader first wants to have a clear overview of the most important things he has to learn and will only then look at the content of these. He wants to know what the purpose of each step in his development process is and wants to stay involved. Regularly check whether the correct leader is still involved and ask him what he thinks – not what he feels; this is a question for the inspiring or social leader.

Motivating the correct leader

Correct leaders are conscientious and serious. They prefer structure, enjoy procedures and work in accordance with protocols. The correct leader is motivated by a neat step plan or by a holiday overview that is neatly developed. Obviously, the correct leader strongly dislikes it when agreements are not kept.

Correcting the performance of the correct leader

Correct leaders first perform tasks exactly as they were intended in the concept, and subsequently professionalize the work bit by bit. Explain to the correct leader exactly what you have observed and how this should be different. Since the correct leader avoids conflict, he strongly dislikes correction meetings and he will avoid discussion.

7.5 Performance-behavior leadership versus traditional leadership

The following table shows the differences between performance-behavior leadership and the traditional leader or manager.

The performance-behavior leader	The traditional leader or manager
Divides his attention equally between performance and behavior	Focuses on performance and spends time on evaluating behavior once or twice a year
Has followers	Has performers
Focuses on continuous improvement	Focuses on the execution of the work
Is authentic and renewing in his behavior	Performs learned behavior
Manages people	Manages work
Works on improving the standard	Works on stability
Looks for new ways	Takes existing roads

The performance-behavior leader	The traditional leader or manager
Aims for stretch	Aims for comfort
Explains the actions for the coming month	Explains the results of the previous month

In addition to these differences, similarities between the performance-behavior leader and the traditional leader also exist. The traditional leader focuses on control, and performance-behavior leadership also includes a strongly developed managerial and controlling side. However, this control of the standards goes hand-in-hand with trust and space to allow employees to act independently within the standards.

The attention traditional leaders have for structures and systems is also an important aspect of performance behavior. However, the traditional leader primarily focuses on the structures and systems themselves, whereas in performance behavior, the human side is just as important. Although the literature often chooses between either the one or the other, both are necessary in practice: the focus on behavior needs the structures and systems, while the focus on performance needs human development. It is "and" instead of "or".

By definition, this means that performance-behavior leaders will need to venture outside their comfort zone in some phases of the implementations of performance behavior, since their behavioral profile may not match the current phase of performance behavior. On the level of safeguarding the standard, for example, the emphasis is on maintaining procedures and structures. In this phase, leaders with a strong dynamic and inspiring profile factor will have more difficulty with their role than leaders with a social or correct profile.

7.6   Performance behavior teams

Within the performance behavior approach it is essential that teams that work together in the organization perform as a team, trust each other and want to exert for the team. In order to reach this state of a collective team in which the individuals are committed to each other, are open and transparent and account for their performance, it is important to identify in which phase the team currently is and to determine how the team is going to develop. In performance behavior we distinguish between four phases in which the team is consecutively: a team of individuals, a team with sub teams, a collective team and finally reaches the phase of a collective team with collective leadership.

Team of individuals

Description

In teams of individuals the individuals don't take initiative, they wait and see if somebody else will take initiative. Agreements that are made are often intentional and not factual. This often results in agreements that are not kept. Meetings are often chaotic of nature and the individuals don't let each other finish talking and do not really listen to what the others have to say. Typical of teams of individuals is that there is no own responsibility, often others are blamed and the individuals complain that they can do nothing about it and emphasize that they are powerless.

Unwritten rules

The unwritten rules of the team of individuals are mainly about the own interest of the individual. Phrases that are characteristic for the team of individuals could be:

- "I did my best, that's enough";
- "It's about effort, not results";
- "If I do my job that is enough. I have nothing to do with others";
- "I have the right to leave in time";
- "They don't listen, so it doesn't matter what you say";
- "Management only thinks about itself and the shareholders, so I will do that as well";
- "You can't trust nobody, everything will be used against you";
- "If work isn't provided to me in the correct way, it is not my fault when something goes wrong".

Development

To develop a team of individuals to the next level it is necessary to create a bond between the individuals and to ensure that everybody is moving towards the same direction. In this phase there has to be focus on content, procedures and skills. It has to become clear how the team handles feedback, how agreements are made and kept. Furthermore it has to become clear what the difference is between having to do something for the team or wanting to do something for the team.

It is important to look back at the past period and to evaluate how this period is experienced by the individuals and if the above mentioned focus achieved improvement in the team. Creating commitment is vitally important. Wanting to do something for the team is very important. This could be stimulated by doing activities with the team that are not work related.

Team with sub teams

Description

The team with sub teams has no collective heart, it displays contradicting behavior and does not like dependency on others. The team has an ambiguous message: "We need you, but do not interfere in our affairs". There are clear subgroups visible within the team which blame each other and compete with each other. Within this team people listen better to each other, are eager to learn and start to learn to give feedback to each other. However, conflicts start to occur between the subgroups, which can be indirect and concealed, but can also explosive, emotional and direct. Finally this team is characterized by resistance towards the supervisor.

Unwritten rules

The unwritten rules of the team with sub teams are mainly about the own interest of the sub groups. Phrases that are characteristic for the team with sub teams could be:

- "We need the others, but only to better ourselves";
- "You said we could decide for ourselves, right? Then do not interfere, because if you do, you do not trust us";
- "See, you said we could do this ourselves, but now you are intervening. You don't trust us";
- "You're never around. This is not delegating, it's just pushing off the work to us. Just what can we do with this?"

Development

The team with sub teams is already better in listening to each other and is eager to learn, however a collective heart is lacking and there is still no own responsibility. The development of the team with sub teams has to focus on increasing the bond between the sub teams and increase the capabilities of the team. To increase the capabilities of the team it needs to become aware and discuss the three main points of communication:

- *Content*: In what areas do we need more knowledge?

- *Procedure*: How are the current work processes running? What are the bottlenecks for these work processes and why? What is going well, and why?
- *Process*: The interaction with each other and with the supervisor, the atmosphere, the informal communication, the handling of critique and conflicts.

In this phase it can be effective to perform a SWOT-analysis of the team. Together with all team members the group discusses strengths and opportunities of the team. Emphasis of the strengths and opportunities during this analysis will result in more cohesion in the group and will create a better bond. The weaknesses and threats should be used as focus points for development.

Collective team

Description

This team can already be called a real team. There is a common objective and the team members have a certain intimacy with each other and feel responsible for each other. In this phase the outside world is considered as "the enemy"; it is "we" against "them". The team is independent and everybody is considered as a colleague and full team member. The team members are proud to belong to the team, take responsibility, try to learn from each other and give each other feedback. In the team the members work with each other on the basis of equality and competence, not on the basis of status. Furthermore the team members solve differences between team members internally and think and act proactively and creatively. Finally they display humor and are able to put things in perspective.

Unwritten rules

The unwritten rules of the collective team are mainly about the strong group feeling within the team. Phrases that are characteristic for the collective team could be:

- "We are better than the other departments";
- "We are better! We are a team, we belong to each other";
- "Not everybody can fit in our team";
- "If you want to join our team, you have to satisfy our demands";
- "We have no interest in ideas that do not fit with the view of our team".

Development

In this phase the team should organize their own team coach meetings. They determine the content, procedure and process aspects that need to be developed. It is possible to provide the team with frameworks that suggest another, more open, way of thinking. In this way the team is stretched to think outside the boundaries of the team.

Collective team with collective leadership

Description

In this phase the collective team has open boundaries, they are able to use the helicopter view and to assess situations that transcend the team level. The team makes choices between interdependency or mutual dependency with other teams and the team is able to change the composition of the team. The team members are all able to work independently, but take into regard the dependency they have on others. The team members strategically handle expectations, act on the basis of trust and handle emotions professionally. Together, this team strives for challenging objectives that are beneficial for the entire organization, not only the team.

Unwritten rules

- "To improve yourself you need others";
- "Our performance is also dependent on others";
- "Together (with other departments) we are strong";
- "We fulfill a function for the greater whole and have to deliver added-value";
- "'We' is broader than our team and more important than 'I'".

Development

In this phase the collective team with collective leadership can be developed further in several ways. An example could be to use a few personal coaches for personal development. In this phase the team knows what the improvement areas are and can point out what needs to be worked on.

Auditing as lynchpin of behavior and performance

Most supervisors and managers find it difficult to steer behavior. Therefore, performance behavior contains an audit system that tests whether the displayed behavior meets the established norm in a number of specific areas.

The audit system is applied on each level within performance behavior: safeguarding the standard, improving the standard and renewing the standard. The content of the audit areas differs per phase, but the structure is the same on all three levels: Auditing occurs on:

1 Preconditions needed to plan, execute, measure and steer performances and behavior;
2 Cascaded objectives which are measured in the right frequency to determine, whether or not the objectives are achieved, together with a same frequency of behavioral measurement;
3 A correct execution plan (plan);
4 A correct execution (do);
5 A correct performance measurement (check);
6 A correct management of deviations (act).

The objective of auditing is to determine the quality of the steering and accountability moments. This is done by measuring the extent to which preconditions are met, by measuring the extent to which participants are prepared for the meeting and by measuring the extent to which participants steer on performance deviations.

The six components on which auditing is performed within performance behavior can be subdivided into basic structures and execution:

> If the quality of all steering and accountability moments is secured by performance and behavior feedback which leads to a corrective and preventive approach to the root cause of performance and behavior deviations, the performance behavior system will have come into operation.

1 *Preconditions and preparation*
   This includes the structures, systems and capacity needed to display the correct behavior, but also the question whether the vision and values of the organization are clear.
2 *Cascaded objectives and behavior*
   These are the objectives and the extent to which these have been correctly translated into the right performance and behavior level on the right steering and accountability level.

Execution of performance and behavior

3 *Plan (Plan)*
   These are the execution plans in which results and run time, but also behavior, roles and responsibilities are clearly described. Auditing "the plan" measures whether the right things are done.

4 *Execution (Do)*

In this auditing component, we measure the quality of the performance of the plan on the macro level. On the micro level, for example, the quality of the execution of the steering and accountability moments is measured on various steering levels. Both provide information about the quality of the execution of the plans.

5 *Measurement and analysis (Check)*

This auditing component measures whether the (deviations of the) performance data is measured and analyzed correctly. Additionally, this component measures whether the right performance is measured at the right level and in the right frequency.

6 *Steer on deviations and interventions (Act)*

Here, it is measured whether the right root causes are converted into corrective and preventive actions.

The audit of the execution measures whether the behavior meets the established norm.

The performance-behavior audit has a few characteristics that simplify the behavioral analysis for the supervisors:

- For each audit question, we work towards a goal value. In this way, the objective is never "the maximum", but a concrete SMART-objective.
- Each audit question has a consideration factor that is dependent on the organization and the context in which the behavior takes place.
- Strive values are indicated in accordance with the *World Class Performance Behavior*-norm with each audit. This is a number that has been established on the basis of branch specific historic audit data. This number indicates the *ideal state* the organization can grow towards.
- DISC-specific behavioral characteristics are linked to each audit-question, so a person's ability to develop specific behavior can be established quickly: when someone does not possess certain characteristics needed for the role he fulfills, it is not useful to invest in training for that specific role.
- Specific competencies and behavioral criteria are linked to each audit question. These are needed to be able to display the necessary behavior in a certain role (for instance, chairman of a steering and accountability moment).
- A few questions to analyze root causes, aligned with audit questions and the audit level, are added to each audit result which can be used to analyze why the desired performance behavior has not been achieved. For example, when someone scores low on naming both a preventive and corrective action, you can ask: "Is the consultation framework visibly present? Does the person follow this consultation framework? Is it explained to the person

what structure the consultation framework has and how he should use it?" These are questions that can be asked when the audit scores are very low. When a person scores higher, but does not yet meet the goal value, the following questions could follow: "What could you do next time to define the preventive action more clearly? Which preventive action belongs to the corrective action you just named? Have the agreements been made in a SMART way?"

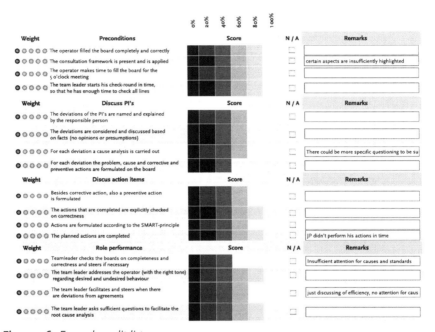

Figure 7.6 *Example audit list*

These performance-behavior audits generate a large amount of performance-behavior data. The audit system automatically converts this data into management information which can be used by the performance-behavior leader to discuss the behavioral pattern of employees. The supervisor indicates what the goal value of the audit in the audit system is beforehand. Subsequently, someone within the organization with the right behavioral profile and the right competencies is trained to be a facilitator. This process facilitator helps to streamline the steering and accountability meetings. He learns to make a choice between an intervention in the process at that moment (For example: "This action is not SMART.") or an intervention afterwards. (For instance: "I observe that you have been late to the meeting four times. What can you do to be on time?") When this fundament of performance behavior is on place, an important precondition for performance behavior has been met.

Figure 7.7 is an example of a performance-behavior audit. This figure shows how the different components score over a period of one month.

Figure 7.7 *Example audit results of one month*

Figure 7.8 shows how the scores relate to the goal values over a longer period of time.

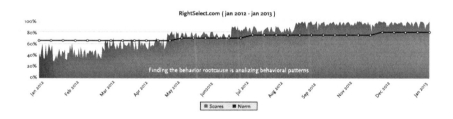

Figure 7.8 *Example audit results over a longer period of time in relation to the goal value*

Figure 7.9 shows an analysis of the behavior of one specific role during steering and accountability moments over sixth months, including the specific DISC-information and the behavioral characteristics from the audit questions. The behavioral profile factors indicate the ability to develop, or the lack of this, in relation to the scores in the audit areas. Examples of these audit areas are role interpretation, preconditions and the way in which the deviations of the performances are considered.

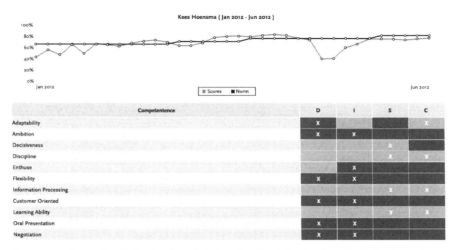

Competentence	D	I	S	C
Adaptability	X			X
Ambition	X	X		
Decisiveness			X	
Discipline			X	X
Enthuse		X		
Flexibility	X	X		
Information Processing			X	X
Customer Oriented	X	X		
Learning Ability			X	X
Oral Presentation	X	X		
Negotiation	X	X		

Figure 7.9 *Example of behavioral analysis in which the behavioral profile factors have been included*

7.7   Facilitation

Facilitation is an integral part of the performance behavior concept that has to ensure that continuous improvement takes place within the organization. It is an important component to assure the correct implementation of performance behavior in the organization and ensures that new practices and new behaviors are anchored in the organization.

Facilitation focuses on the steering and accountability meetings at the different levels throughout the organization in which the performances are accounted for and in which the supervisors steer on deviations. The aim of facilitation is to secure that all established standards are followed during these meetings and to further develop the quality of the meetings. In this way the organization develops its steering and accountability structure which forms the basis of performance behavior. Facilitators are the driving force behind this development and contribute to this development by means of a behavioral analysis on both an individual level as well as on a group level. Subsequently the individual or group is coached to improve the quality of the meetings.

In the previous chapter we already briefly discussed the role of the facilitator. Here we will elaborate further on this role.

The role of the facilitator consists of three different components:

- Monitor: The facilitator monitors the quality of the steering and accountability meetings by means of auditing (also see section 7.7).
- Intervene: The facilitator can intervene during or after the meeting to address deviations. These deviations can be deviations in behavior, performance or deviations in the process.
- Develop: The facilitator makes an effort to develop the individual participants of the meeting by analyzing their behavior, subsequently coaching them and determining a development focus. Furthermore, the facilitator makes an effort to develop the behavior and performance of the group in the same sort of way.

During steering and accountability meetings facilitators observe the displayed behavior of the participants and the way in which the process takes place. This is done by means of the auditing system discussed in section 7.7. When a facilitator comes across any deviations in behavior or from the standards, he can choose to intervene. When planning to make an intervention, a facilitator can make different considerations. For example the consideration to intervene within the group or to address an individual afterwards. This consideration, together with other considerations will be discussed later on.

Besides making interventions, the facilitator also gives feedback to the individuals and the group about their behavior and their development. In this way the individuals and the group become aware of their development and are better able to improve. When providing feedback, always keep in mind that group feedback can be given within the group, but that individual feedback always should be given in a one on one conversation.

After the facilitators have observed a number of steering and accountability meetings the analysis of the available data starts. During this analysis the development focus is determined and advice on development is given to the participants of the meeting.

Now the facilitators start auditing again to collect new data and to follow the development of the meeting and its participants. They then again provide feedback and analysis to stimulate the development.

Interventions

The facilitator has the ability to intervene during the meeting, but he may also make an intervention after the meeting. However, the decision to intervene is not simple. The facilitator has to deal with many different people, with different preferences and should carefully regard the dynamics of the group. To ensure a good intervention that considers the people and the group dynamics the facilitator has to make the following considerations:

- Was the issue an incident (let it go) or is it structural (needs to be addressed)?
- What is the effect of not intervening on the result or process?
- Does the atmosphere allow an intervention at this moment?
- Is this the right timing to make an intervention? (Will it be effective?)
- Is there enough time for the intervention and will I have the participant's attention?
- Learn effect: Is this the right time to start about this issue considering the learning curve of the participant?
- Do I make the intervention now or after the meeting?
- Do I make the intervention in the group or individually?
- What style do I use? Collaborative, assertive etc. (See section 7.9)
- Do I make the intervention based on content or based on the process?

By making interventions the facilitator can directly influence the steering and accountability meeting.

Analysis

After attending several steering and accountability meetings, the facilitators have gathered valuable behavioral information with which they can start an analysis. The aim of the analysis is to determine the next step in the development of the performance behavior, based on the observations from the meetings. During this analysis patterns in the scores of the audit questions are investigated. However, also observed deviations with regard to following the standard are analyzed here. Possible questions that could be posed are:

- What is the trend of the average score of the audits; is it going up or down?
- What are the trends within the different audit questions categories? (E.g. is the score within the 'preconditions and preparation' category going up or down?
- Is/ Are the best scoring audit question(s) from this period, different from the previous period?

- Is/ Are the worst scoring audit question(s) from this period, different from the previous period?
- What deviations with regard to the standard are observed?

After posing these questions the analysis focuses on the deviation between the scores of the last period and the scores of the current period. In this way we can look for the root cause and can go through the PRSS-cycle to formulate an action plan to eliminate the deviation.

Development

The development is the next step after the facilitators have conducted their analysis. We can distinguish between individual development and group development.

With personal development a personal development plan is created. With the help of DISC the participant can get insight into his most important qualities that stem from his behavioral profile. Furthermore this provides insight into the three most important pitfalls that stem from his behavioral profile. By understanding his qualities and pitfalls the participant is better able to understand his own behavior and to positively develop his own behavior. Together with the facilitator the participant now formulates his specific development objective which is tracked on a weekly basis.

The way in which the group develops is determined by the focus that the facilitators give the meetings. After analysis of the observations and available data, the facilitators determine a development focus for the group. This focus could be one of the audit question categories, or even a single audit-question. The facilitators communicate this focus with the group and subsequently intervene during the meeting to pay attention to the development focus when improvement can be made. To determine the development focus the DISC team wheel is used. The DISC team wheel (Figure 7.10) indicates the behavioral preferences of the team members based on their individual DISC assessment. According to the prevailing behavior profiles within the team a development focus is determined.

For example when it shows that, after a DISC assessment, a group is predominantly SC in its behavioral profiles, the interventions could be more DI focused to develop the groups DI (offensive) capabilities. On the other hand, if a group has a more DI profile, the interventions could be more SC focused. Of course, in practice we can measure a more detailed profile, so the interventions are not as black and white as described in the example above.

Desired Behavior

Because the facilitator is the one that addresses participants on undesired be-havior it is critically important that the facilitator himself always displays the desired behavior. To avoid conflict and to be accepted within the meeting the facilitator has to display at least the following behavior:

- The facilitator is prepared for the meeting;
- The facilitator is on time;
- The facilitator communicates when he is absent for a longer period of time and appoints a replacement;
- The facilitator communicates as value-free as possible(no opinions and pre-sumptions);
- The facilitator is proactive (solution-oriented, not problem-oriented);
- The facilitator gives feedback about the development of the meeting.

7.8   Influencing behavior and performance

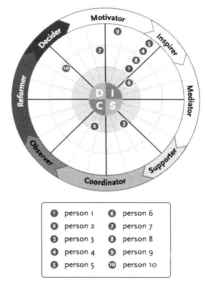

❶ person 1		❻ person 6	
❷ person 2		❼ person 7	
❸ person 3		❽ person 8	
❹ person 4		❾ person 9	
❺ person 5		❿ person 10	

Figure 7.10 *The DISC team wheel*

The way in which a performance-behavior leader influences people to achieve that they will steer on deviations in their performances is one of his most im-portant competencies. Therefore, this book dedicates a section to the influence model. This works as follows:

- A Sender sends performance message (influence).
- B Recipient receives performance message.
- C Recipient decodes message.
- D Recipient responds as follows:

1   No response, or a response that gives no indication whether the performance goal will be achieved. It is not clear whether the influencing succeeded.
2   Response that shows that the sender understood the message and has begun the effort. Influencing succeeded.
3   Response that shows that the sender did not start the effort or started it incorrectly. Influencing did not succeed.

Follow-up actions on responses 1 and 3 are necessary to achieve success. These follow-up actions consist of communicative interventions. To check whether the interventions have the desired effect, you can use the influence rule:

$$E = Q \times A$$

Effectiveness = Quality x Acceptance

Effectiveness is the extent to which the goal has been achieved with the attempt to influence/the message/ the interventions. Quality is the extent to which the message displays the correct tone and content. An acceptance is the extent to which the recipient accepts the message.

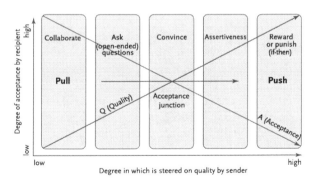

Figure 7.11 *Influence styles with the acceptance line and the quality line*

The starting point of this influence rule is that the message does not merely need to be of high quality; the acceptance of the recipient is also essential in order to achieve the goal. When a sender wishes to achieve a certain objective and the recipient does not want to achieve this objective, conflict arises. In order to ultimately achieve the objective, the sender needs to employ stronger communication. If he employs too heavy means too soon, he evokes resistance (read: negative acceptance). When he does this too late, he will not reach his goal efficiently enough, because it takes too long. If the sender does not adjust his communication at all, he will probably not achieve his goal at all.

The more the sender's steers on quality increases, the more the recipient's acceptance decreases. In the centre of figure 7.11, you can see that quality increases more than the acceptance does. We call this the acceptance junction. At this point, leadership style changes from pull into push.

Figure 7.12 *The five styles of the joystick of influence*

The performance-behavior leader can employ five influence styles, varying from maximum acceptation combined with minimum steering on quality to minimal acceptance combined with maximum steering on quality. Each of the five styles is effective, which means that a style can have results in a certain situation. The goal-orientation of each style depends on the type of meeting, the phase in the meeting and the desired result. If you place the five styles in a circle, you get a joystick with which you can "switch" between the various influence styles in a flexible way.

Influence style 1: collaboration

This style is characterized by exuding and revealing one's own inspiration: it is an enthusiastic style. You try to win the other over for a common cause. You primarily appeal to a person's acceptance; you place less emphasis on the content of the message (which is an effective mean). The collaboration style is about the process and the performance: the common goal. This style is also referred to as the we-style. It can be characterized as a pull-style.

Example

"Let us look together at how we can make sure that you fill in the performance boards completely."

Way of listening

The performance-behavior leader actively listens and appreciates the other's contribution. He attempts to win the other over for a common cause by exuding enthusiasm and speaking in "we"-terms.

Profile style preference

Leaders with the profile factor "inspiring" will be able to utilize this influence style easily. After all, the essence of this style is mainly to convince on the basis of the human factor: collaboration and mutual interest. The inspiring leader will play close attention to the signals he receives from the person he wishes to influence, in order to verify whether he has achieved his objective on the basis of acceptance. Leaders with a social profile will generally also be good at this style. After all, this profile is also people-oriented. Leaders with a dynamic or a correct profile will find this style more difficult, because they are naturally more oriented towards the factual side of influencing and not towards the human side.

Influence style 2: asking (open-ended) questions

This style is characterized by involving the other optimally. You do this by asking open-ended questions, listening actively, stimulating the other to think and attempting to let them find a solution for problems by themselves. This is all aimed at building a relationship of trust in this conversation. This style can be characterized as a pull-style.

Example

"Why have you been late to a steering and accountability meeting a few times this week?"

Way of listening

The performance-behavior leader actively listens and appreciates the other's contribution. He shows understanding for the other person and his situation by asking questions and actively listening to the answers.

Profile style preference

Leaders with an inspiring or social profile will generally be able to employ this influence style easily. After all, this style is mainly about listening well and asking the right questions. A pitfall for inspiring and social leaders is that they can get stuck in this style even when this does not have the desired effect.

A performance-behavior leader needs to realize in time that a certain style no longer suffices and that he needs to switch to a style that is aimed more at quality and less at acceptance, for instance the convince style.

Influence style 3: convincing

This style is characterized by logical reasoning and convincing with facts and numbers. The other person cannot easily deny this. This style, as the name suggests, uses the rational, logical or factual to convince. As you can see in figure 7.11 the convince style sees a change from pull to push: this style contains the acceptance junction. The acceptance junction indicates where the acceptance of the recipient becomes lower than the quality of the message, so that the intensity (power) of the message needs to increase in order to be effective. The first part of the message is still conveyed using the pull-style, but the second part (this depends on the situation, content and shape) can already be characterized as push-style.

Example

"The reason you need to fully fill in the fishbone diagram is that, otherwise, you can miss possible problem areas during the analysis, do you understand?"

Way of listening

The performance-behavior leader hardly listens, or listens selectively. Listening selectively means that you do show that you are listening (via attitude and gestures), but that you only respond actively when the other person says something that matches your message. After you have mentioned all the facts, you really only want to hear the word yes.

Profile style preference

Leaders with a correct profile will apply this style more often. After all, they prefer to employ factual arguments to convince others. When style 1 and 2 did not yield the desired effect, it is necessary to switch to this third style. However, a pitfall for leaders with a correct profile is that they switch to this influence style too quickly – after all, it is in their profile to do so – while style 1 or 2 sometimes still suffices in order to convince others. And when that is the case, it is more effective to use those styles because it brings about more acceptance.

Influence style 4: assertiveness

In this style, the performance-behavior leader exercises influence by naming his wish clearly and firmly. He stands up for his own interests and rights, imposes these on others as a norm, but accepts the other as he is. A constant expectation of obedience is implied. A clear formulation means that it is constantly clear that the I-person wants something. This style is also referred to as the I-style. It is characterized as a real push-style from the performance-behavior leader himself. That is: he exercises influence without needing power or coercion; the influence comes purely from himself.

Example

"I expect that by today you will arrive at a thorough diagnosis developed on paper together with your team."

Way of listening

The performance-behavior leader is a passive listener, since the assertive style is primarily aimed at sending the message.

Profile style preference

Leaders with a dynamic profile will apply this style often. After all, they are naturally assertive and goal-oriented and will therefore communicate in a definite and dominant way. The pitfall of a dynamic leader is that he primarily focuses on the result, push. If he needs to include people in a process, more pull, he will not naturally do this.

When style 1, 2 or 3 does not yield a satisfactory result, it is necessary that the performance-behavior leader is capable of switching to this style to eventually achieve his objective.

Influence style 5: reward or punish (if-then)

This style is characterized by the use of power, exercised in the form of reward or punishments. Reward offers far more possibilities: when the performance-behavior leader promises rewards or challenges, people will often cooperate. Punishments serve to establish boundaries. Someone who apparently does not want to listen, someone who needs a push, might be kept under control via "Punishments". This means that the style is sometimes employed at the expense of the other. The if-then style cannot (structurally) be maintained as a style in the long term, since this style does not elicit ownership but elicits a "guilt-culture".

However, for both reward and punishment it is true that you can utilize them inventively. Not everyone is in the position to negotiate about a pay raise or discharge. This style is a real push-style, including power and coercion, both for reward and punishment in the message. Please note: it is not the actual reward or punishment that is given in this style, but it is the threat of the punishment or reward that can make sure that an employee moves in the direction of the goal.

Example

"If you do not name your performance-indicators in accordance with the consultation framework in the next meeting, I will have to correct you during the meeting."

Way of listening

The performance-behavior leader hardly listens, or listens selectively.

Profile style preference

Leaders with the profile factor "dynamic" or "correct", given their rational motivators, will employ this style more easily than leaders who primarily have emotional profile factors. After all, they are naturally assertive and goal-oriented and will therefore communicate in a definite and dominant way. Leaders with "social" and "inspiring" as a profile factor will have more difficulty utilizing firm language to convey their message.

The performance behavior leader needs to be able to judge whether this powerful style, which is not aimed at acceptance from the other, is really necessary or whether one of the previous four styles can be effective.

Hesitant language, which weakens all influence styles

When performance-behavior leaders in-the-making practice the influence styles, they often attempt to soften their style. On the basis of the situation, they opt for an assertive style but weaken their assertiveness immediately. This occurs as a result of words we call hesitant language: words that express doubt about what is said or how the message will be received. Examples of hesitant language are:

- Actually;
- In principle;
- Possibly;
- Perhaps;
- A bit.

This doubt occurs because our brain actually doubts the situation or the effect. The hesitant language leads to an unnecessary weakening of all five styles, and therefore the hesitant language can even force you to employ a style that is heavier than necessary.

The use of hesitant language is not always a bad thing, but when the power of the influence style increases, it is vital to decrease the use of hesitant language. If we would put this in the "E = Q x A'-graph" of figure 7.11, the line of hesitant language would run parallel to the acceptance line.

7.9   Performance-behavior leadership and culture

It is often assumed that leaders and managers within an organization are capable of "changing the culture" when this is needed. A "culture program" is used, together with the leaders and managers, to enable the "change" within the company culture. Here, a pitfall is that the change becomes an objective in itself. However, change of the culture can never be the objective. It is merely a means to arrive at objectives like performance improvement or cost reduction.

When implementing performance behavior as a system, cultural change is neither an objective, nor a means. It is an inevitable result. Steering and accounting performances and the accompanying behavior at each level within the organization – which is subsequently assessed in a high frequency – is completely new to most organizations and therefore automatically brings about a cultural change.

After all, if an organization learns to work in accordance with standards and the leaders learn, step by step, how to safeguard these standards, a new culture arises in which a much higher level of discipline and ownership is visible than was the case in the old situation when standards were not yet employed.

However, every organization has formed its own specific culture over the years. This culture is determined, amongst others, by the organization's industry, history, employees and operating environment. When implementing performance behavior it is important to assess this culture so that the change trajectory can be fine-tuned based on the prevailing culture and its people to ensure a smooth and effective implementation of performance behavior.

A very useful model that can be used to assess a culture is the Organizational Culture Assessment Instrument (OCAI) model of Quinn and Cameron. The OCAI-model contains four quadrants with different organizational cultures which are the hierarchy culture, clan culture, adhocracy culture and market culture. Each culture differs from the other based on the dimensions flexibility (high – low) and orientation (internal – external), see figure 7.13.

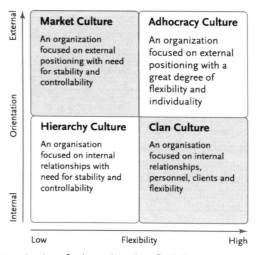

Figure 7.13 *The categorization of cultures based on flexibility and orientation*

A culture does not emerge, or is created, overnight. This is a long slow process which is dependent on a lot of variables. One of the most important variables of culture is the people that work in the organization. Together, these people determine what the shared norms and values are within the organization. They determine what, for example, is appropriate behavior and misappropriate behavior. For this reason it is important to consider the people within the organization when making an assessment of the culture.

As we mentioned throughout the book it is possible to assess people's behavioral profiles based on the DISC methodology. This makes DISC suitable to assess the organizational culture by means of analyzing the prevailing behavioral profiles within the organization. However, the behavioral profiles need to be linked to the OCAI-model. Figure 7.14 shows these links between the different cultures and the DISC behavioral profiles. The behavioral profile 'Social' is linked to the clan culture, 'Inspiring' is linked to the adhocracy culture, 'Dynamic' is linked to the market culture and the correct behavioral profile is linked to the hierarchy culture.

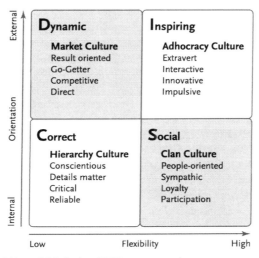

Figure 7.14 *The OCAI-model linked to DISC to assess culture*

The assessment of the organizational culture proves to be a valuable tool to be able to fine-tune the implementation. When the prevailing culture is, for example, a clan culture with predominantly social behavioral profiles this is an indication that a lot of people should be involved in the change process to ensure acceptance within the organization. On the other hand, when the prevailing culture is a market culture with predominantly dynamic behavioral profiles it is possible to move faster and to make decisions quickly. A proper assessment of the culture will provide the basis for a smooth and effective implementation of performance behavior.

In all organizations that have implemented performance behavior both employees and management indicate that the culture has changed. Moreover, both the management and employees indicate never wanting to go back to the past situation. At first, supervisors feared they would lose their autonomy ("What if I can never determine anything for myself again?") and employees feared they would only be allowed to solve problems via a standard protocol and that they would no longer need to think for themselves. They actually found out that the contrary was true. External research into employee satisfaction and employee involvement in firms that implemented performance behavior also point to the positive effects of the implementation. The results of two different surveys showed increases in both employee satisfaction and employee involvement. The first survey included assessment of factors such as work pace, conflict, aggression, reorganization, supervisor support, work variety, receiving/giving feedback, available tools and colleague support. The most significant results from this survey were a decreased work pace, more supervisor support, more feedback, more tools and more colleague support. The second survey assessed factors as process, problem solving, performance, partnering, purpose and people. The latter survey pointed out that the implementation of performance behavior had the most positive effect on partnering, purpose and people.

To conclude we see that when the standard is in place and the leader safeguards the standard in accordance with the structured performance-behavior system, there will arise more space to think about improvements and renewal. After all, less time has to be spent on "standard errors" (that return on a daily or weekly basis) meaning the organization can focus on tomorrow's possible deviations instead of on yesterday's deviations.

At this point the leader has actually created his own space to develop himself as such a performance-behavior leader that no one (including himself) would have expected.

APPENDIX, BIBLIOGRAPHY, REFERENCES, LINKS, ACKNOWLEDGMENTS, ABOUT THE AUTHOR

List of figures

Appendix

Correlation analysis	OEE	HBB	SH	SH/ HBB	DM	DM/ SH/ HBB	DFM	DFM/ DM	SA total
OEE		0,474 0,141	0,620 0,042	0,593 0,054	0,649 0,031	0,735 0,010	0,666 0,025	0,688 0,019	0,745 0,009
HBB			0,696 0,017		0,252 0,454		0,465 0,150	0,341 0,305	0,744 0,009
SH					0,442 0,173		0,636 0,035	0,534 0,091	0,852 0,001
SH/HBB					0,377 0,253		0,474 0,141	0,474 0,141	0,867 0,001
DM							0,790 0,004		0,778 0,005
DM+SH/HBB							0,804 0,003		0,993 0,000
DFM									0,870 0,001
DFM + DM									0,850 0,001
SA total									
OEE		-0,040 0,908	0,143 0,676	0,055 0,872	0,779 0,005	0,409 0,212	0,505 0,113	0,721 0,341 0,534 0,474 0,976 0,012	0,442 0,174

Regression analysis	SH	DM	DM/ SH/ HBB	DFM	DFM/DM	SA total
OEE	52,5 + 0,181 0,000 / 0,042 R-Sq(adj) = 31,6%	54,2 + 0,155 0,000 / 0,031 R-Sq(adj) = 35,7%	48,0 + 0,250 0,000 / 0,010 R-Sq(adj) = 48,9%	45,8 + 0,311 0,000 / 0,025 R-Sq(adj) = 38,2%	50,2 + 0,228 0,000 / 0,019 R-Sq(adj) = 41,5%	46,4 + 0,280 0,000 / 0,009 R-Sq(adj) = 50,5%

List of abbrevations

- OEE - Overal Equipment Effectiveness
- HBB - Heart Beat Board Meeting
- SH - Shift Handover Meeting
- DM - Department Meeting
- DFM - Daily Factory Meeting
- SA total - The total of all steering and accountability meetings

Bibliography, references and Links

Consulted literature

Alblas, G. & E. Wijsman (2005). Gedrag in organisaties. Wolters-Noordhoff: Groningen.

Allessandra, T., M. O'Connor & J. VanDyke (1990). People Smart: Powerful Techniques for Turning Every Encounter Into a Mutual Win. Life Associates: USA.

Baarda, D.B. & M.P.M. de Goede (2001). Basisboek methoden en technieken. Handleiding voor het opzetten en uitvoeren van onderzoek. Stenfert Kroese: Groningen.

Bennis, W.G., Benne, K.D. en Chin, R. The planning of change. Holt, Rinehart & Winston, London: 1970.

Bij, H. van der, M. Broekhuis & J. Gieskes (2007). Kwaliteitsmanagement in beweging. Kluwer: Deventer.

Caluwé, L. de & H. Vermaak (2003). Learning to change. Sage publications, London.

Covey, S.R. (1989). The 7 habits of highly effective people. The Bath Press: Bath.

Dawson, S. (1995). Organisaties Analyseren. Academic Service: Schoonhoven.

Deming, E. W.(200)'Out of the crisis'. The MIT Press.

Emmerik, R. (2007). Kwaliteitsmanagement. Pearson Education Benelux: Amsterdam.

Gay, F. & L. Sweisert (2008). Het abc van persoonlijkheid. Geier learning inc.: USA.

Geer, P. & R. Engelfriet (2004). Hoe vang ik een rat? Uitgeverij Pepijn: Eindhoven.

George, M., D. Rowlands & B. Kastle (2005). What is Lean Six Sigma? The McGraw-Hill Companies Inc.: New York.

Hasselt, H.R. van (1991). Cultuurmanagement, bedrijfscultuur en verandering-sprocessen. Delwel: 's-Gravenhage.

Hoekstra, H.A. en Sluijs van E. Management van competenties. Van Gorcum, 1999

Horn, L.A. (1975). Psychologische aspecten van de organisatie. Kluwer: Deventer.

Jacobi, J. (1973). The psychology of C.G. Jung. Routledge & Kegan Paul Ltd: London.

Juran, J. (1964). Managerial Breakthrough: The classic book on improving management performance. McGraw-Hill

Kanter, R.M. & D. Brinkerhoff (1981) Organizational performance. Recent developments in measurement. Annual reviews: Palo Alto.

Keuning, D. & D.J. Eppink (2000). Management & Organisatie, Theorie en Toepassing. Stenfert Kroese: Groningen.

Koch, A. (2007). OEE voor het productieteam. Uitgeverij FullFact: Lieshout.

Koppen, P. van, D. Hessing, H. Merckelbach & H. Crombag (2002). Psychologie van het recht. Kluwer: Deventer.

Kotter, P. J. (1995) Leading Change. Harvard Business School Press

Lohman, B. & J. Os (2009). Praktisch Lean management. Maj Engineering Publishing: Geldermalsen.

Masaaki, I. (1997). Gemba Kaizen. Kluwer: Deventer.

Mintzberg, H. (1983). Designing effective organizations. Prentice-Hall: Englewood Cliffs.

Nieuwenhuis, M.A. (2006). The Art of Management 1 & 2. Marcel Nieuwenhuis: Oldenzaal.

Pruyn, A & H. Wilke (2001). Sociale psychologie voor managers. Bohn Stafleu Van Loghum: Houten/Diegem.

Quinn, E. R. and Cameron, S. K. (2006). Diagnosing and changing organizational culture: based on the competing values framework. Jossey-Bass: San Francisco

Rampersad, H.K (2000). Total Quality Management. Kluwer: Deventer.

Robbins, S. (2005) Gedrag in organisaties. Pearson Education Benelux: Amsterdam.

Stokes, P. (2003). Filosofie:100 essentiële denkers. Atrium: Rijswijk

Straker, D. (2008) Changing minds in detail. Syque publishing: Crowthorne.

Tak, T. van der & G. Wijnen (2006). Programmamanagement. Wolters Kluwer: Alphen aan den Rijn.

Tidd, J., J. Bessant & K. Pavitt (2001). Managing innovation. Integrating technological market and organizational change. Wiley: Hoboken.

Ven, A.H. van de & M.S. Poole (2004). Handbook of organizational change and innovation. Oxford University Press: Oxford.

Waal, A. de (2001). Power of Performance Management. How Leading Companies Create Sustained Value. John Wiley & Sons: New York.

War Manpower Commission (1944), Job Instruction: Session Outline and Reference Material, Washington DC

Womack, J & D. Jones (1996). Lean Thinking: Banish Waste and Create Wealth in Your Corporation. Simon & Schuster: New York.

Wijnands, N. & H. van den Boom (2008). Scenario naar Lean. Een draaiboek om verspillingen terug te dringen. Uitgeverij Nelissen: Soest.

Consulted articles, notes and memos

Benne, K.D. & P. Shears (1948). Functional roles of group members. Journal of social issues 4.

Butter, R.P. (2000). Marine Safety Rotterdam. Schip en Werf de Zee. January.

Emiliani, M.L. (1998). Lean Behaviors. Management Decision 36/9: 615-631.

Lorenzo, R. (2005). Leaning on Lean solutions. Aerospace America: 32-36. Rabobank kwartaal editie, 2e kwartaal 2009.

Wagenaar, R. (2009). De toekomst van veranderen. Nu zakelijk, 20-8-2009.

Consulted internet sources

www.andredewaal.eu (website of André de Waal, professor at Maastricht School of Management)

www.anp.nl

www.barackobama.com, A call for leadership (website of Barack Obama)

http://changingminds.org, How we change what we think, believe, feel and do (ChangingMinds)

www.encyclo.nl

www.leren.nl

www.nu.nl

www.prism-nigel.blogspot.com

www.teezet.nl

www.wikipedia.com

Acknowledgments

Applying a system as it has been designed is incredibly difficult. One is easily tempted to remove some instruments from the system because this improves things quickly and easily in the short term. However, by doing this, the different parts of the system will no longer be collaborating with each other and the system cannot be considered a system any more.

Naturally, not one correct system, but multiple systems exist. And naturally, you can combine elements from various systems. But the way the system works as a whole is much more important than the functioning of the separate parts. Knowing how the various components are connected and reinforce each other requires a structured and founded approach. Furthermore, the person who implements the system needs to know what the backgrounds of the system choices are. These backgrounds are discussed in this book. The system is developed for and by practice. It is not theoretical, but does rest on theory. Practical theory, suited for the daily practice.

There are many people who have worked on the translation of the daily practice into this performance-behavior book. I would like to thank everyone for his feedback, advice, additions and criticism.

About the author

Neil C.W. Webers (1971) is Head of the Americas region for EFESO and a member of the group executive board. As a management consultant Neil manages global projects for many Fortune 500™companies like PepsiCo, Gerresheimer, Mars-Wrigley and Amcor. He is the founder of the Performance Behavior methodology and author of Performance Behavior (Dutch, first edition 2010, US, first edition 2012) and the Big Improvement Resource and founder of both Flecto and Rightselect.com companies. He integrated his companies in 2012 to the EFESO Consulting Company. Neil is an operational excellence leader with a specialism in performance and behavioral management.

Visit his performance behavior blog: *www.performancebehavior.com*